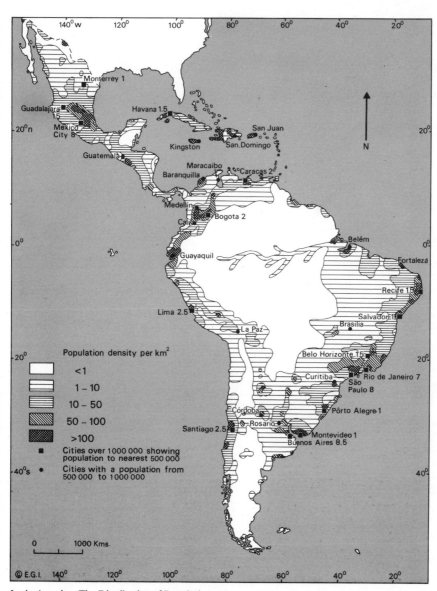

Latin America: The Distribution of Population

Population density per km²

	<1
	1 – 10
	10 – 50
	50 – 100
	>100
■	Cities over 1 000 000 showing population to nearest 500 000
●	Cities with a population from 500 000 to 1 000 000

Monterrey 1
Guadalajara 1.5
Mexico City 8
Guatemala
Havana 1.5
Kingston
San Juan
San.Domingo
Maracaibo
Baranquilla
Caracas 2
Medellin
Cali
Bogota 2
Belém
Guayaquil
Fortaleza
Recife 1.5
Lima 2.5
Salvador 1.5
La Paz
Brasilia
Belo Horizonte 1.5
Curitiba
Rio de Janeiro 7
São Paulo 8
Córdoba
Pôrto Alegre 1
Santiago 2.5
Rosario
Montevideo 1
Buenos Aires 8.5

0   1000 Kms.

© E.G.I.

N

Economies and Societies in Latin America:
A Geographical Interpretation

Second Edition

Economies and Societies in Latin America: A Geographical Interpretation

Second Edition

Peter R. Odell
Professor of Economic Geography and Director,
Economic Geography Institute,
Erasmus University, Rotterdam

and

David A. Preston
Senior Lecturer in Geography,
University of Leeds

JOHN WILEY & SONS
Chichester   New York   Brisbane   Toronto

Library of Congress Cataloging in Publication Data:

Odell, Peter R.
  Economies and societies in Latin America.

  Includes bibliographies and index.
    1. Latin America—Economic conditions. 2. Latin America—
  Social conditions. I. Preston, David A., joint author. II. Title.
HC125.O33   1978   330.9′8   77-12400

ISBN 0 471 99588 6 (cloth)
ISBN 0 471 99636 X (paper)

Text set in 11/12 pt Photon Times, printed by photolithography and bound in Great Britain at The Pitman Press, Bath

Preface

This is not a book on the regional geography of Latin America or even one which attempts to describe and explain Latin American locations of particular sets of economic and social phenomena as an exercise in thematic geography. Books which fulfil such tasks already exist and reading at least some of them constitutes an essential prerequisite to understanding what this book is trying to say about Latin America. The annotated bibliography at the end of each chapter recommends appropriate reading on the various issues involved. But neither is this book a problem-orientated polemic concerned with presenting all that is wrong with the economies and societies of Latin America. Instead it is a book in which the authors seek to present as simply as possible the essential features of the spatial organization of economies and societies in Latin America. The two authors have different interests in Latin America not only with respect to the areas they know best but also to those aspects of its spatial structure with which their work has been concerned. These contrasts in their background interests are reflected in their separate contributions and they intend this diversity of interest to give a book with a wider scope than a single author could hope to achieve. We hope, therefore, that this text will be of interest not only to geographers, but also to other social scientists—in particular, economists, economic historians, sociologists and social anthropologists—who may well find useful, as a background to their own studies, this consideration of Latin American economic and social phenomena from a spatial point of view.

Only the Introduction to the book is a joint effort. Apart from this each author accepts sole responsibility for his own contribution, though each has benefited from the other's willingness to criticize not only his style and presentation, but also his views on particular topics. Each author has, however, been at liberty to accept or reject any criticisms so that the contributions thus remain individualistic in content, form and style. The only significant element of uniformity results from the joint decision to avoid footnotes and specific references and to substitute for them the annotated reading lists at the end of each chapter. This they felt to be more appropriate to a book which can do little more than introduce the complexities of the subject and which aims, therefore, to stimulate interest in more comprehensive statements on various aspects of the spatial structures of Latin American economies and societies.

Essentially, this book is concerned with why human activities have occurred where they do in Latin America. It is also concerned with the consequences of this on the societies involved, for spatial patterns are a visible and measurable reflection of the political, social and economic structures of society in each country. It is also concerned with explaining the pattern of development and underdevelopment in Latin America as a reflection of the nature of the exploitative relationship that exists between Latin America and the world's industrialized nations and that between rich and poor areas within Latin American countries. The spatial patterns affect the progress or otherwise of the societies themselves, thus implying that there are important policy considerations which emerge out of spatial structures. This is but a very recently generally-recognized fact of modern 'interventionist' style governments, even amongst the industrialized nations, and it is still something which remains barely recognized at all in the planning of the development of the non-industrialized countries of the world. Even where it is recognized, however, there is as yet little awareness of what could or should be done about it! Hopefully, therefore, this book may fulfil its intention of making a modest contribution towards a better understanding of some aspects of the spatial structure of societies in Latin America. It may even have a little effect in persuading the policy-makers, and their almost invariably non-geographic advisers, of the significance of the spatial structure of their countries' economies and societies.

The authors wish gratefully to acknowledge all the help they have received in the preparation of this book. For Dr. Preston some of the ideas he presents and the ways in which the material is organized are derived from successive generations of Leeds students who have attended, criticized, and participated in his Latin American course. Many colleagues in their writings, in discussion, and in advice have helped improve his understanding of Latin American society. Most of all, any insight that he may have of rural life is the result of the kindness, understanding, loquacity and intelligence of Latin American farmers, workers, students and 'experts'. Important help in Leeds has come from the understanding of the special needs of a lone Latin Americanist given by two heads of department who, each in his way, have enabled the furtherance of a research career through encouraging a sympathetic university to grant permission for long periods in the field: Robert Dickinson and William Birch were friends and counsellors. Various typists have helped in the embellishment of the manuscript, this year largely Sarah Banks; John Dixon drew the maps with skill and understanding and the Xerox Corporation saved everyone a lot of time. Rosemary, Martin, and Helen provided solace, comfort and encouragement when it was most needed and at other times too.

Professor Odell originally had the opportunity to evolve his ideas from discussions with students of Latin American economic and social geography when he was at the London School of Economics and particularly with John Kirby, Alan Gilbert, Alan Lavell and David Slater who in the years between 1966 and 1972 worked for their doctorates on economic geographical problems in Chile, Colombia, Mexico and Peru respectively and who through their research efforts greatly extended their supervisor's understanding of the spatial processes in the continent. In Latin America itself Professor Odell has benefited from the advice of academics and regional/urban planners in many countries and in various international organizations and he wishes to acknowledge his indebtedness to them. Nearer home, various other people have helped in more mundane but nevertheless essential ways. Preparation of Professor Odell's part of the manuscript was willingly handled by Mevrouw Van der Kaag-de Munnik and Mevrouw Van Reijn-Herscheit, secretaries in the Economisch Geografisch Instituut. The cartographic work for his section was a major task and was done efficiently and effectively by Mr. C. J. Moore, the cartographer of the Economisch Geografisch Instituut—with help from Mr. E. L. van Dijk. Modern cartography necessitates much photographic and reprographic work and this was the responsibility of Mr. R. J. Leusink. And last, but certainly not least, a thank you to Jean and the children. They not only remained at home during his Latin American journeys but also gave him sufficient leave of absence from his familial duties to complete the book more or less on schedule. Needless to say, however, any faults which remain in the text or the maps remain the responsibility of the authors.

Rotterdam/Leeds   P.R.O.
June 1977   D.A.P.

Contents

ix

List of Maps and Plates

Maps

1

Plates (Photographs by David A. Preston except where indicated)   *Facing page 62*

Plate I.   Urban development and growth in Mexico City (Photo: Peter Ward)
Plate II.   The growth and development of a squatter settlement (Photo: Peter Ward)
Plate III.   Negro house, Tumbabiro, Ecuador
Plate IV.   Pimampiro market, Ecuador
Plate V.   Estates and freeholding communities before land reform, San Pablo, Ecuador
Plate VI.   Rosapata, an *ayllu* of Orinoca, Bolivia
Plate VII.   Hacienda Carpuela, Northern Ecuador
Plate VIII.   Escara, western Central Altiplano, Bolivia
Plate IX.   A colonial street, Popayán, Colombia
Plate X.   La Paz, Bolivia
Plate XI.   Mera, Ecuador, 1961
Plate XII.   Newly cleared land, near Puyo, Ecuador, 1961
Plate XIII.   Areas of spontaneous and planned colonization near Caranavi, Bolivia, 1971

CHAPTER 1

An Introduction to the Region

It is necessary to say a little about the area of the world with which the book is concerned. The geographical concept of Latin America does not really need any justification. It exists as perhaps the best-defined world region and, in the post-war period particularly, the idea of Latin America to include all nations and territories lying to the south of the Rio Grande has become widely and formally accepted. Earlier expressions of concern in discussions over the concept of the existence in the continent of non-Spanish/Portuguese-speaking territories have largely disappeared as one after the other of these territories secured its independence and then, normally after a few years of indecision, determined to take political and institutional action to tie itself to the rest of the continent where the 'Latin' countries have, again after some hesitation, decided to accept the newcomers into the Latin American camp. To-day, only the small French Caribbean territories, together with the Netherlands Antilles, which form part of the Kingdom of the Netherlands, and Belize (formerly British Honduras) plus a few other tiny British 'possessions', lie outside the political hegemony of Latin America. Even these remnants of colonialism from 'non-Latin' parts of Europe have many common elements in their history of settlement and exploitation, as well as in their cultural attributes, which tie them in closely with the rest of the continent. Thus, writing in terms of Latin America as 'everything south of the Rio Grande' is to-day hardly going to offend any susceptibilities providing one also bears in mind the corollary, viz. that internal differentiation both between and within the countries of the continent is nevertheless important.

Such differentiation would be axiomatic if one were proposing to proceed in one's analysis on a country-by-country or a region-by-region basis. As indicated in the Preface, however, we are not proposing to do this in this book. Instead the presentation will be concerned with spatial phenomena which, by implication, even if not explicitly, we claim to have some general relevance within the whole of the world region of Latin America. The validity for such a claim lies in the substantive parts of the book. Briefly, here, in introducing the idea of an essential

3

similarity across the continent we would point to the phenomenon of the universality of Spanish or Portuguese influence. Their earlier domination of the social and economic life of the continent has been translated into a continuing influence which is still of significant proportions, most notably through the impact of long-lasting institutions and forms of development such as city patterns and the urban-focused pattern of society, which more than a century of independence has not managed to eradicate. One can also observe the continued, near continental-wide, trend towards urbanization and the concentration of political and economic power in the capital city and/or chief port of each country; or the continuing importance of the extractive type, export-orientated activities in the economies of nearly every Latin American nation; or the continued existence of little-populated frontier regions, with still less developed resources, even in countries where other parts of the national territories are becoming crowded and are lacking in opportunities for rapidly growing populations. Such themes have been and remain enormously important in formulating the spatial structure of the Latin American societies and economies and are dealt with at length in the appropriate sections of the book.

The authors are not, however, unmindful of the tremendous physical and human diversity of Latin America. Their own work and interest in different parts of the continent ensures this and thus they accept the validity of the more traditional geographical books which concentrate on this diversity through their presentation of the countless facts that together go to make up the face of the continent. The authors would indeed go further, and be prepared to argue that it is only as a result of such knowledge that reasonable hypotheses which seek to describe spatial patterns in Latin America are likely to emerge. This is particularly important in a situation in which one is working in alien environments and societies, such that the value judgements implied in the assumptions that must be made before any hypothesis can be tested or any model calibrated are, consciously or not, influenced by inappropriate backgrounds. Knowledge of the 'facts' of Latin America's geography is assumed on the part of the readers of this book and, indeed, at the end of this chapter, the most useful books in the English language in this respect are listed for study and reference purposes.

The authors are not Latin Americans and consequently they look at the continent as outsiders. Their interpretation must thus be different from that of the Latin American as, for example, in the contrasting views of the economic geography of the continent as seen by a Brazilian and a European. The Brazilian sees vast areas of the continent undeveloped not only as a result of a lack of people but also because the colonial powers had little interest in developing agriculture and industry of a sort that would compete with their own domestic industrial interests. The European, on the other hand, sees a half-empty continent with little industry save in a few particularly favoured places, and even there industrial production is seldom so efficient that it can produce goods of a high enough quality to enable them to be exported to other parts of the world.

It is perhaps particularly important to grasp the distinctive characteristics of Latin America's social organization as a prerequisite to understanding the attitudes of Latin Americans not only towards their own problems, but also towards the solutions that others recommend for them. Firstly, Latin American society is much more clearly divided than the society of most European countries. The rich, upper class tends largely to be outward looking and its members esteem most highly goods which come from the 'advanced industrial' countries. Their children, perhaps after completing a university course in their own country, naturally travel to Europe or North America to continue their education either formally or informally. They are often better read in the literature of the Old World than the New. They are also accustomed to social inequality on a scale now largely unknown in Europe and think it quite natural that they should profit from it. The middle class, which is nearly always relatively less numerous in society than in Western Europe or North America, is, on the other hand, strongly nationalistic, believing more than most in contemporary political slogans and convinced of the reality of the economic imperialism of the Great Powers and, in particular, of the U.S.A. It is often an admirer of the freedom which Cuba has gained from the U.S.A., even though it knows little about the revolutionary processes which were involved and is far from being communist or even socialist in attitude. The working class can be divided into the proletarian urban workers and the peasants of the countryside. Both are primarily concerned with self-protection, the former with securing adequate working conditions and wages through labour unions and the latter with small-scale land-ownership and with the maintenance of personal freedom to farm it as they wish. The attitude of bot' groups to other countries is generally one of indifference on the grounds that their concern must be focused primarily on improving conditions at home.

Among the articulate Latin Americans it is important to understand that there is great pride in nationhood and suspicion of outside intervention in any form. Although it is about 150 years since most Latin American countries were formally under colonial rule, a series of political and even military interventions in the affairs of Latin American countries, first by Britain in the nineteenth century and more recently by the U.S.A. during the present century, still serves to remind many Latin Americans that the major powers treat Latin America, like the rest of the Third World, as a series of dependent states whose external relations can easily be manipulated. In more strictly economic terms, as is pointed out in later chapters of this book, much of Latin American industry belongs to foreign companies and was thus developed primarily to benefit the foreign investors rather than the economies of the countries where the industry is located. The nationalization of many foreign concerns in Latin American countries, especially since the nationalization of the Mexican petroleum industry in 1938, reflects these views.

In the light of all this it is unduly ingenuous for Anglo-Americans or Europeans to go to Latin America expecting to be loved. The history of the continent *from the Latin American point of view* has been one of prolonged exploitation by the colonial powers or industrialized nations. And this exploitation is considered by most Latin Americans to be continuing. What, after all, they argue, is the logic of Bolivian tin being shipped as ore to Liverpool for smelting when Bolivia has ample hydro-electric power potential to make the tin locally; or of Colombia or Brazil shipping coffee beans to Europe and the United States when instant coffee could so easily be made exclusively in the coffee-producing countries? Why, too, should Guyana and Suriname ship their bauxite to the U.S.A., Canada and Western Europe to be refined and smelted when they have a vast potential for hydro-electric power development on which locally built plants could operate and at the same time provide job opportunities in countries where there are too few jobs chasing too many people. It is best therefore to approach Latin America not with Eurocentric ideas about what Latin American attitudes towards development, etc. ought to be, but rather in the knowledge that relationships between Latin America and the outside world have not been equally beneficial to all parties. Both these considerations and other differences between the continent and the industrialized countries of Western Europe are so important that they inevitably make the task of the non-Latin American student of Latin America more difficult and expose his research to certain dangers. Two examples illustrate this point as far as geographical studies are concerned.

The first arises when a European-born and trained geographer gets involved in the study and analysis of, say, regional differences within Latin American countries, for this puts him out of his geographical depth in respect of at least three sets of characteristics which make his familiar European-based ideas irrelevant to the regional problems of most Latin American countries. In the first place he has a fundamental familiarity with a situation in which the existence of unused and/or unpopulated parts of national territories has been the exception rather than the rule for many generations; secondly, his experience is of countries whose geographical size is modest, so that, given also their well-developed transport infrastructure, there is little cause for concern about the differential incidence of transport costs in the movement of goods and the time distance involved in people moving around the country; and thirdly, he is a member of a society in which there is a general consensus of opinion in favour of an equitable geographical distribution of incomes and of job opportunities. Useful geographical work by such a person in Latin America thus depends upon his willingness and ability to appreciate and understand the significance of the differences between his own background and the background to the regions he aims to study. This is a process which involves not only learning, but also experience and a 'feel' for the contrasting conditions. Without this, mechanistic applications of, for example, Christaller-type settlement network analysis or of geographical diffusion analysis as evolved in West European conditions, to the different geographical scale and the contrasting spatial organization of society in Brazil or Argentina, seems likely to produce inappropriate results. Similarly with an application of the same types of spatial investment policies as have been used to help the depressed areas of

Western Europe, in the political, social and geographical conditions of the large Latin American countries.

The second example is in the case of urban geographical studies in which hypotheses have generally been based on experience with North American cities. Given this experience, the expectation of the scholar investigating any city structure is that he will find a declining central business district surrounded at best by urban slums or at worst by racial ghettoes. Then, according to the normative models, these will gradually merge into areas which are in a process of social decline until the suburbs proper are reached. There, a gradual increase in affluence and a gradual decrease in housing and population density will reflect increasing distance from the city centre. This model of reality that the North American (or British) geographer carries with him to Latin America is now found to be at best inadequate, and at worst positively misleading, for the typical Latin American city has a centre in which 'all the action' is concentrated and in which many of the socially most acceptable people still prefer to live, with a residence on the central plaza being amongst the most desirable of all locations. The suburbs, if they exist at all in a North American sense, are limited not only because of lower standards of affluence, but also as a result of different life styles. And finally, instead of the grandest suburbs of all on the outskirts of the city, one finds around most Latin American cities the shanty-towns of the 'marginalistas', the recent immigrants to the cities of this part of the world who find their living space on land on the periphery of the city and which is being held unused, often by land speculators, awaiting further urban expansion. The expansion will inevitably enhance the value of the land, which means that, as it is developed, the marginalistas must be driven out to a new and more distant periphery.

Appreciation of the fact that the 'universal' laws of economic and social geography, like the laws of economics and sociology, have in the main been discovered by North Atlantic orientated theoreticans and 'proved' by testing them in this one major world region, emerges clearly for those who work in a world region with contrasting values and cultural attributes, many of which, if they can be quantified at all to fit into the normative theories, proceed to upset the traditional wisdom. Because theory and quantification in economic and social geography have emerged largely out of experience beyond the confines of Latin America, while the authors have spent most of their time and effort in trying to understand this very 'foreign' continent, this book does not depend very much upon accepted geographical theory and laws: instead it is more problem-orientated as it endeavours to describe and explain some of the phenomena and the processes which have resulted in particular spatial structures of society. Some of these at least are, however, worthy of wider attention because of their greater applicability to other parts of the Third World than the spatial structures that have emerged in North America or Western Europe.

But this should not be taken too far. Latin America has not been reproduced elsewhere in the world (except possibly in small parts of Africa and Asia which also came under Spanish or Portuguese influence) and its problems are only in part shared by the other developing continents. Certainly Latin America's collective reaction to its subservient role in the world economy has had implications elsewhere, not least through the work of the Economic Commission for Latin America, whose first Secretary General, the Argentine economist Dr. Raul Prebisch, has had a tremendous influence on economic thought in the non-industrialized world. His work with E.C.L.A. provided much of the initial stimulus for new organizations like the United Nations Industrial Development Organization (U.N.I.D.O.) and the U.N. Commission on Trade and Development (U.N.C.T.A.D.) which, for the first time, brought the views and needs of the world's developing nations into effective focus in international economic and financial affairs. In the more specialized sphere of international economic affairs, that of the world petroleum industry, one has also seen the same kind of 'spill-over' effect of Latin American experience into other parts of the world. The transfer of power in the world oil industry from the international oil companies to the oil-producing countries owes much to the precedents set by countries like Chile and Mexico which took over or controlled the activities of the major American and British oil companies many years ago. Moreover, the attempts by Venezuela in the 1960s to control the rate of oil production so as to maintain prices provided the background to the efforts after 1971 by the other main oil producers in the Middle East and elsewhere to do the same at the general international level. In co-operation with Venezuela through O.P.E.C., their success in achieving all-round higher prices for their oil after 1973 far exceeded expectations.

In other respects, however, Latin America's experience is specific rather than general and thus not particularly relevant to the rest of the Third World. Perhaps Latin America's early political independence from the European metropolitan powers left it too exposed to the might of the United States at a time when there was no countervailing power in the world economic and political system. This political misfortune for Latin America was compounded by the fact of its location vis à vis the United States which assumed that the tenuous continuity of the land mass called the Western Hemisphere, and its physical separation from the world of Europe, Africa and Asia, somehow gave it the right to dictate, both in general and in detail, what was and what was not allowed throughout the region. Elsewhere in the Third World the continued role of European powers through to a period when much of their own economic and political life had been 'socialized', in one form or another, perhaps made the colonial relationships much less definitive and has perhaps even resulted in a greater degree of 'enlightenment' about the political, social and economic organization of society amongst the local élites who eventually took over responsibility for the well-being of their nations. The continuing interest of European powers in their colonies elsewhere in the world paradoxically gave the latter some protection against the United States' one-eyed view of the world and its fixation on the way in which society had to be organized. Equally important, it gave the colonies special economic protection and/or other advantages through such devices as Commonwealth Preference and the French and Dutch economic unions. Latin America has made many efforts to get the United States to agree to similar arrangements in the organization of its trading relationships with the developing parts of the continent—but with virtually no success to date.

But these differences between Latin America and the rest of the Third World compound another set of differences emerging out of contrasting historical and cultural backgrounds. As is shown in the next chapter, most of Latin America has a population which is European or quasi-European in origin so that the non-European elements are relatively unimportant, except in a few nations mainly in the Andes—and even there the European minorities are socially and politically dominant. Thus, the languages of Latin America are international in significance; the dominant religion is one with its roots and most of its other adherents in Europe; sporting activities are dominated by European-style games, and spending patterns and social structures such as the family are recognizably European. In all this, and more besides, Latin America may be distinguished from most of the other countries of the Third World in both Africa and Asia where indigenous cultures have either strongly reasserted themselves over the superficial Europeanness of the colonial period or are in the process of doing so. In other words, European styles and European values are no longer dominant in such countries and one wonders if the pathway to 'development' spelled out by European pioneers has much relevance, particularly when the contrasts are further sharpened by the immensity of the rural population problem in countries like India, Pakistan and Indonesia.

Throughout Latin America these doubts are much less strong and, in general, the student of the continent's economic and social affairs will feel that development is going to emerge, or, indeed, is emerging already, along very familiar lines. Perhaps, in fact, there is some evidence of too much simplistic 'aping' of European and North American-style development forms and processes, but this seldom seems *entirely* inappropriate: merely somewhat out of place and likely to be moulded to fit the style, requirements, and characteristics of the Latin American country wherein they are emerging, in many cases very quickly, within a rapid process of development and change. In other words, the economic and social 'problems' of Latin America seem likely to be solvable within the general framework of methods and techniques that have evolved elsewhere. Given a continuation of expansion in the Western world's economy, such methods and techniques could, within the time-period of the rest of this century, take most of the countries of Latin America outside the framework of the 'Third World' and into the world of the more developed nations; in terms, at least, of the creation of mass consumption economies. Meanwhile, however, there are great, even if not overwhelming, problems that the continent faces in many different ways in the organization of human (and humane) societies.

This book is concerned with the contribution which specifically geographical analysis can make to the understanding of Latin America and its problems. Thus, it is concerned with the following kinds of issues. First, as has already been pointed out, one of the important features of most Latin American countries is that they are generally large and normally have sizeable areas within their national territory that constitute largely unoccupied resource frontiers. The impact of this feature on national political, social and economic policies is primarily a study in applied geography. In spite of this there are few other books which have approached the study of Latin America with this specifically geographical viewpoint in mind. Second, the analysis of urban patterns in Latin America has, likewise, received only passing attention from historians and historical geographers, and little research effort to date has been directed towards analysing the socio-geographical organization of Latin American cities or to comparing the processes discovered to be at work with those known to have been important in European and Anglo-American urban centres. Third, and similarly, analysis of the general aspects of the spatial structure of the Latin American economy on a continental scale has not previously been presented. Such analysis forms the second part of this book which, it is hoped, succeeds in providing a framework around which many more studies of differences in economic growth between regions within developing countries will be attempted.

To the geographer Latin America is not simply a vast world region, but is also one that offers an intellectual challenge: the challenge of seeking to achieve a satisfying level of understanding of the spatial aspects of Latin American economies and societies. The authors hope that this book will contribute to such understanding. But Latin America also presents the geographer, in common with other social scientists, with the challenge of a variety of problems, the solution of which will improve the lot of many people. There are no solutions in this book: but, hopefully, some ideas from which solutions could eventually emerge.

Bibliographical Notes

Familiarity by the readers with the basic geography of Latin America such as can be gained from traditional regional geography texts is assumed. The following brief selection of books in English is intended to indicate how any deficiency in that respect can be overcome, whilst some of the other literature mentioned will be a useful guide to the Latin American scene, in more general terms.

One of the finest regional geography textbooks ever written in the English language is PRESTON JAMES' *Latin America*, 4th Edition (Odyssey, New York, 1969). It is a book which has inspired countless students to a greater interest in the region. More recently, a text concerned specifically with the northern part of Latin America, ROBERT C. WEST and JOHN P. AUGELLI's *Middle America: its Lands and Peoples*, 2nd Edition (Prentice Hall, Englewood Cliffs, New Jersey, 1975) has been published and widely acclaimed. Its treatment of historical aspects and settlement evolution is superior to that of James, although it is not particularly strong in dealing with aspects of economic geography. H. BLAKEMORE and C. T. SMITH (EDS.), *Latin America: Geographical Perspectives* (Methuen, London, 1971) is a book of essays on different parts of the continent by a group of authors with special regional interests. It provides a useful supplement to the above mentioned books as most of the essays are essentially general surveys which pick out main strands in the regional geography of particular countries or groups of countries. However, the essays by ROBINSON, GALLOWAY and CROSSLEY also provide new interpretations of the areas with which they deal. More specifically on matters economic and social is J. P. COLE, *Latin America: an Economic and Social Geography*, 3rd Edition (Butterworths, London, 1976). This surveys the main features of the geography of each country's economy and society and is useful as a reference book for 'chasing up the facts'—as well as for the slightly unusual treatment it accords to problems of space and geographical connectivity, etc. One textbook that is both readable and has adopted a usefully distinctive approach is ALAN GILBERT's *Latin American Development* (Penguin, Harmondsworth, 1974). Gilbert focuses particularly on regional growth and development and is concerned with the government of development; he provides a valuable synopsis of a great deal of information but lacks a clear sense of the political forces that control development.

For students of Latin America in general and for browsers in libraries the large volume edited by CLAUDIO VELIZ, *Latin America and the Caribbean: a Handbook* (A. Blond, London, 1968), is still invaluable as background reading even though it is now over ten years old in its treatment of the issues. It contains a large number of essays about each Latin American country and about a variety of topics of importance. Thus there are articles on the cinema, architecture, football and music as well as about inflation, foreign policies and peasants, inter alia. There are not many books that appeal to the general reader on social and political problems but the English translation of JACQUES LAMBERT, *Latin America: Social and Political Institutions* (University of California Press, Berkeley, California, 1968) is full of insight and is intellectually stimulating. More readily available are the two volumes by MARCEL NIEDERGANG, *The Latin American Republics* (Penguin Books, London, 1976). For many years the author was the Latin American correspondent of *Le Monde*—generally considered to be the only Western European newspaper which has taken a continuing, serious interest in the continent. There are two small books for quick reading that provide a good jumping-off point for further study. One is STEPHEN CLISSOLD's *Latin America: a Cultural Outline* (Hutchinsons, London, 1965) which tells interestingly about the continent and its people and which, for instance, refers to Latin American literature that aids understanding of the continent. It includes a list of English translations of some of the more important works in Latin American literature. The second is GEORGE PENDLE's *A History of Latin America* (Penguin Books, Harmondsworth, 1966). This gives an evening's reading on the history of the continent in an engaging way.

This book will be read and used almost exclusively in the English speaking world and amongst groups with little or no knowledge of the Spanish or Portuguese (or, indeed, other) languages. For this reason nothing in any language other than English has been listed here though the authors themselves are indebted to a range of contributions by Latin American, European and French Canadian authors. Similarly only literature in the English language has been included in the bibliographies at the end of each chapter. Those bibliographies are meant to be used so they do try to indicate a selection of additional literature that readers will either find stimulating and/or essential to an understanding of the issues concerned.

PART I

Major Themes in the Social Geography of Latin America

by

D. A. PRESTON

CHAPTER 2

Human Groups and Their Landscapes

Introduction

The human population of Latin America is markedly similar to that of both Western Europe and Anglo-America. This is particularly true of the cities which are similar in size and in the ethnic variety of their inhabitants to those elsewhere. In no sense is the quality of life for the middle and upper strata of the urban population markedly inferior to that in European and Anglo-American cities. There are also marked similarities in tastes and in aspirations for such urban dwellers although the structure of employment is not the same. Differences between urban populations are as great within Anglo-America and Western Europe as they are between either of these areas and Latin America. The Anglo-Saxon and Latin population differences in Europe may indeed be more pronounced than any comparable differences in Latin America.

The so-called mañana attitude with which many English speakers characterize Latin America is largely the invention of impatient and ignorant foreigners, unable and unwilling to understand that not all the world does business and takes decisions in the same way as themselves. Latin Americans, to their credit, are almost invariably courteous and often find North Americans and northern Europeans arrogant, brusque and discourteous in their dealings with foreigners.

In attempting to understand the relations between human groups in Latin America and the landscapes that they have made, the most important characteristic to remember is that all of Latin America has in the past been governed by foreign, European, powers and that even today the majority of the continent does not enjoy full control over its economic and political life which is dominated to varying degrees by the U.S.A., U.S.S.R., Britain, France and the Netherlands. It is in this sense that Latin America has more in common with Africa than with Europe, for they share a common past of colonial domination. This past and the present reality of life in Latin America suggests that, in this chapter, we should be concerned with the role that different social groups, sharing common values, play in relation to their subordination to outside influences.

Despite the process of external domination for the past 480 years we believe that important differences between regions and even nations in Latin America are embodied in the social and cultural characteristics of their inhabitants. The two parts of the island of Hispaniola, for example, have a common history of colonial oppression and both have been occupied by the U.S.A., but their most striking difference is in the predominant hispanic mestizo population of the Dominican Republic and the almost completely Afro-American French-speaking population of Haiti.

The patterns of settlement and the distribution of population do not greatly affect the domination, social, political and economic, of the city by the metropolis, the town by the city, and the hamlet by the town. Control is exercised down the settlement hierarchy and although Latin America may be legitimately studied through an examination of the methods by which such domination is exercised we prefer to analyse the major characteristics of the visibly different social and cultural groups. The strongest cultural differences occur indeed among groups which are subject to the oppression of the white and mestizo population—the Indians and the Blacks—and it would be unrealistic and disrespectful not to recognize their cultural distinction.

Political life and economic decision-making are concentrated in urban centres, but predominantly in the largest cities where there is a culturally amorphous proletariat comprising largely immigrant wage-earners living in peripheral informal settlements whose livelihood is often in the informal economic sector, that is, as peddlers, salesmen, providing a variety of services and each person often earning money in many different ways. The nature of urban life for the lowest class in society reduces cultural differences between individuals and groups and the middle sectors, the bourgeoisie, likewise subscribe to norms of behaviour that are Latin American but which are similar to those of Anglo-American middle-class society. A substantial part of such people work for companies or institutions where foreign influences are predominant. By contrast in rural areas such influence, though important, is indirect and the individuality of human groups at a community and regional level is both more noticeable and more highly valued. Local values may still predominate rather than those of similar people in metropolitan and foreign centres, despite the dissemination of alien urban values by the process of rural schooling directed by school teachers from the cities. In this chapter, therefore, we shall look at the human ingredients of Latin America and try to show how each of the major cultural populations has created a distinctive cultural landscape.

The Amerindians

The Americas were peopled later than other large continents. When Man entered North America, at least 25,000 years ago, the Pleistocene Ice Age had finished and Man was clearly distinct from other ape-like creatures. He was, however, little more than a flint-chipping hunter when he crossed into the New

World from Asia by way of the Bering Straits which were then largely land because the sea level was lower at that time. Early sites of man's activities have been discovered in southern Chile that were occupied as early as 8800 B.C., which would suggest a relatively rapid rate of travel southwards. But the population grew very slowly and by the time of the Spanish Conquest the population density of the Americas was still low. Only southern Mexico and the central Andes had more than ten persons per square kilometre.

The Americas, then, are noted for having been occupied at a relatively late stage of human evolution and for having a generally low population density. In addition, all the New World centres of advanced civilization were in Latin America rather than in Anglo-America and they also generally developed later than in the Old World. Mountain areas are particularly important in this respect for they provide a variety of habitats for plants and animals. In a dozen miles, down a steeply sloping valley, one can move from the limit of cultivation, where even coarse high-altitude grasses seem to have difficulty in growing, to cloud forest where the trees are laced with mosses and plant life seems abundant and exuberant. The abundance of regions offering such variations in the tropical areas of the Americas allowed early inhabitants of the American mountain areas the opportunity to experiment with a wide variety of plants and to grow those varieties that they believed most useful for food and clothing. The plants that were domesticated included maize, kidney and lima beans, squashes *(cucurbitae)*, tomatoes, capsicum (peppers), white potatoes and a variety of fruits including the pineapple.

These distinctively American crops were not only important to farmers in the New World. Travellers brought seeds back to Europe in the sixteenth century and, within a short time, many of the crops became important in the agricultural economy of Europe. The potato spread rapidly in the cool moist parts of northern Europe and in some places became a staple crop within 200 years. Tobacco and maize were likewise New World imports for which a demand developed that resulted in their being grown in many parts of southern Europe. Maize in particular spread rapidly in the Old World and had reached China by the 1570s.

Besides these achievements in the use of the plant and animal world, the Amerindians in the two main centres of civilization—Central and Southern Mexico and the Central Andes—also developed the arts of astronomy, weaving and modelling to an advanced degree as any visit to the Latin American collection of a major museum will demonstrate.

The most important changes in the pattern of life for the native population of the whole continent resulted from the arrival of the Spanish and later the Portuguese. The most dramatic effect of the Conquest was not a result of the new ways of the lords and masters of the land but rather of the diseases that they brought with them. The native people did not have the resistance to European diseases that the conquerors had acquired as a result of generations of contact with them. Measles, smallpox, influenza and typhus caused large numbers of deaths and the valley of Mexico was ravaged by a smallpox epidemic even as early as 1520, before the conquest of the area was complete. The population also suffered losses through the battles that accompanied the conquest and such events as the civil wars in Peru (1535–68) cost many indigenous lives. Conditions in the mines developed by the Spaniards in Mexico and Peru were responsible for many deaths. Forced labour used for public works also resulted in a high death rate. It has been estimated that over 85 per cent of the population of Middle America was wiped out in the period 1519–1650. Estimates for population change in the other densely populated area, the Andes, are little more than informed guesses but it does seem likely that the population declined there too and recent estimates suggest that 70 per cent of the population of the Peruvian lowlands may have died off within 50 years of the Conquest.

Despite the sharp decline in the Indian numbers in the main population centres of Latin America during the early colonial period the Indian still remains the predominant human group in large areas. The Indians of the tropical forest lowlands were less affected by the Conquest and many, indeed, scarcely knew of it. The most important changes for the lowland Indians came during the nineteenth and twentieth centuries with the exploitation of the forests for special commodities such as rubber and the colonization of the temperate lowlands of Argentina, Uruguay and Chile by European immigrants.

At the present time the most noticeable Indian areas are in the highlands of Latin America. Figure 2–1 indicates in which zones they predominate. While the Indian areas of the highlands are relatively well known, those of the forested lowlands are much less populated and the Indian areas correspondingly difficult to identify. A major difficulty in delimiting the areas of Indian population is in the definition of what constitutes an Indian. In some areas a person who wears a poncho, short trousers and native sandals in the fields will wear a suit, tie and shoes to attend a meeting in the capital, and most national censuses have abandoned questions about use of native languages. Indian migrants often can scarcely be recognized working in a gang on a construction site. In principle, however, Indians occupy the lowest social stratum and live in the less desirable and less accessible places save where they form the majority of the rural population. In the forested lowlands Indians are scarce and confined to the more inaccessible areas or live in pockets of forest to which their government has confined them. Their place in society is even more marginal than that of the highland Indian and because of this greater degree of isolation many are unable through illiteracy and lack of Spanish to have any effective contact with national governments. Their births and deaths are unrecorded and voting rights in local and national elections negligible.

The social place of the Indian is distinctive. In those countries such as Guatemala, Ecuador, Peru, and Bolivia where Indians predominate in the rural areas, the term *indio*, or one of its many variants, is pejorative. The rural people are spoken of as being 'only Indians', or 'poor Indians' and children are told not to

Figure 2–1. Distribution of racial groups in Latin America

behave like an Indian. They occupy the lowest place in the social scale. It is customary for people who appear to be of mixed blood, to deny any recent Indian ancestry. To remark that a person, such as a government minister, looks very Indian, is to cast doubt on his virtue, honesty, manhood and respectability.

In a country such as Mexico, where Indians form maybe 60 per cent of the population and where considerable national self-confidence exists, there has developed a pro-Indian feeling which tends to glorify the Indian cultural heritage at the expense of the Spanish. This does not always mean that Indians as a present-day group are necessarily highly esteemed, they may be referred to as being but a pale shadow of the 'noble savages' that existed once upon a time, but the ideal (however unrealistic) of Indianness *(indigenismo)* is nonetheless real.

It is possible to portray a very gloomy picture of the role of the Indians in Latin America. They are almost exclusively agricultural people, and thus where onerous land tenure systems exist it is more likely to be Indians who are bought and sold with the land rather than mixed-blooded *(mestizo)* people. But there is an increasing range of opportunities for Indians to leave their traditional environment and find paid employment, particularly in small towns and cities. In some areas, such as near Otavalo in Imbabura Province, Ecuador, the Indians have remained as owner-occupiers of their land, have engaged in small-scale textile manufacturing and sell a proportion of the goods themselves. (Plate I.) They have maintained their traditional dress even though some travel by bus, lorry, or even plane as far afield as Rio de Janeiro and Caracas selling scarves and shawls. At least one pop-group in Ecuador is composed of Otavalo Indians! In Bolivia, the Revolution of 1952 together with large-scale agrarian reform has resulted in the virtual abandonment of the term Indian for the rural population and instead it is now referred to as peasant *(campesino)*. In many places this rather dramatic change of nominal status has been accompanied by some degree of social progress.

Afro-Americans

Africans were among those who were first to set foot in the New World in the period after the first voyage of Columbus, for negroes accompanied Balboa when he discovered the Pacific and Cortés when he entered Mexico. Before the Conquest the Spanish and especially the Portuguese had contact with African slaves. The Portuguese had traded along the West African coast since the early fifteenth century and the first African slaves were brought to Lisbon in the 1440s. Slavery was a human condition to which the Spanish and the Portuguese were accustomed, and their attitude towards slaves in the Iberian colonies was more liberal and relaxed than that of the Dutch and British in their possessions in the Caribbean and North America. The Portuguese in particular often allowed their slaves more opportunities to gain their freedom and the interbreeding of Portuguese and Africans proceeded rapidly in Brazil.

Imports of blacks from Africa were made necessary by the decline in native population already referred to, by the general scarcity of native population in the lowlands, and by the labour demands of the plantations and mines that became established as the colonies developed. Although there was plentiful Indian labour to be had in the uplands there were difficulties in exploiting it on a very large scale. The Spanish Crown and the Church were concerned with protecting the indigenous population and although their legislation was only partly effective, as witnessed by the evidence of brutal treatment provided by Bartolomé de las Casas, the exploitation of the Indians was controlled. Few such Christian thoughts extended to Africans. They were used in large numbers on the estates of the Religious Orders, and the Jesuits were probably the owners of the largest numbers of slaves in the Americas.

They had many uses besides those as labourers in mines and plantations. Many were personal servants and bodyguards and others were bought because of their special skills. Some of the Africans were metalworkers more skilled than any that existed in Europe of that period and were purchased to make metalware which was sold. Slaves were expensive; the heavy losses on the voyage from Africa and the low reproduction rate of slaves in the new environment resulted in high prices at all the slave markets. Perhaps curiously, much of the profit from the slave trade went not to the merchants of Seville, Cádiz, or Lisbon but to traders from Britain and the Low Countries. From 1492 until the ending of the slave trade it is thought that between 5 and 8 million Africans were brought to Latin America. The majority of slaves were brought from Angola and the Congo and included a wide variety of tribes. The mixing involved during the capture of tribesmen, the transport to the slave market, sale, transport to the New World, and their resale at least once more, ensured that slaves from the same tribes were seldom able to keep together and this resulted in a loss of much of their native culture in the course of a single generation. What African traits remained were a mixture of half-forgotten practices and beliefs from a wide range of tribes, in particular from those most recently arrived in the New World. Their religions were more resilient and in Brazil witch-doctors practised in many areas where there were slaves; young freedmen were sent from Brazil back to Africa to be trained in the secret arts and to return to the New World as *bona fide* practitioners of witchcraft. Slaves and free Africans had their own organizations which arranged religious ceremonies.

The main areas where intensive lowland agriculture was developed after 1550 in the New World were those to which the largest numbers of Africans were imported; these included N. E. Brazil, the Caribbean, and to a lesser extent the Caribbean and Pacific Coasts of Venezuela, Colombia, Ecuador and Peru. The Africans spread inland from these areas and escaped and shipwrecked slaves colonized some of the more remote zones, such as the Pacific coasts of Colombia and the province of Esmeraldas, Ecuador. The Caribbean coast of Central America was colonized sporadically by the British in the seventeenth and eighteenth centuries and their African slaves remained, but the present African complexion of the population originates more from British West Indian workers who came to work on banana plantations and those who spread out into neighbouring areas after having worked on the Panama Canal. In the Caribbean, Jamaica, Haiti and the small islands of the Lesser Antilles all have a predominantly black population as a relic of their colonial past.

Initial settlement in the larger Caribbean islands during the fifteenth century was exclusively by the Spanish, and their interests in the area were associated with the hope of finding precious metals. When what minerals there were had been exhausted by the middle of the sixteenth century, attention turned to the growing Empire of the American mainland. The shortage of labour that resulted from the virtual disappearance of the native population on the islands as a result of disease had made agriculture there unattractive.

After 1620 the attention of the British, Dutch and French turned to the Caribbean, in particular to the eastern Caribbean islands unoccupied by Spain. By 1640 most of the smaller islands were occupied by one or other of these three European nations. In 1640 large plantations based on the cultivation of sugar were established in Barbados and, based on the import of African slaves, this land-use system spread to many Caribbean islands. By the end of the eighteenth century Africans outnumbered Europeans by 5:1.

In Brazil, early colonial agricultural development on the north-east coast, centred around São Salvador and Recife, was based, as in the Caribbean, on sugar cane plantations and African slave labour. Africans were imported in large numbers for sale in São Salvador after 1538 and in Recife after 1574.

The largest single concentration of blacks in Latin America is in the old heartland of Brazil in the North East. By the eighteenth century settlement, and with it slaves, had spread south towards Rio and west into Minas Gerais. During the last 75 years, among the large numbers of people moving to the growing urban and industrial centres, there have been many blacks. As. As a result the areas in Brazil with the heaviest concentration of blacks are in the large cities and on the north-east coastal agricultural area.

Although the negroes were imported as slaves, their relations with other inhabitants of the continent are quite distinct from those that have developed in Anglo-America. Escaped slaves impressed the forest Indians by their size, colour and powerful magic. The shipwrecked slaves who settled in the forest region of north-western Ecuador and the Chocó of Colombia lost little time in organizing the local Indians to work for them. On the other hand freedmen were common in all Latin American cities and slaves were able to obtain positions of moderate power in many of the colonies. At the present time, although it is true to say that the colour problem is not as acute in Latin America as elsewhere, it is unrealistic to ignore the fact that racial discrimination exists. Even in Brazil, where a greater degree of racial harmony exists than in many areas, the working class people of the north-east are predominantly black and skin colour lightens with ascending social class.

The contribution of Africans to the Latin American landscape is variable. The plantation as an institution and as a land tenure system was developed by Europeans, although based on the use of African labour. The slaves did introduce some African plants that are now used widely, particularly in the Caribbean. These included the congo bean, okra, millet, and the mango. Vacant land is widely regarded by Latin American blacks as available for agriculture, and squatting is a common form of land occupation in the Caribbean. Some writers believe this to reflect native African attitudes to vacant land.

Following the breakdown of the slave-based society, starting at the end of the eighteenth century, many negroes left the coastal plantations, took to the hills, and established themselves there on unoccupied but poor land as farmers.

In their music and regligious beliefs the Africans have profoundly influenced Latin America. Some Latin American dance rhythms, such as the samba, derived from the quizomba of Angola, are in fact of African origin and the use of drums in the music of lowland Latin America is indicative of African influence. The black Caribbean and Brazil are still areas where African-derived religious beliefs flourish. Such beliefs, too, are not confined to the lower classes and many maintain that a former President of Haiti owed the length of his despotic rule to his communion with the gods of Voodoo.

Although the land-use patterns of many of the Caribbean islands bear the imprint of the colonial masters more than of the present, predominantly black, inhabitants, the distinctive cultural tradition of the black Americans has contributed much to the complex civilization that we describe as Latin American.

The Europeans and Others

The influence of the Europeans, and smaller numbers of settlers from the Middle East and Asia, on Latin America has been greatest during the colonial period and then from 1850 to 1940.

The Spanish conquered Latin America remarkably quickly and with very few men. In a couple of generations most of the continent north of 30°S was explored, albeit cursorily. Even the length of the Amazon was traversed, although by accident. The landscape was transformed as a result partly of the changes in population that resulted, but most of all by the foundation of new towns and by the development of mining. The native population continued their traditional systems of agriculture except where supplies were needed for towns, mines, or for export.

The number of colonists was small. Between 1493 and 1519, 5481 settlers were recorded in the archives in Seville, a further 13,262 in the period 1520–39, and a total of 54,881 from 1492 until 1600. These included administrators, clergy, soldiers, merchants and many others seeking their fortune in the new world. Relatively few of these people were bent on founding agricultural settlements. The Portuguese in Brazil were a notable exception to this rule and the settlement of Spaniards in agricultural areas in the Central Plateau of Costa Rica and in Antioquia in Colombia was unusual and gave rise to a land tenure pattern of small, family farms that occurs rarely in those parts of Latin America settled during the colonial period. Cattle and sheep herding as developed particularly in central and northern Mexico caused great changes in the rural landscape, as did the concentration of the native population into towns, *reducciones*, which the Spanish Crown ordered for their more efficient control. The Church was instrumental in changing the settlement pattern of large areas. Major examples of this are the northern regions of Mexico and the centre of South America, where the Jesuits had large *reducciones* from Bolivia to Brazil. The old culture of the New World was in many places, particularly on rich agricultural land and near the major towns, supplanted almost totally by new things from Europe.

The orderly grid-pattern towns founded during the sixteenth and seventeenth centuries were dominated by graceful churches built with Indian labour and decorated by newly Christianized native artists. Roads were scarred with the tracks of Spanish carts drawn by mules or oxen introduced from Europe and the upper classes of the local inhabitants even affected Spanish-style dress. The degree of cultural change may be assessed by this description of the Indians of the Chota Valley, Ecuador, written probably in about 1580, some years after the Conquest. 'All the Indians that have plots of coca have horses which they ride like Gentlemen and they come and go to the fields on horseback; and most of them have oxen with which they cultivate their plots and very few of them do not have a pair of oxen; they are great butchers, they like eating meat (beef) . . .'

At the beginning of the nineteenth century the continent of Latin America was sparsely settled south of a line from Santiago in Chile to São Paulo in Brazil. In southern Chile the warlike Mapuche (Araucanian) Indians prevented settlement until 1877 and the Indian menace rendered settlement in Argentina south of the humid Pampas, and south of the Mendoza–Buenos Aires highway, hazardous without Indian approval.

During the nineteenth century though, the pattern of world trade changed with the industrialization of western Europe and the attendant rapid growth of its cities. There were political upheavals too: the abortive 1848 Revolutions, as well as major catastrophes such as the Irish potato famine, which allied with a grossly unjust land ownership system, denuded rural Ireland of a sizeable part of its population. On the one hand, industrial and urban development demanded supplies of raw materials and food, and on the other there were powerful forces uprooting people and encouraging them to migrate to new lands. Not all the European emigrants were rural folk: the Pogroms in Russian Poland later in the century sent Jewish people, largely from the towns, to the growing cities of the New World as well as to some of the growing industrial towns of western Europe.

The nineteenth century, for most countries of mainland Latin America, was the beginning of the Republican period. The yokes of Spain and Portugal were thrown off and new respnsibilities were undertaken. One of these was the effective occupation of the newly delimited national territory. The Brazilian Emperor Pedro I, for example, pursued an active immigration policy and as a result of his encouragement some 20,000 Germans came to Brazil in the period 1824–59.

Immigration into Latin America can conveniently be divided into three categories: those who were colonists, attempting to settle in previously only sparsely populated areas; those who came primarily to meet demands for labour in the booming rural areas; and those who came to set up businesses or seek work in the towns. Those attracted under the first category included religious minority groups, such as the Mennonites, who sought isolated areas in which their society could develop unaffected by the stresses induced by close proximity to modern urban developments. The Mennonites settled the western Paraguayan Chaco and part of eastern Bolivia, and the Welsh settled in the Argentinian Patagonia. Others attracted to colonize new areas were German-speaking people and some Italians who pushed back the frontier of settlement in both South Chile and the southern states of Brazil. Many of these settlements only introduced the immigrants to a new set of hardships that replaced those which had originally caused them to leave their homelands. Few people became rich and many fled to the towns for greater security and a better life. The ports of entry, such as Buenos Aires, and growing commercial centres like São Paulo provided a wealth of opportunities and attracted both new arrivals and disillusioned farmers.

Most immigrants who came to Latin America came to work either on existing farms or in the cities. In the Caribbean the gap in the labour force left by the freeing of the slaves was filled by indentured labourers, largely from India and Java. In Peru, Chinese, and later Japanese, were employed in the canefields. In most cases, many of the workers returned home as their contract provided, but a proportion remained, normally leaving agriculture and setting up stores in local towns. Others bought land and developed intensive horticulture quite unlike the existing agricultural systems. The Japanese in the Chancay Valley in coastal Peru, for example, became pig breeders on an extensive scale. In Southern Brazil too, the Japanese immigrants had an important impact on the rural landscape, introducing both new crops and a new, more intensive, agriculture.

In the newly-growing coffee belt of São Paulo and the Pampas of Argentina agricultural expansion was made possible by Italian immigrants who worked as sharecroppers or labourers, but never had the chance to buy land. When fresh areas were opened for expansion many of the labourers moved out to farm new land as colonists, but large numbers congregated in the main cities. Besides the Italians and the Germans, a number of other immigrant groups had an influence out of all proportion to their numbers. The assistance that Britain gave to some of the newly-emerging Republics, partly as a result of the enlightened foreign policy of George Canning, made British immigrants welcome and in Argentina, in particular, British investment was involved in a wide range of activities, including railways, banking, ranching and meat packing. It is no coincidence that two of the upper-class suburbs of Buenos Aires bear the same names as their counterparts in London at that time: Ranelagh and Hurlingham.

Some immigrants specialized in certain occupations. For all their lack of previous experience, Irish immigrants in Argentina found sheep herding a very profitable occupation and the number engaged as shepherds increased from some 4000 in 1852 to 35,000 in 1870 and they were responsible for more than half the Argentinian wool clip. Levantine people are noteworthy in many Latin American capitals and they are frequently involved in the hotel industry, manufacturing and running small general stores. La Paz, Bolivia, for example, has a large cotton mill owned by a Sr. Saïd. There are shops with names such as Galería Beirut and a flourishing Club Libanés on the main street. German-speaking Jewish people are responsible for many jewellery shops, restaurants and money exchanges in Latin American cities.

The contribution of the Europeans to Latin America can be seen at two levels. Firstly, the whole development pattern of the continent was moulded by the Spanish and Portuguese during the colonial period, and the towns and cities still bear witness to this. The rural population was reorganized to work on large estates for the benefit of the ruling class. During the nineteenth century, however, new development was achieved much more with the aid of foreign immigrants and foreign capital in Argentina, Uruguay and Southern Brazil and, to a lesser extent, in the cities of the rest of the continent. The development of Caracas, for example, is closely related to the wealth acquired from Venezuelan oil. The new Americans brought special skills, enthusiasm, and a determination to start a new and successful life that materially improved the fortunes of both they themselves and the countries whose citizens they had become. Their impact on the landscape was complex for they came from so many countries. No town in Peru is without a Chinese restaurant, and no city in Argentina is without its Italian ice-cream. Traffic in Porto Alegre in Brazil is endangered by the number of bicycles: reminiscent of Germany or Scandinavia.

As a result of the variety of origins of the new settlers, and often because in any one area there were settlers from several countries, there are few areas in Latin America whose rural landscape bears the imprint of people of a single national origin. More often the landscape—pattern of settlement, land use, land tenure and territorial organization—does appear to be influenced by Dutch, French, German or Japanese cultural traits but is still distinctively Latin American with an added ingredient. In Southern Brazil or Southern Chile rural house styles in some places may seem thoroughly Germanic, for many of the first European settlers came from German-speaking parts of Europe, but they grow maize alongside potatoes and they are subject to Brazilian and Chilean law: their children speak Spanish or Portuguese and are similar to other young people in Latin America. A French geographer who studied foreign settlement in southern Brazil was indeed more impressed by the similarities of the settlements and agricultural organization of people with different cultural origins than by their differences. In the islands of the French Caribbean (Martinique and Guadeloupe) the problems that beset the population are essentially those common to most of the Caribbean islands, and the agriculture is broadly similar to other Caribbean islands. The greatest differences are linguistic. The large towns are visibly French influenced. The majority of the vehicles are French. The town houses are unmistakably French, but down on the waterfront and in the vegetable market the scene reverts once more to being distinctively Caribbean rather than French.

The most important feature of the Latin American population is its heterogeneity. In few places in Latin America is the rural landscape other than a complex amalgam of varied influences.

The Mixed Groups

Few women came from Europe with the early colonists. Thus the men took Indian women as their wives and mistresses. The product of these unions, people of mixed blood, known by a variety of terms, added a new racial element to the population. Many of them were brought up in the households of the conquerors, others were forgotten and lived with the native population and were absorbed by them. These people of mixed origins became more numerous as time went on, and it was not surprising that they should have acted in many ways as intermediaries between the Spaniards and Indians. In Brazil there was similar free interbreeding between the masters and the slaves, and in the Caribbean too. The charms of half-caste women were said to be far superior to those of either white, Indian, or negro and the brothels of colonial Brazil seem to have always had women of various colours, to cater for all tastes.

A considerable problem faced a person of mixed parentage. He was accepted by neither Indian nor Spanish groups and his place in society was insecure. Particularly during the Colonial Period, even those who appeared to be of pure white parentage would seldom be favoured for a job if a Spanish-born person could be acquired. Likewise a person with very Indian features would seldom achieve status in his own community since his ancestry was known and not respected.

But the population of Latin America is now predominantly non-Indian and people of mixed race predominate in most countries. In part, the increase of this group has not been the result of continued interbreeding but rather of social status replacing racial origin as a means of categorizing people. It is now possible for Indians to come to Lima or Mexico City, cut their hair, learn to speak Spanish in the locally accepted way, dress differently and thus become non-Indian. The terms used to describe people of this social status are varied and with main regional variations in their precise meaning, but *mestizo, cholo,* and, in Yucatan, Guatemala and the rest of Central America east of Mexico, the term *ladino* are the most commonly used.

In general, people belonging to the mestizo group may be generally identified as speaking Spanish, wearing factory-made clothes and being more conscious of being a member of a nation-state than an Indian whose dress is determined by local tradition and who identifies himself most clearly with his ancestral community.

In areas of predominantly Indian population the geographical distribution of mestizo and Indian population is clear. The Indians predominate in the highland rural areas, the mestizo in the towns of the mountains and throughout the coastlands. This is partly because there were originally few Indians on the coastlands but more because the lowlanders seem to have suffered even more than the highland people from new diseases. It was to these areas too that different immigrant groups came to work in the fields or trade in the towns. As a result the coastland people are a much more complicated racial mixture than those in the mountains, for Indians, Chinese, Japanese and Europeans predominate in different localities within the same area.

Where people of different racial origin live in the same area, social position seems to be of greater importance than skin colour or racial type. In this sense a colour bar does not operate. On the other hand, there is a variety of evidence to show that the poorer people tend to be black or have dark skins and the richer to be whiter.

By comparison with North America, however, what racial prejudice does operate is of minor importance. The mixed-blooded people therefore have fewer barriers to social mobility than they have, for example, in the Union of South Africa, and this social mobility has also encouraged a greater degree of geographical mobility.

To indicate the complexity of the racial pattern in a small area it is illuminating to describe the settlements of the Chota valley in northern Ecuador (Figure 2–2). The Chota valley lies at 1800 m in a deep flat-bottomed valley between the eastern and western ranges of the Andes of northern Ecuador. It is traversed by a shallow braided river course which is liable to some flooding. With the aid of earth-lined irrigation channels, water is brought to the sugar cane fields that predominate in the valley bottom. Much of the land is in large estates and the Jesuit fathers imported negroes in the sixteenth century to work on their estates. In one tributary valley of the Chota is a small village, Ambuqui, inhabited by mestizos who have their own smallholdings but have access to little water for irrigation. They are extremely poor and the majority of their houses are of daub and wattle construction with tall thatched roofs, very similar to the houses in the negro villages (Plate III). Apart from the poor mestizos of Ambuqui, all the land in the valley bottom was until recently farmed by negroes working as virtual serfs on large estates. The main market of the valley is in the small mestizo town of Pimampiro, on a high terrace area 450 m above the valley floor. The land around the town is farmed by mestizo smallholders although three estates also exist. Tomatoes are the most important crop. Some dozen kilometres away from Pimampiro, into the hills, are Indian communities where maize is grown. At the market negroes come from the valley and Indians from the hills, and both sell to wholesalers who come from the large towns (Plate IV). They also trade with one another. By contrast with the

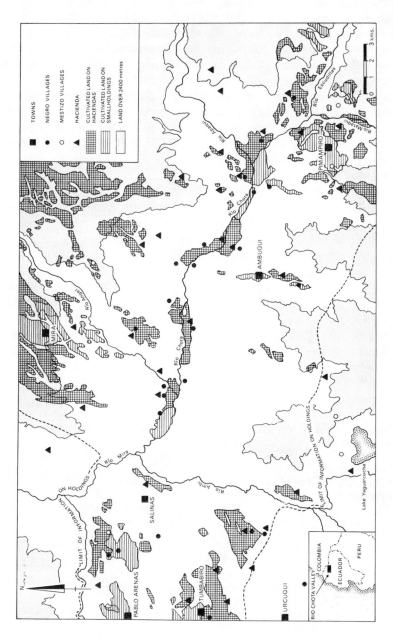

Figure 2–2. The Chota valley region, Ecuador, 1961

poor folk of Ambuqui, the mestizos of Pimampiro are moderately prosperous. In the town there are a dozen or so Indian families and also a few negroes. No form of discrimination is made by the local people between the mestizo negroes and Indians on racial grounds. Thus three distinct ethnic groups live close together, producing different goods but not necessarily differentiated in accord with any pattern that might be expected. Some mestizos are poor farmers, others are rich merchants. Class is more important than race.

Each of the different groups who came to live in Latin America since the last Ice Age came with a different cultural heritage. What can be seen now in the continent is a partial fusion of all who have gone before. It is always dangerous to imagine that the negroes of Bahía, the Chinese of Lima or the Italians of Buenos Aires have recreated in the New World a facsimile of their ancestral environment. Some things they dropped as being inapplicable in the new land, other items they copied from local Indians, and still more were adopted from those who were socially superior to them. What results may still seem distinctively African, Chinese or Italian but what one sees is an amalgam where some elements appear to predominate over others. A Nigerian, Cantonese, or Neapolitan person might indeed be more impressed by the Latin American nature of what he saw rather than its 'foreign' component.

Now, Latin Americans, like most people, are more concerned with social position rather than cultural identity. A peasant in Ecuador aspires to owning a lorry, not to becoming a white man, a Panamanian aspires to being able to buy a car or a television rather than changing his colour, and in this sense race is not an issue in Latin America, however much individuals may sometimes feel that they have been discriminated against because of their facial features or skin colour.

Bibliography

(Only works in English have been included in this and following Bibliographies. These publications will also refer the interested reader to some literature in Spanish and Portuguese which is relevant.)

BENNETT, W. C. and BIRD, J., *Andean Cultural History,* American Museum of Natural History, New York 1964.
A concise, illustrated account of the evolution of the major Andean civilizations. Available in paperback.

WOLF, E. R., *Sons of the Shaking Earth,* University of Chicago Press, Chicago, 1959.
A brilliant, readable account of the social history of Middle America from the arrival of the hunters from Asia to the apogee of the Spanish Empire. Invaluable, stimulating and very relevant to the whole of Latin America. Available in paperback.

STEWARD, J. H. and FARON, L. C., *Native Peoples of South America,* McGraw-Hill, New York, 1959.
Useful summary and updating of the monumental *Handbook of South American Indians.* Excellent chapters of contemporary Indian society.

JEFFERSON, MARK, *Peopling the Argentine Pampas,* American Geographical Society, New York, Research Series No. 16, 1926.
An account of the settling of Argentina by Europeans: of great interest, value and readability.

LEWIS, OSCAR, *Five Families*, John Wiley, New York, 1962; *Children of Sánchez*, Penguin Books, Harmondsworth, 1964.
Pioneering accounts of the life of poor Mexicans as told by themselves. Provide a brilliant but savage view of what life can be like in Mexico. *Five Families* is an account of a day in the life of five Mexican families of different social classes and occupations. *Children of Sánchez* is the Sánchez family's account of their life.

FREYRE, GILBERTO, *The Masters and the Slaves*, Knopf, New York, 1946.
Verbose, extravagant but brilliant analysis of Brazilian society indicating much of the role of the African in Brazilian life.

GILLIN, JOHN, 'Mestizo America' in Ralph Linton (ed.), *Most of the World*, Columbia University Press, New York, 1949.
A useful and informative account of the mixed-blooded people and their varied role in Latin America.

MÖRNER, MAGNUS, *Race Mixture in the History of Latin America*, Little, Brown, Boston, 1967.
Excellent introductory essays on the human components of Latin America.

BASTIDE, ROGER, *Black America. A study of African Civilizations in the New World*, Duckworth, London, 1971.
Serious study of African influences in the New World centred around religion.

WAUCHOPE, R. (ED), *Handbook of Middle American Indians* (9 vols.), University of Texas Press, Austin, 1964 onwards.
Invaluable source material for a study of human populations on Mexico and central America.

CHAPTER 3

Types of Rural Environment

Major Features of the Latin American Rural Environment

In Europe many of the regional variations of the agrarian landscape are the result of sequent occupance by different peoples over several thousand years. In the New World, by contrast, the landscape has been fashioned predominantly as a result of occupation by immigrants from Europe during one, or at the most five, centuries. Despite this comparatively short period of occupation by relatively recent immigrants, the influence of the indigenous pre-Columbian inhabitants on the contemporary rural landscape is important only in a few areas where population densities are low, for example in parts of the Amazon basin.

In many instances the pattern of cultural change is influenced by the physiography. Relief is an important factor in explaining differences from place to place in the density of the population and in material culture and its associated patterns of settlement and land use. The major physical barriers to communication in Latin America—the Andes, the Mexican Sierra Madre and the eastern margins of the Brazilian Plateau—have hindered free movement of people and thus increased the possibility that local and regional cultural differences can exist. In addition these mountains have often given rise to the existence within a hundred kilometres of several very different physical zones. In an hour one can drive from barren high-altitude vegetation at the limit of cultivation, through temperate mountain basins, and then down to arid tropical desert on the coast or to steaming jungle in the continental interior.

There is a very important division in Latin America between traditional and modern forms of social and economic organization and this division can be related to geographical factors. By traditional organization is implied those forms of social organization which place great importance on past practices, where both the family and the community are important units and where respect for the past is an important element of individual attitudes. In traditional communities agriculture has changed little, ancient techniques of cultivation are used, communal land tenure remains in evidence and innovations are treated with suspicion. Traditional economic organization within a community customarily implies a minimum of transactions with outsiders, there being a high degree of self-sufficiency within the community with barter often replacing cash sales and purchases. By contrast, in a more modern rural economy, cash is widely used, a higher proportion of goods is sold and the motives behind many agricultural decisions are commercial. The social organization of a more modern community shows a greater degree of contact with other communities while the norms to which individuals conform are those widely accepted in many different rural areas. The importance of the family as opposed to the community is considerable and, as a result of a greater awareness of changes over a wider area, innovations are less unwelcome.

The division noted between traditional and non-traditional societies is easily recognizable as part of that which differentiates town from country. The same differences can be noted between rural areas and are closely associated with isolation. Physical isolation, distances from markets, or from central urban services, influences the degree to which rural people make use of such services. Rural communities close to a town or city can scarcely not be affected by such proximity. In some cases traditional agriculture, land-use patterns and even land tenure are less susceptible to change because less potential for change exists. Llama herders high in the mountains within ten miles of La Paz can do little else with their land on account of altitude and the low potential for development of the area where they live. Thus both isolation and land capability are associated with the degree to which a community is modern or traditional. This, in turn, is an important influence on the patterns of land tenure and land use as well as the systems of agriculture which are of central interest to geographers studying rural settlement.

It is vital to realize that it is not enough to know that some areas grow maize and others wheat, and that big farms predominate in some areas and smallholdings in others. The understanding of the rural landscape comes from an appreciation of why these areal differences occur and what other related differences there are. While sociologists and anthropologists are centrally concerned with the organization of society and with the nature of interpersonal and intergroup relations, the social geographer is also concerned with society, but most essentially with those elements of society which influence man's use of the land, the form and function of his settlements, and his methods of farming. The rural (and urban) landscape can only be adequately explained in these terms through an understanding of some aspects of social organization. A recurrent Latin American problem, to which a solution can be sought in this way, is that of the co-existence of very different types of farming and settlement in a region which is physically homogeneous.

Areas of advanced commercial agriculture may be juxtaposed with communities of subsistence indigenous agriculture and even in a region so agriculturally renowed as the humid Pampas of Argentina, farms rearing prize Hereford cattle on high-quality artificial pasture may be situated next to large estates with scrub pasture and half-breed cattle of poor quality.

One cannot describe adequately the full range of variation that occurs in Latin American rural areas and a more useful approach to an account of the human geography of these areas is through the construction of a simple classification of types of rural environment that can be recognized throughout the continent.

A Typology of the Rural Environment

Classifications of cultural types have been made by those social scientists who are concerned more with differences in social organization than with the relations between man and the land that he both occupies and exploits. In any geographical classification of the rural environment it is necessary to consider not only the social organization, particularly with reference to the organization of labour and the relations between land owners and their workers, but also land tenure, the economic organizations that are associated with farming and the techniques of agricultural exploitation that are employed by different groups of rural people.

From a consideration of these factors, five types of rural environmental organization can be clearly distinguished:

1. Freeholding rural communities
2. Family farms
3. Estates
4. Industrial plantations
5. The smallest farms

We shall use these five types as a means of indicating the main characteristics of rural settlement in Latin America and thus seek to bring some order to the complexity of the rural scene. It must be understood however that this typology is nothing more than a tool, an aid to the understanding and, by its nature, it can only be used to explain a proportion of the variation in Latin American rural landscapes; some cases doubtless exist of areas which do not match any of these types, but this is a danger inherent in the use of any system of classification.

A. Freeholding Rural Communities

A rural community is a group of people inhabiting an area of variable size whose name is that used to identify the human group. Almost all rural people will tell you not only the name of the locality where they live, but also the name of the larger area and group of families: the community to which they belong.

The distinctive feature of this particular type of rural group is that its individual members are owners of much of the land that they cultivate and are thus freeholders. In addition, the community as a corporate body is also a landowner, since common land also exists that can be used by any or all members of the community, to which they have no claim as individuals but only as members of the community. The freeholding community is distinctive by being, together with the estate, the type of rural settlement with which the greatest degree of conservatism is associated. This notwithstanding, freeholding communities have been increasingly subject to change and very great variations can be observed among them.

Although freeholding communities are typical of areas of Indian population this is not always the case, but, in general, freeholding communities will most frequently be found in areas of highland Indian population (see Figure 2–1). Freeholding communities will also be commonly found in areas peripheral to the main zones of highland Indian population, particularly in the northern and southern Andes of Colombia, Venezuela, Chile and Argentina as well as in highland Middle America and lowland Yucatán.

a. Communal land tenure is rare. Cultivable land is regarded as such a sufficiently valuable commodity that it is almost invariably held by individual families and divided among heirs on the death of the father. Even in those rare instances where cultivated land is owned by the community and divided up and farmed by each person individually and then reverts back to the community after cultivation ceases, there is usually other land that is unquestionably the property of individuals: for example, the houseplot. However, pastureland is more frequently owned by the community as a whole and no-one can claim a right to graze his animals over one area and to exclude the livestock of other people from it. Similarly, water in streams and rivers is often held to be common property, although in practice it seems frequently to be appropriated by a few for their exclusive benefit. Often the exact status of land is difficult to discover if no titles are held either by individuals or by the community. Even if the community does hold documents that define individuals' exclusive rights to land, they do not always help to clarify exactly which land is involved.

Typically the amount of land occupied by each family in the communities is very small and seldom capable of supporting the whole of the family. Some members are thus forced to engage in other activities, such as petty commerce, to supplement their income. This is by no means universally true and in some localities communities have vast areas of relatively poor land, isolated from roads and therefore seldom of interest to the acquisitive individuals who robbed the traditional communities of their lands in so many other areas. In the Central Altiplano of Bolivia, where rainfall scarcely exceeds 200 mm, communities may cover 400 square kilometres and in one community, Escara, it was calculated that an average family would possess 0.46 ha of cultivable land and another 230 ha of scrub where sheep and llamas are grazed. The land here, however, is so poor that even these large areas are barely enough to support a family. Even where land is scarce some individuals may have very much more cultivable land than others.

More recently created tenure forms include the *ejido* communities formed in Mexico after the Revolution of 1910. Of the two types of *ejido* the most common is that where the land is farmed by individuals but where ownership is vested in the community as a whole. Other *ejidos* (only one in twenty) are collective farms in which large fields are maintained where the people work collectively for the benefit of all in common. In socialist Cuba the new land reform has called into existence both state farms, where the State owns the land and employs wage labourers, and collectives, not very unlike the collective *ejido* or the Russian *kolkhoz*.

The systems of land distribution that exist in peasant communities generally tend to ensure that families have parcels of land in areas of different agricultural potential. In Aymara-speaking areas of southern Peru and Bolivia the cultivated areas away from the dwellings are often called *aynokas*. In each of these, every member of the community has several plots of land, some of which will be on good flat alluvial terrain whilst others will be on poorer, sloping, thin-soiled hillsides.

The process of gradual dismemberment of the freeholding communties, which has continued off and on since the colonial period, has resulted in their being now largely confined to areas that are either isolated or of poor soils. Thus in the broad inter-Andean valleys it is not uncommon for the valley bottoms to be occupied by estates and the communities remain clustered on the hillsides. (See Figure 3–1 and Plate V.) In some parts of central Peru, however, the uplands are in estates, and the lowlands are occupied by free communities. As will be seen later, there are a variety of advantages to communities existing close by estates which provide a supply of work opportunities for the poorer freeholders.

b. Self-sufficiency is seldom a goal. It has been previously suggested that in areas of traditional agriculture a high degree of self-sufficiency is common. While this is frequently true, it is important to realize that it is only realistic to compare relative levels of self-sufficiency, for no community can produce all that it needs.

Nor is it realistic to regard self-sufficiency as a goal towards which agriculture and, therefore, land use is oriented, because individuals are concerned primarily with having enough goods to maintain a standard of living appropriate to their status in the community, rather than merely avoiding having to buy or trade goods outside the community. Whether they can be self-sufficient is a function of the land that they have available for agriculture, the extent to which it is physically possible to produce a large proportion of goods needed and the level of their aspirations. Within a community it is axiomatic that some individuals (and families) are more dependent upon cash income than others, although it would be rare to encounter anyone who had no cash income and produced all that was necessary for his subsistence.

Although freeholding communities are distinctive by frequently being very traditionally oriented, they have been increasingly subject to a rising demand for goods produced outside the community. Throughout the highlands of Latin America, radios, factory-made clothes and footwear are now widely purchased,

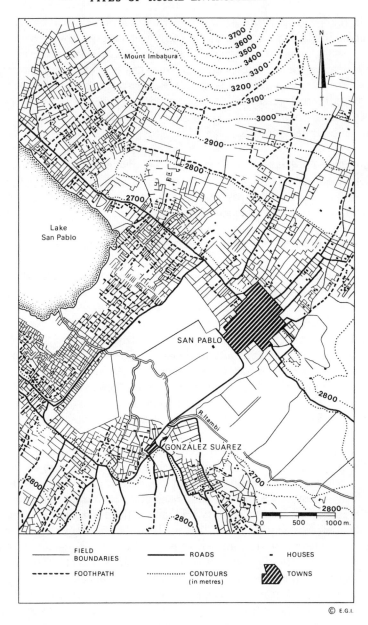

Figure 3–1. Estates and freeholding communities, San Pablo, Ecuador, prior to land reform

while in the flat land of the Altiplano of Peru and Bolivia bicycles are likewise ubiquitous. Some communities, particularly near to large towns, are very much more subject to change than others. Recent research in Bolivia has even suggested that freeholding communities with very little land per family are less traditional than others because shortage of land necessitates seeking alternative sources of income, often through migration. In other more isolated areas however the view of the freeholding community as a repository of traditional values and practices remains substantially correct.

c. Traditional agricultural systems prevail yet change exists. The most striking aspect of the systems of agriculture employed is that they have often been subjected to only minor changes over a long period of time. Traditional crops predominate in the field, whether they be beans, maize and squash as in Central America or potatoes, quinoa and maize as in the Andes. European imports, principally wheat or barley, are often of greatest importance in the estates rather than in the communities.

The land-use patterns however are relatively unrevealing if we seek to use them to differentiate this type of rural occupance from others. The system of agriculture, that is the techniques of cultivation employed, and the sequence of land use in successive years, is what distinguishes this form of rural settlement from others most clearly. In the context of a traditional society there is only limited incentive to vary agricultural techniques. There is a wide range of varieties of the principal crops to suit all conditions. Maize and potatoes in particular should not be thought of as single crops, for each community may use half-a-dozen varieties of each product regularly, and another half-dozen under special circumstances. For example, each variety of potato is known to thrive under a particular set of conditions and a farmer thus has a rich variety of alternative crops available to him. The use of new crops can serve several alternative purposes: to provide for new tastes that a family has developed or to produce a surplus for cash sale or to meet an extra need (e.g. fodder) on the farm. Maximization of production is usually sought within the cultural norms of the community, alternative practices are held to be risky and, unless there is a surplus of production available, new techniques, crops, or methods are unlikely to be employed. Fallowing, for example, is widely practised as a necessity either to avoid soil exhaustion or to conserve moisture or a combination of each. There is evidence which shows that the period of fallowing, which in some parts of Latin America may be as long as 25 years, is also a reflexion of the supply of land. Where there is little available land, fallowing is for a short period and has even disappeared completely; in other areas with plenty of land, fallowing for long periods remains common. But we have already indicated that the view that the freeholding community is the bastion of conservatism is no longer true, particularly in those areas where there is adequate land for experimentation and where contact with the dynamic life of the cities through migration encourages a more modern attitude to farming.

Thus freeholding communities can be found which have turned to new forms of agriculture (often growing vegetables) that have made their members the most prosperous farmers of their region.

d. Communities as social organisms. The role of the community in the organization of agriculture is far from negligible. Where communal lands remain, they are administered by the community or its nominees. Agricultural activities which involve the cultivation of successive fields wherein all families have land, may similarly be communally organized. Families, groups of families, or even the whole community may nominate individuals to guard crops against thieves, encroaching livestock, or even evil spirits. Where communal cultivated land remains it may be cultivated with the labour of the whole community. Individuals are also frequently accustomed to call on relatives and neighbours for labour for harvesting, housebuilding or other major tasks, in return for which the obligation to labour similarly in return is recognized. These ancient systems of working the land may be sometimes supplemented or even replaced by the non-traditional form of hired labour.

Freeholding communities guard their land jealously. An assault on the land of a member by someone from another community is often held to be an attack on the community as a whole and the assaulted family can count on everyone's support. Disputes within the community may be submitted to elected community officials for solution before they are presented to external legal authorities.

Social sub-zones within communities may also be more clearly recognizable than in modern rural societies, and extended families occupying contiguous areas, or groupings within the community, such as moieties, may occupy distinct sections of the community land. In central and southern Peru, as well as in much of highland Bolivia, rural communities are sub-divided into *ayllus*, each occupying separate territory. The ayllus have their own names and even their own subsidiary posts of authority. The farmland of people of each ayllu is usually separate. They are small sub-villages within the community, in many ways like the *capulli* into which the larger villages in central Mexico used to be organized.

A further feature of socio-geographical concern is the mobility of members of these communities. Many writers have viewed traditional peasant or Indian communities as relatively static and subject to little change. It seems now however that although many elements of community life change little, the individuals who make up the community are mobile. In many areas pressure for land has forced some young men to travel far in search of work; heads of families, throughout highland Latin America, are accustomed to travel to lowland areas to work on the sugar or banana plantations to earn money for ceremonies at home such as marriages, or patron saints' days. Slack periods of the year have likewise long been used for trading jouneys, often to exchange local produce for goods from a different climatic zone. More recently urbanward migration has affected many rural areas.

B. Family Farms

The salient characteristic of the foregoing settlement type was the importance of families belonging to a cohesive socio-geographical entity: a community. Family farms however are found in areas where all land is individually owned and where the most important unit of land holding and agricultural exploitation is a farm that is small enough to require normally only the labour of the nuclear family of the operator, that is the farmer, his wife and children. Such a definition does not exclude farm holdings where extra labour is employed at peak periods but its essence is that the use of such extra labour is unusual.

It is also important to realize that differences between farmers are much more adequately expressed by levels of production than by area of land controlled. Thus it is unrealistic to think of a family farm as being of a particular size. In an area of irrigated horticulture one hectare might adequately support a family, while maybe 250 hectares of high-altitude pasture and cultivable land might be necessary to support the same size of family at a similar level of living.

The parts of Latin America where such farms predominate are frequently those that have been effectively colonized within the last hundred years as well as those atypical areas of much older colonization such as the Central Highlands of Costa Rica or the Antioquia area of Colombia. Argentina and Uruguay, as well as the southern states of Brazil, are typically zones much of whose rural population is based on family farms. For example it was estimated that in Argentina in 1960 one-third of all families engaged in agriculture were operators of family farms. Areas of recent colonization are also characteristically formed of largely family-sized farms, in part because colonization is more often carried on by individual families than by corporate groups.

a. Ownership is not the commonest tenure. In Argentina, where family farms are more widespread than elsewhere, as many such farms are operated by non-owners as by the owners themselves. Frequently the pattern of ownership will reflect the excessive concentration of land in the hands of a few families which is common in regions such as the Andes, but this is not necessarily to be seen in the way the land is used. Some landowners prefer to split their large holdings into a number of family farms which are rented, frequently on short leases, to would-be farmers. A considerable variety of forms of lease exists. In some cases the rent is paid in cash, in others in a proportion of the harvest and, in the past, some landlords stipulated the cash crops to be cultivated. Legally tenure is not always secure; occupiers may not have title to the land they farm, or the renters may only have a short lease which discourages investment in improving the land for improved yields in the future.

Family farms are also found in areas where for one or more of a variety of reasons large estates have never developed and where the local population has become less Indian in its cultural attitudes. The areas of family farms in some places may be traced back to grants of land given to common soldiers and other lesser folk during the period following the Spanish Conquest. In the Chancay valley north of Lima, for example, although much good land was broken up into medium-sized estates which were awarded to members of the nobility, who normally chose to reside in Lima, grants of land were made around small towns to people of lesser importance to encourage the development of more middle-class farmers, who would live on the land and farm it themselves.

There is not enough evidence to suggest that this was a widespread occurrence and an alternative course of events to explain this phenomenon could have been the spontaneous settlement of immigrants from the Old World, in the seventeenth and eighteenth centuries, and later fusion with the local Indian population creating a rural population of people of mixed blood. In highland Ecuador, the northernmost province of Carchi and the southernmost one of Loja are predominantly inhabited by mestizos occupying small and middle-sized holdings. Both areas are sufficiently far from Colonial centres that there might have been little demand on the part of the nobility for grants of lands in these regions.

b. Production for national markets predominates. A standard comment made by social scientists about freeholding communities is that their surplus production seldom reaches the national market and their economies are not externally orientated. Family farms, on the other hand, more commonly grow crops for sale and expect to purchase a much higher proportion of goods for their own consumption than do workers on traditional estates or people living in freeholding communities. This is partly the result of their different social evolution. Family farmers are more in contact with regional and national centres than are other rural people. They are likely to have relatives in the centres, whilst they themselves belong predominantly to the cultural group that is distinguished by having clothes of factory-made cloth, by wearing shoes and by using a wider variety of manufactured goods in their houses. In order to have the money to buy these goods, which are necessary to maintain their standard of living and status in the community, crops must be grown to be sold for cash. This tendency is further stimulated by the need of those farmers who rent their land to have money or surplus produce with which to pay their rent. Thus both cultural and economic factors combine to encourage the family farmer to produce cash crops.

The concentration on cash crops results in the susceptibility of these farmers to market fluctuations and to exploitation by middlemen. Although small-scale producers in freeholding communities are frequently grossly exploited by merchants and storekeepers, this only affects a small proportion of their livelihood. Family farmers on the other hand may depend for their very existence on the sale of coffee, bananas, or vegetables. Family farmers are seldom able to store their harvests and thus all sell their crops to merchants at roughly the same time: the market is oversupplied and prices fall. A sack of coffee that could normally sell for sufficient money for a month's food will then only produce enough for two weeks. The effects of market fluctuations are often exaggerated to rural people by merchants, who exact a high margin of profit by informal artificial price-fixing agreements.

An economic problem which affects family farmers and which is a powerful hindrance to their economic progress is the lack of funds to effect improvements. Often the volume of production from each farm is insufficient fully to warrant even simple devices for improving the quality and thus the value of what they produce. Coffee growers in Colombia, who are typically small-scale producers on family farms, have difficulty in constructing adequate drying floors for the coffee and likewise in the provision of water for washing the berries. Here the lack of community solidarity often makes the logical conclusion, the formation of co-operatives, difficult to achieve. Family farms are sometimes even remarkably similar to traditional freeholding peasant communities in their economic orientation and, in some isolated pioneer areas, such as some of those in Santa Catarina and Rio Grande do Sul states in southern Brazil, family farms exist which, for want of adequate communication with the outside world, are as internally oriented as peasant farms in highland Peru. Here attempts at producing a saleable surplus were frustrated not by the lack of a market but more by lack of means to send the produce to market.

c. Cash cropping by primitive methods. The emphasis on the production of cash crops has already been mentioned but it should not be thought that, because family farms are more market-oriented, they are necessarily modern in other ways. Although in some areas, particularly where vegetables, fruit and flowers are produced for a market, family farms can achieve high levels of productivity and efficiency, these types of holding are more frequently characterized by low levels of efficiency and the use of archaic forms of production. Fertilizers and improved varieties of seed are adopted only by a deviant minority and reliance for a good harvest is placed more on a suitable combination of weather for growth and ripening than on giving Nature a helping hand, in part because farmers do not have enough capital to buy such seeds or goods.

A feature of cash cropping in many areas of the world where small farmers predominate is an excessive reliance on one crop. This obviously makes the income of farmers even more susceptible to price fluctuations, but even where several crops predominate one is usually the most important throughout the region and fluctuations in the price of this one crop have more effect on farmers than changes in the prices of others. Coffee producers in Colombia are a particularly good example of this dependence on a single crop, and on a smaller scale this situation could be duplicated in many other parts of Latin America. Rare indeed is the farmer described in the Lake Patzcuaro area of Mexico who observed what vegetables others in his area planted for cash and then planted different vegetables himself, thus trying to ensure that he would not produce a crop with which the market might be glutted.

d. Family and community. If emphasis was laid, in the description of freeholding communities, on the importance of the community rather than the family, it should not be supposed that the community in areas of family farming is of no importance. Many areas of family farms are associated with small quasi-urban settlements but there is nothing comparable with the agro-town of Mediterranean Europe. There has been a system of regional government in parts of rural Latin America since long before even the Vikings came upon the New World. But the administrative unit which includes family farms is more often identified as a national political division rather than as a cohesive social entity such as the freeholding community. The organization is often looser; some people living in a particular parish or canton may be unaffected by, or uninterested in, belonging to it, but for the majority it is the social and political unit through which they are connected to the provincial and national government. In areas of recent colonization, social organizations are quickly formed and petitions drawn up for the creation of new civil regions.

The looser social cohesion of these areas permits a greater degree of geographical mobility. Family opinion rather than community attitude is likely to affect the decision to migrate. The social environment of a community of family farmers is often conservative and one where innovations are adopted hesitantly and after long periods of preconditioning. Young people in this environment often feel very discontented and constricted, and some of those communities which have experienced most emigration are those where family farms predominate.

C. Estates

One of the distinguishing characteristics of Latin American land tenure is the excessive concentration of good farmland in the hands of a small number of families. In countries such as Colombia, Chile or Brazil, between one-half and three-quarters of the agricultural land is owned by a few aristocratic families. In some regions as much as 90 per cent of the land may be owned by less than one per cent of the population. The estates, variously known in Spanish as *haciendas*, *estancias, fundos* etc., are also distinctive by being virtually feudal social enclaves, where all power is in the hands of the landowner and personal liberty is an alien ideal, unpractised and little-known. The corresponding lowland form of tenure, the plantation, was distinguished originally by employing slave labour and by producing cash crops, principally sugar cane, and has evolved in some rural areas into impressive semi-industrial undertakings. By contrast the highland estate has changed little except where agrarian reform legislation has changed existing structures, as in Mexico, Bolivia, Peru and Chile.

The large estates were characteristic of the highland areas of Latin America: particularly in Central America, and in the Andes from Venezuela to Chile. Now many estates have been sub-divided through fear of land reform or as a result of legislation and in many Andean areas large haciendas have less importance than formerly. The Brazilian highlands as far south as Paraná state are also characterized by large estates but social conditions there are somewhat less oppressive than in the Andes. In parts of Argentina, particularly the north-east and, to a lesser extent, in the humid Pampa, large estates occur but they are frequently associated with less rigid social conditions than those in Brazil.

a. *The land does not belong to those who work it.* The land in a large estate is owned by a family or an individual and he has a legal title for this land. Despite the apparent simplicity of this form of ownership, some land is rented by the landowner to his labourers in return for a wide variety of services. Only rarely and recently have rural workers been able to have either a formal labour contract or title to the small plots of land leased to them by the landowner for their house and farmland. They thus have no security and no effective rights in law. Exploitation by landowners is therefore widespread and even where laws do exist to protect estate workers (such as in Ecuador) they are virtually unenforceable. This may be compared with the insecurity of tenure resulting from a lack of legal evidence of ownership that afflicts many rural people with smallholdings in different parts of Latin America, and in the Caribbean.

Although the working population on large estates have little security they were nonetheless bound to the land in a variety of ways. The *yanacona* of Peru, the *huasipunguero* of Ecuador and the *inquilino* of Chile were all rural workers who owed services to the landowner in return for which they had the right to the use of a small parcel of land. Now they are smallholders working occasionally as day labourers. However, in Peru, for example, the exact definition of *yanaconaje* varies from province to province and even from one property to another. But while the majority of workers on the estates occupied a lowly position and received a small plot of land in exchange for as much as six days labour a week on the estate, others had different tasks, such as shepherd or carpenter, in return for which they received payment in kind, or the right to plots of land. Some estates even rent large sections of land to others who want to farm but this means only a change of master as far as the workers are concerned. In other cases, land is share-cropped by an enterprising worker, or by someone from a nearby settlement. As a result of this variety of arrangements, the apparent simplicity of a land tenure pattern comprising large estates and few landowners is illusory and a single property may have people cultivating different areas under a wide variety of tenurial systems.

b. *The economic goal is normal production with minimal investment.* The main advantage of ownership of a large estate for many people is the social prestige and economic security that it brings. Capital invested in land tends to increase in value and, where currencies lose value quickly and devaluation is a routine occurrence, as in most countries of Latin America, a safe haven for investment is highly regarded. Socially, investment in industry is less prestigious than investment in land and, in many Latin American countries, politicians and prominent public figures tend to buy land rather than stocks and shares.

Although those investing in land are frequently powerful and respected persons, they seldom wish to invest in making the land already acquired more productive, so that little money is available to carry out improvements and better farming systems. Moreover, the rate of return from land ownership is not expected to be high and little incentive exists for increasing output. Many estate owners are concerned more with maintaining output at its present level rather than increasing output or productivity. Labour is seldom in short supply and need be paid virtually nothing. The workers are frequently required to produce small payments such as eggs and to transport the landowner's share of the harvests to the owner's town house. In Bolivia some owners maintained shops in the town stocked with produce, delivered regularly from their estates at no cost to themselves. With advantages such as this high rate of return for little effort, it is not hard to imagine the lack of incentive to increase production further.

An important feature of the production from estates is that it is predominantly geared to a local or national market. Relatively rarely, as in the coffee estates of Central America, Brazil and some parts of Colombia, is production destined for export. The less archaic estates in eastern Bolivia and the River Plate lands frequently employ paid labour in contrast to the semi-feudal obligations that restrict the Andean estate worker. The conditions of work and the rates of pay are however still very different from those experienced on modern coastal plantations.

c. Traditional agricultural systems are common. Although dairy farms near to the major cities may employ a limited degree of modern technology, a sizeable proportion of the total agricultural production from estates is the result of the application of old-fashioned, even pre-Conquest, methods. Yields of crops grown on estates are very much less than on properties of a similar size in comparable areas of Europe although ecologically the estates are situated on the best land. Mention has already been made of the characteristic landholding pattern in Ecuador where large estates occupy valley bottoms and Indian communities crowd the inferior land on hillsides. But despite these natural advantages the land use is frequently geared to minimum investment and traditional agriculture. (See Figure 3–1 and Plate V.) Pastureland is commonly on high-quality alluvial soils even though grain or vegetables sown on the same land would yield higher returns. Even where the landowner has adopted improved methods, for example perhaps high-quality wheat is sown with fertilizers, the workers still cultivate their own plots with hand tools to grow traditional indigenous crops such as maize, potatoes and beans.

In parts of Bolivia the system of agriculture before the agrarian reform of 1953 involved the peasant cultivating the whole arable area of the estate using traditional methods and the produce from the landlord's land, which maybe amounted to one-third of the total area, was delivered to him: but all decisions regarding cultivation were taken by the workers. One problem that estate owners face is the proliferation of their workers: each mature worker's son may petition the landowner for a plot of land in return for work duties. In several instances in Ecuador, Peru and Bolivia so much of the land was taken up in workers' plots that the landowner found the area of land cultivated for his benefit diminishing each year. The alternative to this is expelling workers and their families. In one area of Bolivia where an estate owner decided to give up arable farming and change to sheep rearing, he evicted dozens of families from the land, leaving them without any means of support.

d. The landowner as a father figure. Apologists for the estate owners describe the workers as children who depend on the landowner to such an extent that if he were to leave they wouldn't know to whom to turn. There is little doubt that the closeness of the bond between worker and master is an important feature of this landholding system. At baptisms, weddings, births and deaths the master (landowner) is called upon to be an honoured guest. He is the godfather (and father too in some cases) of the children of the estate and is the person who may order the police to release any of his men put in jail for being drunk on market day. The coin has another face though, for it is he too who calls the army to quell any sign of mutiny and to shoot squatters if they refuse to move. The landowner has the ear of the police, the lawyers, judges, priests and politicians and little can effectively be done to counter his will.

The master–worker (*patrón–peón* in Spanish) relationship is the main characteristic of this system. Seldom does any social class exist besides that of rulers and subjects. The overseers in some areas are intermediaries, in the Andes often being socially superior *mestizos*, but in other places the overseers are elected regularly by the workers themselves. Although the estate labour force is part of the estate as a social entity, within it many of the traditional social habits remain. Traditional agricultural ceremonies are held and traditional posts of authority exist within the group. This is particularly true in those parts of the Andes where estates were created during the last hundred years out of freeholding communities. Freedom is a scarce commodity. Although workers may be ejected summarily, equally their labour may be valued and escaping workers caught by the police and returned to be punished, often brutally. The landowner acts both as a cushion and a barrier against the outside world, for he introduces no modern methods, often discourages education and punishes those who seek to leave his land.

D. Industrial Plantations

The rural settlement type most typical of the colonial empires of European powers in the lowland tropics is the plantation. The Dutch, French, British, Spanish and Portuguese established similar systems of farming tropical lands geared to the supply of goods for export. Major industries in western Europe of the seventeenth and eighteenth centuries were supported by supplies of sugar, indigo, cotton or tobacco, while the slave trade that provided the labour for this farming system likewise made the fortune of many a European merchant.

In Latin America the plantation became established throughout the Caribbean, on the shores of Central America, on the north-east coast of Brazil and in the irrigated valleys of the Peruvian coast. It was a feature of colonization and during the late nineteenth century it was replaced in some areas by more modern, efficient, almost industrial undertakings. During the last 70 years this process of modernization has continued and there are now clearly two separate types of plantation. The colonial plantation is becoming progressively less important and for this reason, and because it is extremely well described in many books and articles, the main emphasis here will be on modern plantations, of the sort that are known as *usinas* in Spanish America (or *usinha* in Brazil) as opposed to the old *ingenio*. The traditional plantation was commonly family-owned and employed numbers of slaves, later indentured or hired labourers, to cultivate the land and to work what machinery was needed. A strong link often developed between the plantation owner and the workers even though the one exploited the other. As demand for tropical produce gave rise to increased production in many areas of the world, plantation owners found it increasingly difficult to sell their goods at a competitive price and they either sold their land or amalgamated it with other estates and introduced more mechanization. Foreign companies became interested in tropical produce, especially bananas and sugar, and invested money to open up new land for plantations and in buying up old plantations to form larger units. They were concerned with productivity and tried to establish factory-type relations with workers, paying them well but not allowing them land to cultivate. Mechanization was accelerated to reduce the labour force and skilled technicians were employed to supervise the processes of production. As a result, in many areas plantations of a traditional type were succeeded by larger, more efficient, more highly-mechanized holdings employing labour on a much more impersonal footing. A more recent modification of the plantation is the transformation into state farms, as has happened in Cuba, as a result of which the direction of the plantation and the profits from its operation are appropriated by the State which manages it on behalf of the workers, or into collective farms as in Peru since 1969.

The plantation is distinct from the estate, although also a colonial form of institution and land tenure, by being predominantly located in tropical lowland areas and by being a land-use system geared to the production of large quantities of one commodity for export. The modern forms of plantation are distinctive in being the principal way in which business corporations invest in Latin American agriculture. In a continent where massive investment in agriculture is unusual this alone makes the modern plantation a noteworthy phenomenon.

a. Corporate ownership predominates. Whereas in the other types of rural holdings that have been described a variety of forms of tenure can be encountered, the plantation is characteristically owned by a family or corporation and its land is not leased. The workers on highland estates produce much of their own food and part of the rationale of the system is that it is unnecessary to pay them much in the way of wages. In order for maximum use to be made of the land and also to avoid accepting a permanent labour force, workers on modern plantations are provided with housing, usually of a relatively primitive nature, and are paid either a daily wage or a wage varying according to the amount of work they do. By contrast, the traditional plantation was accustomed to give rural plots of land to the workers and in this way was superficially similar to the estate. The slave-worked plantations frequently had quite large areas farmed by the slaves who were sometimes allowed to sell produce from their plots on payment of a percentage of their takings to their master.

Major landowners in the Caribbean used to be the leading banana companies, the largest of which by far was the United Fruit Company. They have been accustomed to cultivate only a part of the land that they own, particularly in Central America. In part this was the result of changing fortunes in the banana trade but at least until recently large reserves of land were kept unused, allegedly for future expansion. In many areas this unused land has been invaded by squatters who maintain small family farms untroubled by their precarious legal position. By 1971, however, the United Fruit Company had disposed of much of its unused land in Central America.

b. An externally-oriented economy. The aims of plantation owners were primarily to produce a surplus of one particular crop for sale overseas or to a major national market. The methods of agriculture demanded a lot of workers and frequently some small degree of mechanization as, for example, for crushing the cane in the case of sugar. In areas such as the Guianas the volume and value of production was such that landowners where possible built their own roads or else used river transport.

The continuing demand for crops like cotton and sugar into the nineteenth century ensured the continued existence of the plantations, but cotton came into competition with that produced in Anglo-America, and increased competition made it more difficult for the smaller units to survive. In sugar areas, small estates often contracted to supply cane to the large mills in place of the small crushing mills powered by donkeys or by hand that were relics of the pre-industrial past. In other cases large mills bought up surrounding plantations to ensure for themselves an adequate supply of cane of the correct quality.

The new plantation crop of the present century was the banana and it became associated with large-scale operations with a highly complex and integrated supply and marketing operation. The United Fruit Company, in addition to its huge banana plantations, also owns railways, telegraph services and a modern and efficient shipping line. In only two areas in fact are large quantities of bananas produced for export in medium-sized estates and family farms: in the Turbo area of northern Colombia, which developed during the middle 1960s and in lowland Ecuador, the world's major banana-exporting region.

The tendency towards the predominance of major producers, already noted for sugar, has been repeated for example in the establishment of near-monopolies in the production of bananas and tobacco. Here major companies seek to maintain their position in the market by preventing the growth of minor competitors and refusing to buy the production of peasant farmers who have no alternative outlet for their produce. This has been one of the most serious charges levelled against the large companies of the capitalist industrialized countries although there are signs that in the newly-developing areas the companies are concentrating on marketing and on taking measures to ensure a high-quality crop rather than engaging in agriculture themselves. In the Turbo area of Colombia, the United Fruit Company has associated itself with the newly-developing area of banana cultivation on the Caribbean coast, not by establishing large estates but rather by helping farmers in return for guaranteed deliveries of bananas to the U.F.C. for shipment. In Ecuador the same company handles part of the packing and shipment of bananas and has little direct contact with growers. As labour becomes progressively more expensive and labour unions become more active it is reasonable to expect an increase in mechanization and in productivity. The greatest improvements in Latin American agriculture in the last 25 years have come not from the underprivileged peasant sector but more from the highly-capitalized and already productive plantations.

c. Twentieth-century agriculture. Because production is geared to the provision of a single cash crop a great deal is invested in the land; drainage is carried out or irrigation water provided and fungicidal spraying from the air is commonplace. Investment in experimentation may even be carried out and new varieties of crop or fertilizers tried out. Emphasis may likewise be on ease of harvesting as much as productivity.

The resulting land-use pattern shows a high degree of uniformity. Rotation may not be carried out and vast areas of cotton, cacao, sugar or bananas are the result. Housing is confined to areas of limited use for agriculture and often there is a central complex with offices, workers' housing, machine sheds and the warehouses for packaging or treating the produce of the area.

For access to markets, ease of communication is important and the central settlement complexes of plantations are frequently sited on the coast where there is a harbour, on a navigable waterway, or on major rail or roadways. Particularly in banana-producing areas efficient port services have grown up which have developed and are now used for a wide range of trade quite apart from that associated with the plantation.

d. Personal relations diminish in importance. As the methods for treating the crops become more efficient and streamlined, so too does the treatment of the labour force. The labourers are paid according to piece rates, they buy most of what they eat from local stores, and may even know little about agriculture other than what is related to the particular task in which they engage. Alternatively the labourers may be migrants from the mountains who work for a season cutting cane, picking cacao pods or coffee beans. The traditional paternalism that marks the old plantations as much as the highland estates has been replaced by a more industrial relationship between foreman and labourer. The migrant workers often seek to establish the customary relationship with the managers, perhaps by asking a foreman to be a godfather to a child, but a paternalistic concern for workers is not typical of social relations in plantations.

Large numbers of labourers are required and a degree of specialization of jobs occurs, thus allowing differentiation between the workers on the grounds of status and skill. Migrant workers who return regularly often become semi-skilled at one particular job, earn more money and may even decide to stay. Workers on the modern plantation are free in ways which workers on highland estates are not. They are seldom tied to their work by debt or other obligations, and often they move to buy land in areas not far from where they have worked on plantations. But this freedom is both beneficial and detrimental to the interests of the workers. While he is free to leave, so also his employer is free to dismiss him and where the employer is a large company occupying a wide area, there may be few other chances for employment, particularly if the worker is dismissed for political reasons and blacklisted. A major characteristic of plantation labour however is that there are only brief periods when a lot of manpower is needed and, particularly in areas of sugar cane growing, for much of the year labour needs are slight. Thus in major sugar-producing areas, such as in Cuba before the Revolution, rural workers may be employed for only a few months each year during the sugar harvest and have to spend the remaining part of the year in penury, or in a completely different form of employment. It is partly for this reason that temporary migration from the highlands in the Indian parts of Latin America is regarded as a particularly satisfactory way of supplementing the income of highland peasant farmers and providing short-term labour at harvest periods.

E. The Smallest Farms

While the categories that we have examined previously are the most easily identifiable forms of rural occupance it is necessary to identify, in addition, some of the characteristics of the smallest farm units which employ many of those in the poorest sector of the rural population. It is not always easy to separate farmers in this category from those in freeholding communities or those who are workers on large estates since the categories are not mutually exclusive and an individual may be both a member of a freeholding community and a tenant on a nearby estate as well as even working on a plantation in the lowlands in the slack season.

Data from a major study of seven countries, reported in Barraclough and

Domike (see Bibliography), show that in Ecuador, Peru and Guatemala in the 1960s almost 90 per cent of farms were too small to support a nuclear family with two adults; in Colombia over 60 per cent of the farms and in Argentina and Chile around 40 per cent were of this size. Such farms are frequently referred to in Latin America as *minifundia* and are different from family farms not just in size but in the consequent necessity for some members of the family to obtain a living by working elsewhere or by non-agricultural work at home. The form of tenure by which these smallholders occupy the land is varied and frequently precarious. This category included tenants, squatters and those who have title to their land since the principal criterion of this category is the adequacy of the land occupied to provide a living at the typical levels of incomes, markets, and levels of technology and capital currently prevailing in these areas.

Farms of this size have arisen because of the prevailing practice in Latin America of dividing the land between each of the heirs and thus even a farm comprising a house and 1000 square metres of field might be divided among three or four people, although it is also common practice for some heirs to sell their rights to those other heirs who are most keen to have the property, which does diminish slightly the tendency for already small farms to diminish in size. The process of sub-division by inheritance affects farms of all sizes and in some areas large estates have become family farms in two or three generations by inheritance and the sale of land.

The land use system of the smallholdings involves the intensive use of crop and grazing land, sometimes with soil erosion and deforestation as a result. The fallow period may well be shorter than on similar land farmed in larger, family farms with lower yields as a result. The basic purpose of farming minifundia is to provide as much as possible of the food necessary for the family, and only a very small proportion of the farm produce is sold. Income for those items that need to be purchased such as salt, oil, clothing and tools must come from other sources, either domestic handcrafts such as weaving, hat-making, or carpentry, or work for cash on other farms in the area, or the performance of useful services such as midwifery, magic, or playing in a band for a fiesta. Farms of smallholders are seldom consolidated into one plot of land, rather they will comprise several parcels of land spread over a couple of kilometres distance from the house.

Because agriculture is necessary to provide food for the household but can rarely provide a surplus for sale the adoption of new crops, new seed varieties, and new methods of cultivation is believed by many smallholders to be very risky since a partial crop failure could disrupt the family economy. Research in a wide variety of circumstances has shown that, other things being equal, farmers with more land are more likely to be innovators than those with less land. A further disadvantage of smallholders is their dependence on the market in order to earn the money with which they buy the necessities that they do not produce. If the demand for occasional labour locally dries up, perhaps as a result of a change from cropfarming to livestock, the workers have immediately to find work elsewhere. Similarly, if the price of straw hats (a common cottage industry in some areas) falls sharply, farm families realize that the return for their work is not enough to buy what they could previously.

Patterns of Change

Although the rural environment in Latin America affords most opportunities to observe traditional society and the survival of ancient customs or artefacts it is also subject to considerable change, however halting may be government efforts to encourage the spread of certain changes. The building of new roads and the improvement of existing ones, the introduction of new crops and agricultural practices, and the increasing contact of the rural population with city life as a result of migration have all played an important part in bringing about changes in farming and farm life as well as within the small towns and villages in rural areas. These and some other changes are examined separately in later chapters; here it is useful to add a dynamic element to the views hitherto given to rural life in order to show some of the new situations that are responsible for changes that affect rural people and whose importance is not likely to diminish in the foreseeable future.

Improvements in communications are important because they allow movement in two directions—not only may people and their goods and ideas travel along the road to reach the previously isolated villages, but also villagers may use these new highways to leave home to travel elsewhere either temporarily or for good. It is customary to believe that new highways and improved communications provide benefits to those areas whose isolation has been ended, but this assumes that rural people are generally hampered by isolation and that the benefits of increased accessibility accrue equally to the previously isolated families and to other highway users. In fact, it might very well be that lorry and bus owners and merchants in the newly accessible city markets benefit more than the rural families. Communications, which include radio and telephone, enable the influence of urban-based ideas and institutions to reach rural families and lead them to act in ways that benefit urban merchants and, because of the nature of the political economy of most Latin American states, to become dependent on people outside their village. This dependence is a result of selling surplus goods to outsiders for cash and becoming accustomed to buying items with the cash and subsequently needing cash in order to satisfy what has become a necessity rather than a luxury. Storekeepers and others part of the outside world lend money in order for the villager to make his purchases when he has nothing to sell in return and the village becomes dependent on him in a way that was previously little known. Even when the highways reduce the cost of getting goods to market, a three-day mule journey may be replaced by a half-day bus journey for which cash is paid and the merchant to whom the goods are sold may not offer a very good price or his scales may be very wrong so the farmer faces a dilemma which occasional local trading usually avoids—the need to sell having made a long journey at some cost. Improvements in communications are not necessarily harmful to rural people but it is important to realize that they are not necessarily beneficial since they open up rural communities to outside exploitation. Improved communications do offer villagers a wider choice and so long as the choice is open and village freedom is unimpaired they can allow rural people opportunities for improving their levels of living even without greatly changing relations within the community.

The Green Revolution

The spatial dimension of improved communications is clear—rural areas become closer together, less effort is needed to bridge the distance between settlements and between parts of a nation. The spatial dimension of the other factor of change which must be considered is more complex. While improvements in communications take place throughout Latin America and fundamentally alter spatial relations, the introduction of high-yielding varieties of food grains together with the use of artificial fertilizer and other chemicals to increase yields and control pests (a group of changes often known as the Green Revolution) has a more discontinuous distribution but an equally great impact on those rural communities where these changes have taken place. Research on high-yielding varieties of wheat, centred in Mexico, resulted in the dissemination of new, rust-resistant varieties during the 1950s and of even better dwarf varieties since 1963. Mexican wheat yield rose from 0.94 to 2.9 tonnes per hectare over the 1950–70 period and production rose such that Mexico became a wheat exporting country. Parallel work on rice in the Philippines led to similar genetic improvements in rice varieties and both improved wheat and rice spread widely although rice yields did not jump so dramatically. The improvements in agricultural technology have not been limited to food grain, nor indeed to those parts of the world where the new varieties were developed and where they were most widely used. In considering the repercussions of the Green Revolution we need to consider the whole range of options available to farmers wanting to consider increasing output. It may seem obvious that farmers will want to increase output but this is only true when the farmer is accustomed to produce a marketable surplus. If he is mainly concerned with producing food for his family's consumption he may prefer to ensure that his harvest will be adequate, that is minimize risk, rather than maximize production if this involves a higher risk. Thus, if a set of new techniques and crops are made available to farmers, not all will avail themselves of them and their adoption will not always affect the farmers in the same way.

Experience in a number of countries, including many outside Latin America, has shown that the new technology has been initially tried most frequently by those farmers who produce a surplus and are market oriented, thus by those who are most advanced in peasant communities. The profitability of farming using the new technology encourages the proliferation of farms which use a lot of money or which rely more on wage labourers than on family or tenant labour and such farms, which can easily reinvest their profits to assure higher yields, may have both higher yields and higher profits per unit of area than a small family farm. A further important change in the structure of the labour force is a decline in permanent attached labour and an increase in mobile attached labour. In general it seems that the agricultural innovations associated with the Green Revolution, where they have been successful, have tended to proletarianize the rural labour force, sever its attachment to the land, and to favour particularly those farmers who had already more than average amounts of land. Far from enabling the rural poor to enjoy a better living it has made it more difficult for them to rent land and, by increasing the well-being of the middle peasant stratum and the capitalistic farmer, has made the poor even poorer by comparison.

Equally serious is the question of whether the technology that is used to ensure higher yields is appropriate. A condition of success of the wonder seeds is the application of large quantities of inorganic fertilizer and the treatment of the growing plants with insecticide and fungicides, all of which are expensive. The quality of the advice given to the farmers is often poor and couched in general terms making it difficult for them to discern its relevance to their own particular situation. They are sometimes advised to adopt innovations which subsequently are either inappropriate or unsuccessful and in all cases which increase dependence on external linkages.

Local Resource Use Systems

Patterns of change in rural environments are often associated with resource use problems. In order to appreciate the nature of the use of natural resources and to demonstrate how imbalances in resource use can be identified it is useful to look at two distinct rural areas whose future is jeopardized by resource scarcity, to discover how this has come about and how the strategy that the communities have adopted to overcome the increase in population has resulted in serious ecological problems.

Farmers and turtlehunters in Nicaragua. On the Miskito coast of eastern Nicaragua are a series of villages of Miskito Indians, partly English-speaking, who live from both farming and from hunting and fishing. They are considerably acculturated as a result of a variety of outside cultural influences over a long period of time and also, in part, as a result of the men working in the past for companies using the forest resources of the hinterland. The variety of resources used by the inhabitants of one village, Tasbapauni, has been studied by Bernard Nietschmann in some detail and from his work this summary account is derived. Villagers cultivate both plots of land on the beach ridges up to 20 km away on foot and fields across the lagoon behind the beach ridge up to 35 km distant. From these fields they produce a variety of root crops and bananas which provide the carbohydrate element in their diet. In addition, pineapples, papayas, and breadfruit

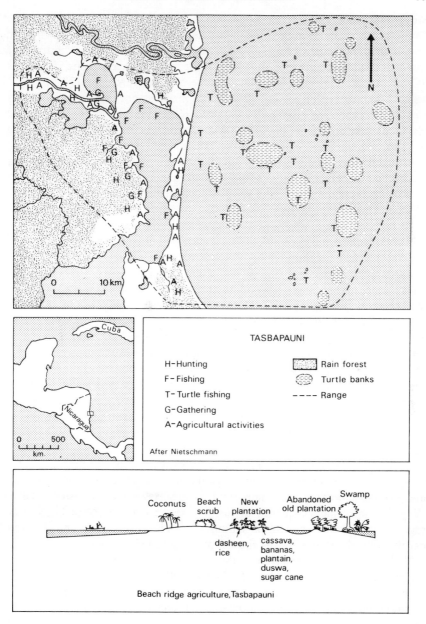

Figure 3–2. Natural resource use on the Miskito coast

are grown while rice and coconuts are also grown largely for sale for cash. Domesticated animals are of little importance in local subsistence activities. Hunting, both in the forest swamps and especially in overgrown former cultivated land where deer and peccaries may be found, is the major source of meat, together with fishing. By far the most important source of meat (providing 70 per cent by weight) is the green turtle. The green turtle provides not only large quantities of meat (a medium-sized green turtle will yield 46 kg of meat) but also calipee, a cartilaginous substance from the inner shell margins that is the basis for green turtle soup as consumed in England and the U.S.A.

In addition to what a family produces, including often important amounts of foodstuffs received and given between them, about 25 per cent of calories consumed are bought from village shops—such items as sugar, flour, rice, beans, coffee and meat.

Important changes were identified in the Miskito subsistence system that represent a distortion of a system that was previously better able to provide a satisfactory level of living without undue stress on natural resources. The major group of changes were associated with an increasing importance being given to cultural values accepted by national as opposed to local society which has given rise to an increasing proportion of the production being used to sell goods in order to buy items produced elsewhere. In order to have a larger surplus for sale it may be necessary to increase production beyond previous subsistence levels, to cut down on the amount previously distributed amongst people in the expectation of later reciprocation, and to reduce the amounts consumed. For example, turtlemen are spending more time to catch more turtles for sale away from the village; with the money they buy largely carbohydrates and turtles become progressively more difficult to find. As money becomes more important so families become more dependent on prices in the market that are often determined largely by external factors. The domestic and village economy becomes more unstable. The agricultural economy is changing similarly. Fallow periods become shorter as a consequence of an increased population and some commercial crops such as rice and coconuts become more important at the expense of subsistence farming. Wage labour replaces exchange labour. As a result, many of the ecological advantages of the previous system of shifting cultivation will be lost and the land be capable of yielding less just as the sea becomes devoid of turtles.

Full justice cannot be given to the complexity of Nietschmann's analysis of Tasbapauni community ecology but it parallels in a number of ways what has been observed in many parts of the world where commercial motives make demands upon the natural environment that cannot be met except in the short term. Why do commercial organizations develop on the basis of the supply of a commodity which is known not to be abundant? Their justification is that investment can quickly be repaid and a quick profit made before the resource is depleted after which investors are satisfied, a natural resource ruined, and dozens of village economies completely disorganized.

Indian farmers in Chiapas, Mexico. The agriculture practised by Tzotzil Indian farmers in southern Mexico contains many elements of the aboriginal agriculture that developed after the domestication of plants in Middle America several thousand years ago. The increase in population in association with a national economic and political system which encourages the development of cash economies has led to the development of new ways of exploiting the environment among the members of one group and of seasonal labour migration in another village, but in much of the area a further consequence is continuing soil erosion.

In the community of Apas, as elsewhere in highland Chiapas, shifting cultivation based on maize and beans is the predominant cropland use and only 20 per cent of families have no land of their own nor are expecting to inherit land. Farmland is located at about 2000 m above sea level but some cropland is as high as 2800 m, above which forest and scrubland predominates. Stands of evergreen oak and pines are now only encountered in the most inaccessible areas. The rainy season lasts from May until October with the harvests generally being completed

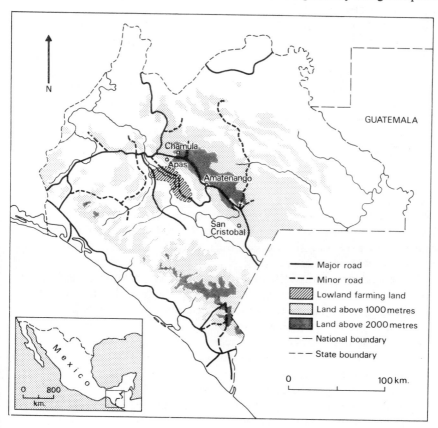

Figure 3–3. Chiapas State, Mexico

by February after which livestock graze over the fields. Fields are cultivated for varying lengths of time and likewise fallow periods vary between 5 and 15 years. Since the early 1960s significant changes in farming have been analysed by George Collier who concluded that farming intensity has declined except where most rapid regrowth of vegetation during fallow period takes place. Many of the soils in areas formerly cultivated have been impoverished and infestation of maize plots by grasses takes place more rapidly than previously. Thus, although population is increasing, the area farmed in the highlands has not increased proportionally and may even have decreased. In the case of Apas this is made possible only by the use of land in the hot lowlands of the Grijalva basis to the south where, since the early 1950s, Indians have come to rent land which may yield three times as much maize per unit area as fields at home in the highlands. Although lowland farming is associated with the employment of additional labourers it still provides four-fifths of the necessary food income for a highland family. Thus lowland farming enables families to continue to live in the highlands who otherwise might be forced to work and possibly live elsewhere.

In the nearby community of Chamula similar demographic problems have been solved differently but with a dramatic degree of soil erosion as a consequence. In part this is said to be a consequence of the farming of very high land on which the regeneration of vegetation is slow. Here Chamulas have developed a system of long-term shifting cultivation where agriculture gives way to horticulture as yields fall with intensive cropping of potatoes, cabbage and broad beans, with sheep becoming increasingly important as grass invades and their wool is valued for sale and the dung for checking the declining fertility of the fields. As the cycle progresses grassland predominates, wells dry up and run off increases with progressive soil erosion; heavy rains erode paths and gullying develops as families move away to farm fresh plots elsewhere. To supplement income from farming, Chamulas have a flourishing craft industry which, in itself, further strains resources with the cutting of more timber for furniture, firewood and charcoal. Others travel to work on commercial farms in the lowlands where people from these villages have long since developed a range of contacts to ensure regular employment when they are available.

We may ask why should the Indians want to hold on to their highland lands when there are opportunities for earning a living elsewhere? Equally cogently one may ask in what way is the farmer's perception of his environment so defective that he does not recognize and avoid the exhaustion and erosion of his land. Collier suggests that the degree of attachment to his land makes increasing land fragmentation necessary and the Tzotzil attitudes towards natural phenomena allow them to ascribe declining fields to supernatural causes which are beyond their power to prevent. The demand for labour for cash makes it possible for the family to remain in the ancestral homeland while the men bring back money with which to buy the necessary extra food.

Comparison with Miskito resource use is instructive. In both cases increasing population is a major factor and solutions are sought which would avoid a permanent depletion of the community by emigration of entire families. In both areas serious resource depletion is occurring, of marine resources in Tasbapauni and of soils in Chiapas, but, in the former case, active external market forces are encouraging the resource depletion while, in the later case, it is the unwillingness of farmers either to move or to develop alternative uses of their resources that results in the Chamulas participating in marketing their labour elsewhere and the Apas farmers growing much of their maize on rented land in the adjacent lowlands.

A General Conclusion

It is misleading to hope that the stereotypes that have been described offer any more than a panoramic view of the reality of rural Latin America. Some areas surely fall into none of the broad categories that have been described. Above all it must be realized that most areas of the continent are changing, some very rapidly. Two such aspects of change, relating to the establishment of new land tenure systems with agrarian reform programmes and the increase in colonization of new lands, are dealt with in a succeeding chapter. Change however is a universal process. An important element of change can be described by the elephantine term *embourgeoisement* that French social scientists have used. This describes the gradual assimilation of urban 'middle class' capitalist values by rural people. This process affects rural workers who live nearest to major urban centres and who are in areas where commercially-oriented agriculture predominates, and this includes a substantial proportion of Latin American farmers away from the Amazon basin. Even in highly traditional social areas such as highland Latin America, young men in rural areas are increasingly aware of urban values and modern methods of business even if their fathers resist many changes. Thus, while it is unrealistic to suggest that a majority of agricultural holdings in Latin America are, in a Western European sense, modern, there is nonetheless a much stronger trend towards change than was discernible a generation ago.

Bibliography

WAGLEY, C. and HARRIS, M., 'A typology of Latin American subcultures.' In D. B. Heath and R. N. Adams (Eds.), *Contemporary Cultures and Societies of Latin America*, Random House, New York, 1965, pp. 125–147. The original article under the same title appears in *American Anthropologist*, **57**, 42–69 (1955).
A valuable and, in its day, pioneering attempt to describe the features of Latin American society according to a classificatory system. Of considerable relevance to geographers and particularly relevant to the understanding of rural society.
BARRACLOUGH, S. and DOMIKE, A, 'Agrarian structure in seven Latin American countries', *Land Economics*, **42**, 391–442 (1966).
An analysis of seven major studies of the land tenure and associated problems in Chile, Brazil, Argentina, Colombia, Ecuador, Peru and Guatemala. Of considerable importance although strongly slanted towards economic considerations.

CARTER, W. C., *Aymara communities and the Bolivian agrarian reform*, University of Florida Press, Gainesville, 1965.
Based on research in several former estates and freeholding communities near to La Paz.

ICAZA, J., *Huasipungo*, Dennis Dobson, London, 1962.
A novel written in 1934 by an Ecuadorian deeply concerned with communicating the conditions under which the Indian population live on large estates. Well written, shocking and informative.

KELLER, F. L., Finca Ingavi—a medieval survival on the Bolivian Altiplano, *Economic Geography*, **27**, 37–50 (1950).
A useful account of the organization of a Bolivian estate before land reform.

PAN AMERICAN UNION, *Plantation systems in the New World*, Washington, Social Science Monographs No. VII, Pan American Union, 1959.
A collection of essays by leading students of the plantation in different parts of the New World.

HUTCHINSON, H. H., The transformation of Brazilian plantation society, *Journal of Inter-American Studies*, **3**, 201–212 (1961).
Excellent, well written account of the old and new socio-economic forms of the plantation as they have evolved in N. E. Brazil.

DESSAINT, A. 'Y., 'Effects of the hacienda and plantation systems on Guatemala's Indians', *América Indígena*, **22**, 323–54 (1962).

HILL, A. DAVID, *The Changing Landscape of a Mexican municipio: Villa Las Rosas, Chiapas*, University of Chicago, Chicago, Research Paper in Geography No. 91, 1964.

NIETSCHMANN, B., *Between Land and Water. The Subsistence Ecology of the Miskito Indians, Eastern Nicaragua*, Seminar Press, New York, 1973.

COLLIER, G. A., *Fields of the Tzotzil. The Ecological Bases of Tradition in Highland Chiapas*, University of Texas Press, Austin, 1975.
Two fascinating studies of human ecology as viewed by a geographer and an anthropologist which are discussed in this chapter.

DENEVAN, W. M., 'Campa Subsistence in the Gran Pajonal, Eastern Peru', *Geographical Review*, **61**, 496–518 (1971).
An interesting and thought-provoking analysis of the subsistence base of a group of forest Indians in the Peruvian jungle which may be usefully compared to the two studies of the Miskito and the Tzotzil.

FORMAN, SHEPARD, *The Raft Fishermen. Tradition and Change in the Brazilian Peasant Economy*, University of Indiana Press, Bloomington, 1970.
A fourth case study of the disruption of the balance between Man and the physical environment and of the social forces ('modernization') that are threatening raft fishing communities in N.E. Brazil.

HEWITT, CYNTHIA, *Modernizing Mexican Agriculture: socio-economic implications of technological change 1940–1970*, United Nations Research Institute for Social Development (UNRISD), Geneva, 1976.

CHAPTER 4

Characteristics of the Urban Environment

The large metropolitan cities of Latin America are like other cities of similar size in Europe or Anglo-America; towns on the other hand are quite unlike towns elsewhere, even in Spain and Portugal. The impact of Spanish culture on the New World was often greater in the towns than in the country. Social pride and personal preference led many of the early settlers to stay in urban centres, no matter how small they were, and the results of commercial activity were often to be seen most clearly in the town buildings. The once-rich mining town of Potosí had 30 churches, reputedly one for each new mineral find made.

Chronicles of the travels of the Spanish invaders in the mainland America often read like a list of towns *(villas)* founded, each after a few days march and a battle with the local Indians. Some of the towns were on new sites that proved to be unsuitable and were moved once or even several times until by trial and error a good site was chosen. Other settlements though were on the site of old Indian towns or forts; Mexico City on the site of Tenochtitlán is the most notable of these. Urban living was not widespread prior to the coming of the Spanish and many centres were of predominantly ceremonial significance. The majority of the population lived outside the town. Industry and mining before the sixteenth century were generally on too small a scale to have been associated with the building of sizeable towns. The towns that the Spanish founded were planned in an orderly fashion, with a rectangular street pattern quite different from that of towns in Spain. A Royal Ordinance of 1523 went so far as to lay down the steps to be followed when a new town was laid out and this to some extent accounts for the similarity in the pattern of colonial towns. Many of these towns remain today as monuments to their architects and builders and even those that have expanded well beyond the limits of the colonial settlement have kept the major public buildings of the central plaza intact.

The towns built during the colonial period show the greatest socio-geographical difference from those in the Anglo-Saxon world by being oriented not to a central main street but to a square *(plaza)* in the geometric centre of an orderly grid of streets. The centre of many an English town is the High Street, and in the U.S.A., Main Street, but this is seldom true of Latin American towns. To be sure, North American towns often have central squares, where the courthouse and other public buildings are located, but commercial and social activity centres primarily on those roads where most of the shops are located. In Latin American towns, where the colonial street pattern remains, commercial activity is more dispersed; some administrative centres are located on the plaza as are cafés, bookshops etc. Revolutions frequently start in a crowded meeting in the main plaza, and the evening social gatherng, particularly in small towns, is uniquely focused there. It is there that people gather for firework displays, parades and a wide range of activities.

Urban centres vary not only with the origins and aims of their past and present inhabitants but in relation to their economic role in the urban system of the region and nation of which they are part. Urban geographers are accustomed to speak of an urban hierarchy: something analogous to the 'pecking order' that has been observed in social groups of animals. At the top of the urban hierarchy is the metropolitan centre, the primate city, which performs a wider range of functions than any other city and which is more populous than any other urban centre. According to the criteria used, a number of levels in the hierarchy can be observed. This hierarchy is also related to the nature of the economic and political relation between urban centres. The larger centres attract more economic activities and are better able to influence political decisions in their favour than smaller centres. People tend to migrate from smaller places to larger ones and the destiny of every settlement is closely associated with decisions that are made by superior authorities in larger centres. Although local initiative is important in development, many such initiatives are stifled for political reasons by larger centres in whose interest it is that smaller towns do not grow sufficiently to threaten their superiority.

It is most instructive, however, in Latin American circumstances, not to take any one system of urban classification but instead to distinguish three clearly different urban settlement types: the rural market centre, the colonial town and the metropolitan centre, since each represents situations that occur in Latin America in many different forms. Once again it is emphasized that many towns may have some of the characteristics of more than one of the types; for example the centre of Lima has some of the characteristics of the colonial town, concentration of administrative offices and ceremonial centres around the main square, a uniform grid pattern of the streets; but perhaps 80 per cent of its inhabitants live away from the old centre of the town and the business centre of the city is in the newer, rather than the older, section of the city.

RURAL MARKET CENTRES

Small towns varying in size from maybe 300–1000 inhabitants are an important element of the urban system. They are socially distinctive because their in-

PLATE I. Urban development and growth in Mexico City. A *ciudad perdida* located alongside a railway line running through a part of the city. The two-storey houses behind the shanties are part of a different suburban development (Photo: Peter Ward).

PLATE II. The growth and development of a squatter settlement. Isidro Favela, Mexico City, 1974 (see also Fig. 6.1). Some of the streets have been paved, some homes have a second storey, trees along the sides of the street are growing and the area has something of the appearance of a rather bedraggled suburb (Photo: Peter Ward).

PLATE III. Negro house, Tumbabiro, Ecuador. Few house styles are truly typical of particular ethnic groups but many houses in negro communities in the inter-Andean valleys appear distinctive. Here the roofing material is sugar cane leaves on a lattice of poles (as seen on the left-hand house), the walls are of packed earth on a pole frame as can be seen from the right-end wall of the near house, set, in this case, on a stone base for solidity. The interior consists of one room but there is an outside 'veranda' covered by the roof where people sit to do minor jobs or just talk. A wooden barrier at the doorway keeps itinerant pigs out of the home. Rather unusually there is an outside oven at the end of the veranda.

PLATE IV. Pimampiro market, Ecuador. The characteristically mestizo town of Pimampiro is situated near to areas inhabited by negroes, mestizos and Indians and its market is a meeting ground. In the middle foreground is one of a number of open air eating places operated by Otavalo Indian women whose husbands are butchers and pig dealers. Beyond, seated on the ground, are negroes from the Chota valley selling tropical fruit and beyond them, to the left, are stalls selling clothes and hardware owned by mestizo merchants from Pimampiro and from other larger towns in the vicinity. The lorry visible is from an estate and is selling potatoes produced there.

PLATE V. Estates and freeholding communities before land reform, San Pablo, Ecuador. This illustration relates to the map Figure 3.1 and is a view towards Mt. Imbabura looking across the eastern end of the San Pablo depression. The lake is just off the photograph to the left centre; the town of San Pablo is barely visible amid the eucalyptus trees on the right centre. Large estates occupy the well-watered bottom land where dairy cattle graze large fields. Beyond and on the slopes of the mountain (an extinct volcano) on poorer land are the Indian *parcialidades* (freeholding

PLATE VI. Rosapata, an ayllu of Orinoca, Bolivia. Freeholding communities in the Central Altiplano are situated in an area of exceptional poverty. The view is across the salt flats of Lake Poopó looking towards the eastern Cordillera 100 km away over which cumulus clouds are developing. Largely communal pasture land borders the salt flats; the villages themselves, near the hillfoot, are on sandy but fertile land where good crops can be grown only when there is adequate rainfall. Here some land is subdivided amongst community members each year for cultivation. Most cropland is on the stony hillsides where fallowing for as long as 15–20 years is practised.

PLATE VII. Hacienda Carpuela, Northern Ecuador. In the bottom of the Chota valley, in N. Ecuador, irrigation makes cultivation possible. Much of the land is owned by large estates such as Hda. Carpuela. Sugar cane for the estate is being grown in the foreground to the left of the Pan American Highway. Futher away are the small fields of the estate workers, the *huasipungueros*, where avocado pears (hence the many trees), sweet cucumbers, tomatoes and aniseed are grown. The village of the negro *huasipungueros* is uphill from the main irrigation channel on barren land. The dusty hillsides are grazed by wandering herds of goats and donkeys. To the left of the village, across the road, is the estate house.

PLATE VIII. Escara, western Central Altiplano, Bolivia. The town, also shown on Figure 4.1, lies at the foot of a rocky hill of volcanic origin. The church and associated chapels date from the sixteenth century. The town contains a mixture of poor peasant thatched cottages and improved tin-roofed houses but each stands in a plot large enough to allow some crops to be grown. Shops are visually indistinguishable but civic pride has led to the main square being embellished by a bandstand, a flag pole and concrete benches. Beyond the town is dry dusty land used for growing quinoa (a native grain) and beyond that is poor scrub pasture on which sheep and llamas graze.

PLATE IX. A colonial street, Colombia. House fronts in colonial towns are often bare of ornament save for window grilles and middle-class homes have no imposing doorway. Life is oriented towards the central patio.

PLATE X. La Paz, Bolivia. The capital of Bolivia nestles in a basin below the Altiplano. The Central Business District lies in the valley bottom and the major commercial establishments along longitudinal highways. Shanty towns cover the hillsides above the city but the vacant land there is owned by the municipality through whom the migrants can buy it. The smart suburbs are lower in the valley—the north American colony, for example, is in the transverse valley in the centre of the far right of the photograph.

PLATE XI. Mera, Ecuador, 1961. Towns within zones of colonization spring up quickly and have neither many conveniences nor much visual merit. Timber is cheap therefore houses are of wood and they line the only street. The forest begins at the end of the back garden. Plentiful bars for weary colonists give the town a 'Wild West' look. A military camp lies to the right of the road in the picture.

PLATE XII. Newly cleared land, near Puyo, Ecuador, 1961. Some trees are left standing, often for shade. In this site bananas and coffee are being grown amid burnt tree stumps. The colonist at first has only time to build himself a simple home.

PLATE XIII. Areas of spontaneous and planned colonization near Caranavi, Bolivia, 1971. Although limited areas of good land can be cultivated near to the River Coroico it will be appreciated that the majority of the land is sloping and some on slopes approaching 15°. Much of the land is planted to bananas and also cacao, coffee and citrus fruit.

habitants are clearly superior to the rural population of the surrounding areas but, on the other hand, their inhabitants feel inferior to people in the large regional and national urban centres whose inhabitants include a much greater variety of social classes than do small towns.

The inhabitants of the small towns are seldom predominantly farmers, rather they make their living from providing services to the rural people, particularly by buying and selling goods. Some families may own land but seldom does all their income come from farming. Typically, for example, the husband and his sons might farm but his wife would maintain a shop that could provide much of the family's cash income.

Rural market towns are thus distinguished from smaller urban nuclei, hamlets, or villages, by their clearly urban nature and the acknowledged difference between the townsfolk and the rural population. These towns can be differentiated from the larger centres by their size, lack of urban-located industry, the limited range of services that they offer, and the fact that they serve a restricted geographical area. Such small towns are often isolated and relatively inaccessible by comparison with larger and more important centres.

A. Town and Country

The social distinction between rural and urban people is very sharp. It is clearly mainly people of a lower social position who work on the land. The towns are inhabited, so townsfolk would say, by people of substance: merchants, small landowners and shopkeepers. The representatives of authority, the police and local political representatives, live in the town and certainly never in the countryside.

The countryman, for his part, whether he likes it or not, has to go to the town to buy paraffin for his lamp, matches to light it and beer for his daughter's christening. The people who are most likely to buy his crops or to lend him money to buy a pure-bred ram or bull are from the town. If a farmer is disliked by people in the town they can refuse to sell him anything and refuse likewise to buy anything that he wishes to sell. It seems in short that although there is a symbiotic relationship between town and country, each needing the other, it is the townsman who derives greatest benefit from this and the countryman is very much at his mercy. The exploitation that takes place is amply indicated by the frequency with which peasant revolts are directed against neighbouring small towns. In the period following the 1952 Revolution in Bolivia, the peasants in part of north-east Potosí, both those living in freeholding communities as well as those on estates, besieged the nearby town of San Pedro de Buenavista, where the townsfolk had thoughtfully armed themselves with automatic rifles. The peasants accused the townsfolk of trying to encroach on their land, and of charging unnecessarily high prices for goods in their shops. A bloody battle ensued at the end of which the surviving peasants were forced to retreat.

Figure 4–1. Escara, Bolivia. (From a field plan by Rosemary Preston)

If the people of small towns are powerful in their own areas, they are still in part subservient to the regional centres, in particular provincial capitals. In most Latin American countries positions of authority from Prefect (of a province) down to local postmaster and holders of rights to sell alcohol (frequently a government monopoly) are held by people in favour with the national political regime. Thus townsfolk who aspire to a position of importance need to be allied with the correct political group and with those who make the minor appointments. Therefore the people in the larger regional centres look to their friends and relatives in the capital to help their nomination, while people in the small towns look to friends in the regional capital who, they hope, will gain important positions and who will then nominate *them* to positions available in the smaller towns. What happens effectively is that a social hierarchy of towns is established where people in each town depend upon others in higher-order towns for their patronage. The small towns, therefore, dominate the countryside but are themselves subject to the larger towns.

The population of the small towns is far from homogeneous although the majority of the people belong to the lower and middle sectors of society. A proportion of the inhabitants are labourers with no land of their own, or servants of those families rich enough to have servants. Some work as apprentices or workers in the minor local cottage industries such as shoemakers, tailors or hatmakers. The most distinctive social element in the small towns, however, is the middle class: shopkeepers, small landowners and merchants, for they are seldom found in the countryside. All this group are distinguished socio-geographically by being much less tied to their home areas than the rural farmers and they are much more likely to have contacts in the larger towns and cities and to make journeys there regularly themselves. They are thus far more integrated into national, political, and economomic life than the farmers.

B. Physical Aspects of the Towns

Many of the small towns are of relatively ancient origin and were founded during the colonial period. Thus their form and the buildings they contain reflect many of the conditions under which the town was first founded. A rectangular street pattern is common with the centre of the town defined clearly by a square on the edge of which is found the church, often built during the colonial period, and other public buildings such as the offices of the mayor, the local traffic inspector, and maybe the policeman, as well as a school. Figure 4–1 and Plate VIII show the plan of a small town of 400 inhabitants in an arid area of the Bolivian Altiplano.

Few houses are of two storeys except around the main square and along the principal road. In very poor towns there may even be no houses with more than one storey. Roofing materials are also an indication of the social aspirations of the inhabitants. Thatch predominates throughout the poorest towns, and in the houses of the poor around the edge of any town. Depending on the availability of materials tile is common as well as slate or stone in mountain areas. A recent innovation carrying with it increased prestige is the use of corrugated iron as roofing material. Walls are built of mud and straw pressed together in a wooden frame; more recently mud bricks have become widely used. Increasingly houses are painted, and where white predominated, now pastel colours appear. In the rural towns in Bolivia that have been spontaneously developed by the local workers, it is very noticeable that pinks and blues occur together with the more traditional white. In the smallest towns it is common to have garden plots where crops can be cultivated, as can be observed on the plan of Escara (Figure 4–1). Small market centres in recently developed colonization areas in tropical lowland areas and in places such as the three southernmost states of Brazil are very different. Settlement in general is initially concentrated along the roads and only at a very much later stage does it spread away from the highway. As a consequence service facilities tend to be scattered along the highway and only slowly does a market centre become identifiable. This process has been described in detail as part of the colonization process in the inner areas of Santa Catarina and Rio Grande do Sul in Brazil as well as in Bolivia and Ecuador. Under such conditions the development of clearly identifiable rural market centres is confined to locations where highways meet or at bridging points of rivers, where produce is gathered by merchants before being sent to the major urban centres.

Amenities not found in the country make any town distinctive and it is often such things that attract rural people to live in towns. The local *pensión* offers hot baths, distinctive in the town maybe, but unheard of in the country; water comes from a faucet and not from a well; sometimes light at night comes from the town's generator which enables the local bar to have a refrigerator to cool the beer. The school is only a hundred metres away and the doctor and priest may, with luck, be close on hand for the living and the dying.

Land within these small towns is often controlled by the town council even though householders have the right to land that they occupy. In part this arises through the very common lack of a legal title to the land on the part of the townsfolk, but it may also be seen as a remnant of traditional pre-Columbian social organization when communal rights to land were more widely in evidence. Town councils may now see the common good as sufficient reason for enforcing a change in property boundaries to permit the widening of a road or the construction of a football pitch. This is illustrated by a case that was encountered in the village of Escara (Figure 4–1). A town sports club had decided to erect a basketball pitch in the town using part of the garden plot of a member of the club and of an old woman whose land adjoined. The Town Council agreed to this and both those whose land would be used were offered alternative plots on the edge of the town. The old woman refused but the pitch was built nonetheless and used until she had a wall built across the pitch in order to mark her original plot.

C. The Town as a Central Market

In rural areas all towns act as market centres to some extent. Where the surplus of agricultural production is small the market function of such towns may not always be apparent; in one small town in northern Ecuador, for example, the Sunday market consisted of two old women selling potatoes and beans. But a lot of transactions take place in shops, where a man might trade 3 kilos of potatoes for a couple of bottles of beer. Even if the town itself is not a major collection point for crops and livestock from the surrounding region, merchants may use it as a temporary base while buying local produce and the town derives some benefit from this.

As a supplier of manufactured goods also the town is important and, in particular, items of everyday use, such as flour, salt or matches are in constant demand no matter how poor the surrounding rural area may be. The profit margins on goods sold in town stores vary in relation to the availability of other sources of similar goods. Thus in isolated areas of Brazil goods may cost double their price in São Paulo, a difference which is not wholly accounted for in the extra cost of transportation. On the other hand, in northern Bolivia knitted goods smuggled from Peru are cheaper in the small towns near the frontier than in La Paz. The cost of smuggled goods to the merchant increases with every customs post that has to be passed, where either a bribe is necessary or some goods are confiscated. Thus the cost of goods rises rapidly with increasing distance from the frontier according to the number of customs posts. Smuggled Argentinian champagne in Bolivia costs 50 per cent more in La Paz than in Cochabamba, over 500 kilometres nearer to the frontier. The competition for the sale of coca leaves (for chewing) however is sufficiently great that no major differences in price occur between the city of La Paz and the small towns 80 kilometres away.

Rural people can avoid using their local town for buying and selling by travelling further to another centre. This takes time and may lead to relatively little cash benefit. The small towns are a crucial stage in the flow of agricultural goods from the areas of production to the centres of consumption and are likewise the principal agents through which manufactured goods and basic necessities are sold to the rural population.

The rural centres should be seen as numerically important small towns that link the rural population with the urban life of each country. They occupy one of the lower positions in any urban hierarchy and they are very numerous. By reason of the great contrasts between urban and rural living the towns are archaic in their social structure, undemocratic in their use of power and monopolistic in the abuse of their role as market centres. Despite this, to the rural population they are trendsetters and farmers often aspire to becoming town dwellers. In short, the rural towns are the main link in Latin America between the backward rural areas and the more progressive and dynamic urban sector.

Small towns that are rural market centres are predominantly populated by families that earn their living by providing services—shopkeepers, petty bureaucrats etc.—and by farmers who chose to live in a town. Such towns are remarkable for having very little industry and thus very few wage-earning proletarians. Industry does not grow up easily so far from the major population centres and, when it does occur, it is small-scale and short-lived, as well as often associated with political patronage or local initiative. Efforts to stimulate small-scale co-operative effort which would involve many people working individually and obtaining raw materials and selling the products collectively have had relatively little success except in the short term. Traditional industries such as hat-weaving and leather-working are at the mercy of fashion and depend on a steady demand unassociated with advertising. Urban-fashioned tastes, on the other hand, are more commonly for factory-made goods that are made in cities. Rural industrialization is not common, it runs counter to the interests of the existing urban industrial centres, and those charged with implementing it are seldom capable of envisaging sufficiently small-scale, labour-intensive projects to affect the rural employment situation.

COLONIAL TOWNS

Many of the towns founded by the Spanish and Portuguese during the colonial period still exist at the present time and have changed relatively little during the past three centuries. Other towns founded during this period became important centres, developed industries, and have grown in size and character to such an extent that they are physically indistinguishable from other cities of similar size of more recent foundation. The towns of the colonial period that have survived with little change, particularly in their central areas, are sufficiently distinctive, both physically and geographically in terms of their internal arrangement, to merit special attention. In addition some elements of the social problems of colonial towns still influence the social geography of both small rural towns and large metropolitan centres.

Physically the colonial-type towns are larger versions of the small rural centres. Built on a rectangular street pattern, centred on a large and often well-kept plaza with other squares in the outskirts of the town, and with the principal buildings in the centre, the colonial-style town seldom appears modern to the visitor. Such changes as do occur usually take place behind the old facades of the buildings and the palatial structures around the central square may pass from being a personal palace to becoming the offices of the regional development corporation. The Governor's palace may become the centre of the regional bureaucracy while the archbishop's residence may be turned into a museum. Houses remain small, seldom exceeding three storeys around the central square and diminishing in size to a single floor within 200 metres of the town centre.

Houses were characteristically built around an interior patio and the street entrance of larger homes was often an archway wide enough to permit a carriage to enter. The side of the house facing the street is usually unadorned and if windows open on to the street, they are protected by elaborate wrought-ironwork. (Plate IX.) The houses of the nobility frequently had ornate balconies overlooking the main square where the family could watch the demonstrations and displays that have traditionally taken place there. Most towns had, and continue to have, market buildings, usually away from the centre, in order that the sale of goods can be controlled and taxed for the financial benefit of the municipality. Streets are frequently surfaced with cobblestones although perhaps the square and main thoroughfares will be given a modern smooth surface. High pavements of stone are sometimes reminders of the period when the streets were awash in the wet season and pedestrians were high above the splashes made by passing vehicles.

Colonial towns, such as Popayán in Colombia (80,000 inhabitants), serve people from rural districts and other smaller towns from a large area. Its amenities make it very distinct from the small market centres to the visiting rural worker. It is here that important political figures live, and where there are firework displays on national holidays. To buy a major item like a mechanical cultivator, or even a bicycle with three gears, it may be necessary to come to the big town. Even the poor who live in these towns have access to a greater variety of amenities. There is drinking water within 100 metres, a school offering more years of education than any in the countryside, a medical dispensary and a priest or even a bishop ready to hand for those in need.

A. Top People Live in the Town Centre

A widespread principle of social organization in space is that the upper classes tend to live in certain zones of the periphery of towns while the labouring groups live in or adjacent to the centre of the town. Although this generalization is most true of British and Anglo-American cities it is also true in many other countries. However, a most distinctive feature of the social geography of the colonial towns is that the arrangement of people of different social status in the town does not conform to the social patterns of modern towns. Various urban ecologists have described the ideas underlying this feature in detail. In the towns founded during the Spanish colonization it was customary, when the town was first laid out, for the leading citizens to be allocated plots around the main square, around which would be the church and the principal public buildings. Lesser citizens built their houses on the available land further from the centre. In newly-developing urban nuclei in colonization areas a similar pattern can be noted and without doubt this type of social zoning is common in newly established towns: only at a later stage in development do the social élite move outwards. In Spanish America the socially privileged were seldom so numerous that they could not all be accommodated in and around the main square; moreover there was seldom any of the rapid industrialization that might render parts of the town close to the centre less desirable to live in. As a result, even to the present day many towns can be observed where this type of zonation exists (Figure 4–2). Often, naturally, the social pattern has begun to be eroded. Rich people now aspire to owning a modern house and living away from the centre of activity, on the periphery of the town, along shaded avenues and where land is available to build houses for their children. The old mansions in the centre are too large to be occupied by a single modern family and in any case the value of land in the centre has often now become so high that only business concerns or the regional government organizations can afford to buy or rent it.

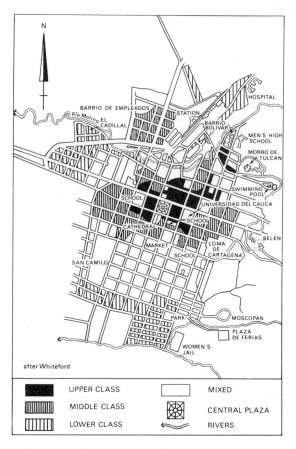

Figure 4–2. Popayán, Colombia

B. Barrios and Neighbourhoods

Social areas within towns or cities known as neighbourhoods in the U.S.A. or *quartiers* in France are called *barrios* in Latin America. In the old colonial town the origin of the distinctive nature of the barrio lay in the colonial period when ordinances laid down where people of certain social origin, in particular Indians, should live. The creation of sub-units in the colonial period has often contributed to the barrios being ingrained in the plan of the town, each barrio having its own church and on occasions its own central plaza. The famous *diablada* of Oruro in Bolivia (a procession of dancing groups) is composed of groups each from a particular workers' guild or barrio within the town. Such segments of the towns, like neighbourhoods in Anglo-America, retain their identity and have their own name. Today in a large town they may even have their own football teams.

C. Colonial Towns in a Modern World

Although colonial towns were in part arbitrarily founded by the conquerors, those that have survived as viable urban centres in the present century are those that fulfil important economic roles as regional centres. The extent to which changes have taken place in a particular town may thus be said to be as much a function of the change in the region which the town serves as within the town itself. The coastal areas of Latin America are more prosperous and modern than the highlands and the colonial centres of the coast. Towns such as Trujillo in Peru or Panama City have been transformed by spreading residential areas, expanding slums and developing industries. By contrast, in the mountains agriculture has changed relatively little and the volume of business in the urban centres has grown only slowly and Popayán (Colombia), Cuenca (Ecuador) or Salta (Argentina) remain colonial towns in atmosphere and appearance, even though they have outgrown their colonial boundaries.

Change in the towns of this category comes more on their periphery than in the centre. New suburbs grow but they are grafted onto the old urban plan without necessarily transforming the old pattern. Gradually, however, the new suburbs include homes for the old upper class who formerly lived in the town centre, as has been indicated above, but this is only a stage in the slow process of urban evolution which has come belatedly to these towns.

As economic centres these towns collect goods from surrounding rural areas and from the small towns that have a lower rank in the urban hierarchy. These goods support some industries, such as flour milling, but much of what they collect is passed on directly to the major markets—the metropolitan centres. These transactions provide employment for a part of the middle-class, white-collar group in the town. The town also is a centre for the distribution of manufactured goods, received from the major industrial or commercial centres, for consumption in the town and for sale to the rural people who come to town to trade. Because of these commercial functions the town contains not only an aristocracy whose chief source of wealth and power is the ownership of land and the manipulation of sources of political patronage, but also a solid group of citizens who live from retail and wholesale trade, from the management of small industrial establishments and through employment in government offices. In the small towns, by contrast, there are few people who can aspire to being well within the middle class and certainly only a handful who could be classed as white-collar workers. The colonial city then is an historical anomaly, a town that has not grown or changed sufficiently to have thrown off its past. It is located more often in backward highland areas than amid the hustle and bustle of the coastlands, but it nonetheless offers a quality of living and a range of opportunities, both social and economic, which are the envy of villager and peasant.

METROPOLITAN CENTRES

The colonial town is a distinctively Latin American phenomenon: the metropolitan centres of Latin America are basically similar to such areas in other highly urbanized parts of the world. Four urban agglomerations: Buenos Aires (8 million), Mexico City (10 million), São Paulo (6 million), and Rio de Janeiro (4 million), are among the two dozen largest urban centres in the world, and another thirteen urban areas have a population in excess of 1 million.*

Perhaps one-third of the population of Latin America lives in towns and cities with over 20,000 inhabitants, and of these one-third live in the four largest metropolitan areas mentioned above (see Figure 4–3). In Argentina, Cuba, Chile and Venezuela over half the population live in towns. The proportion of the population living in urban areas is perhaps less important than their role in the economic and social life of each of the countries. People living in cities, particularly large metropolitan areas, are better educated, earn more and are more involved with national political life than people from the small towns and the countryside. It is in the cities that major decisions are taken which affect the lives of everyone in the nation. As a result, in the past and to some extent at the moment, people outside the big cities are jealous of the fortune of the city folk. This is of course not peculiar to Latin America but these feelings are particularly bitter in countries where there are few very large cities. They are also of great importance in encouraging people to migrate to the cities. In Colombia, where there are four cities with over half-a-million inhabitants, Baranquilla, Cali and Medellín rival Bogotá for the jealousy of the non-urban population. A considerable amount of inter-city rivalry occurs too but this frequently consists of the smaller urban centres complaining of the growth of the capital or primate cities.

The concentration of a sizeable proportion of the population in cities is by no means a recent phenomenon. Even during the early colonial period there were only a small number of urban centres, usually the administrative centre of a Viceroyalty, or Audencia, and the more wealthy and aristocratic Spaniards maintained residences there even if they travelled widely or it they owned lands elsewhere. It was often the failure of the Spanish crown to establish other impor-

* Including Santiago (3.1 million), Bogotá (2.8 million), Caracas (2.2 million), Havana (2.4 million) and Lima (3.2 million). In each case the population refers to the total urban area and not just to the administrative unit of the city itself.

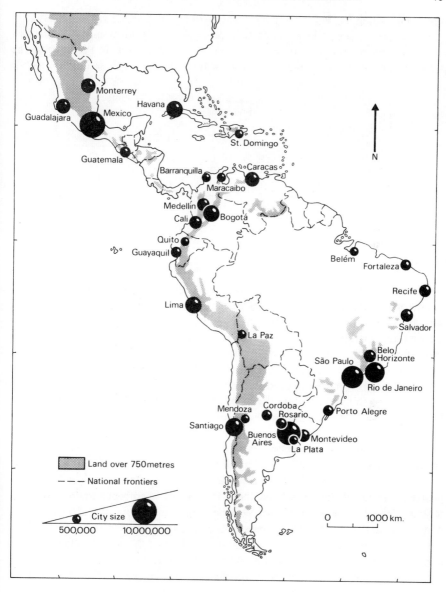

Figure 4–3. Big cities of Latin America

tant towns which has led to the concentration of population, power and prestige in a few centres. It seems however to be a principle of city growth that the largest cities grow most rapidly, exluding of course new towns. Thus in Peru during the period 1961–72 the following rates of growth occurred.

Table 4–1. Population increase in Peru 1961–72 (numbers in thousands)

Area	1961	1972	% increase
Greater Lima	1436	3158	120
Urban population*	3262	4988	53
Rural population	5209	6766	30

* Excluding Greater Lima.

A. The Physical Aspects of Metropolitan Centres

Buenos Aires is by far the largest city in South America, and indeed the Southern Hemisphere. Its 7,000,000 inhabitants occupy 120 square kilometres. It was not a colonial centre of importance but it epitomizes the nature of modern metropolitan centres. Founded on the south bank of the estuary of the River Plate in 1536 and again, after initial failure, in 1580, the colony prospered little and the town saw only limited prosperity until after 1778 when trade by sea with Europe was permitted. Prior to this goods were sent overland through the Andes to Lima in order to be shipped to Spain. By 1800 the town had barely 40,000 inhabitants, but the latter half of the nineteenth century saw the development of the Pampas and a flood of immigrants from Europe. By 1900 the population had leapt to 821,000 and by 1925 to more than 2,000,000. After this the built-up area expanded beyond the limits of the City of Buenos Aires until in 1960 the City had a population of 3,000,000 and the whole metropolis contained over 7,000,000 people. A result of this growth has been the spread to embrace townships on its margins (see Figure 4–4), the development of a new port over 50 kilometres downriver, and the increasing congestion of traffic in the centre of the old city. Radial boulevards were built across the grid pattern of the streets in the 1930s to improve the condition of the centre but, as in the largest cities of western Europe, the improvements have little more than temporarily alleviated the congestion of the city thoroughfares.

Although inevitably each city is unique, the problems of Buenos Aires are those that beset Rio, Mexico or São Paulo. The nature of the city government in Latin America has often permitted idiosyncratic solutions to commonplace problems and certainly the architectural solution to many city building problems has been visually and aesthetically attractive as well as unusual. An obsession with the French urban design of the Napoleonic period has often led to the creation of wide

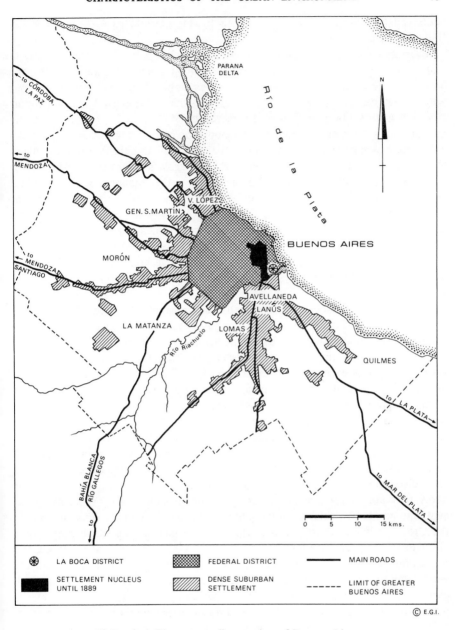

Figure 4–4. The metropolitan region of Buenos Aires

boulevards and focal points like the Plaza de Mayo in Buenos Aires or the Plaza Bulnes in Santiago de Chile.

A distinctive feature of all Latin American cities but particularly the big cities is that their history is often reflected in their street names. National heroes are honoured and even poets and authors are remembered in newly named streets. Some street names change to follow current fashion and every Latin American city now has its Plaza or Calle John F. Kennedy. Dates of note are also commemorated in street names, an urban phenomenon rare in Anglo-American cities.

In recent years the visible changes in the metropolitan cities are those familiar to all of us in our own large cities. (Plate X.) The growth of large multiple stores in city centres, the replacement of old office blocks with gleaming new towers in the central business districts, and the rapid growth of shopping centres in the middle-class suburbs. In the middle and upper-class suburbs the house style is more heterogeneous than in Anglo-America or Europe. Colonial-style homes (built after 1960) that would not be out of place in Beverly Hills, California, stand cheek by jowl with rococo extravaganzas looking like gingerbread castles. Gleaming, daring, modern plateglass houses stand beside copies of Anglo-American ranch-style homes.

If the well-off of Latin American metropolitan centres live comfortably in attractive if ornate homes, the poor too have made their mark on the urban landscape. The population increase in the big cities has comprised mainly poorer people. They lacked the resources necessary to obtain their own homes and, like urban immigrants everywhere, they settled first in poor overcrowded lodgings in the decaying areas around the central business districts of the main cities. As a family established itself in one of these reception areas its members found some sort of employment and learnt more about city life, then they usually moved out to occupy their own piece of land in one of the rapidly developing squatter settlements on poor unused land on the edge of the city. A sea of poor shanties occurs on some parts of the edge of most large cities in Latin America. In Rio they are called *favelas,* in Lima *barriadas,* in Medellín *tugurios* but, whatever their name, they are the predominant housing for the urban poor and especially for recent immigrants. All cities are attempting to help the newcomers. Some cities help them to negotiate titles for the land they have illegally occupied, all make some effort to provide teachers for the new schools, main sewage, water and electric power, but few manage to re-accommodate more than a small proportion of the worst housed. But to the rural-born migrants, even those living in a shack with cardboard walls and a tin roof, being able to earn enough money to live is preferable to being a poor peasant, owning no land and with little prospect of being able to earn money. By rural Latin American peasant standards, the workers of the big cities are well-off and that is why more migrants arrive each day to the cities. The shanty towns are located on the least desirable land, often on steep hillsides as in Rio, or in Santiago, along rail tracks, and although initially the houses are flimsy, insanitary and inadequate they are improved over time and paper walls are replaced by mud bricks, and whitewashed two-storey structures are by no means unknown in long-established squatter settlements.

B. Ecological Patterns in the Big City

The zonation both into physical areas and by social groups is very different from that in the rural market centres. There the central plaza marked the geographical centre of the town and where those with highest social status lived. Those with a lower social position lived further away from the centre. This is clearly quite contrary to the prevailing theories of urban social ecology. In Anglo-American cities the centres are non-residential business districts, and people of highest social status live far out on or beyond the city limits. In reality the big city and the small town are such completely different places to live in that it is hardly surprising if the social geography of each is distinct. Smaller cities such as Mérida in Yucatán have begun to change from the small town pattern towards that of the big city: many of the upper class, both the new rich and the aristocracy, have moved to smaller but more modern homes on the edge of town and offices and shops have taken over the mansions of the rich. The rural immigrants likewise cannot always find somewhere to live in the city and thus live in newly urbanized areas on the edge. The development of neighbourhoods *(barrios)* has been a logical result of the segregation of new housing of different people of differing social status on the edge of the city. In the large cities industry has needed more space to grow and this has further increased the complexity of the urban pattern. As the arrangement of land use in the growing cities has changed so, by and large, has it come to resemble more closely the urban patterns of large metropolitan centres in the northern hemisphere.

Latin American towns and cities are the most rapidly changing part of the continent and thus it is as important to understand the patterns of social class and land use in the old and the new towns and the directions in which change is taking place as it is to be able to describe in detail the urban pattern of any one urban centre.

Conclusion

Although the types of urban settlement where the majority of the Latin American urban population live have been analysed there has been no mention of several highly distinctive types of urban settlement which are of significance in certain parts of Latin America.

In other chapters some indication is given of the role that extractive industries play in the Latin American economy. Associated with extractive industry, distinctive urban settlements have developed; on the one hand mining settlements of the colonial period, some of which seem to have avoided many of the rules that colonial period urbanists were supposed to follow, and, on the other hand, more recent 'company towns' located on oilfields, mining areas, or near to large sugar, cotton and banana plantations.

The colonial mining towns were located, naturally, close to major mines, even if no suitable site for the development of a town existed. Some, like Zacatecas in Mexico, are huddled in narrow mountain valleys, others, like Potosí in Bolivia, are at exceptionally high altitudes (4000 m), but they have in common the fact that relatively few such towns retained their importance over the centuries. Ouro Preto in Brazil is typical of many old mining centres in that it remains a city with narrow streets, old churches and other fine colonial period buildings but it has ceased to be an important regional centre, having been long since outstripped by Belo Horizonte.

More modern mining centres are frequently associated with the ownership of the mine, or mines, by one company and the associated company towns thus have a degree of homogeneity that might otherwise be lacking in their visual appearance. Such towns as Chuquicamata in Chile, or Toquepala in southern Peru, have all the characteristics of a company town but in addition they are like the colonial mining towns in that they are located away from major routeways and often, as in the case of Chuquicamata, far from densely populated agricultural zones. Major oil centres also spawn a host of small company towns, such as El Tigre, San Tomé and Anaco in N.E. Venezuela, but also, when associated industries are located there, more diversified industrial complexes often locate around existing minor regional centres. Maracaibo in Venezuela, despite its old centre, owes much of its rapid growth to its position on one of the continent's most developed oilfields and its character is more that of an oil centre than a regional capital; Tampico on the Gulf coast of Mexico has likewise developed from being a minor regional centre to being a major industrial town with services and housing of a better quality than might have otherwise been expected. San Pedro Sula in northern Honduras is a similar type of town whose growth is closely linked with its proximity to the main headquarters in Honduras of the United Fruit Company. Its traditional though prosperous central area contrasts with the smart houses, gardens and paved roads of the white-collared workers and the company town of La Lima, 11 km to the east—the actual HQ of the United Fruit Company—might not be out of place in Florida, so smart and clean does it seem. Above all, this type of town and those previously mentioned are enclaves of development in an underdeveloped region and there is a prosperity unexpected in such an area which contrasts sharply with the poverty of the surrounding rural areas.

Apart from the influence of foreign companies on the urban scene in Latin America, a modern development of note is the establishment of wholly planned new cities in sites where no settlement previously existed. The most visually impressive of these is Brasília but the rapidly developing centre of the industrial complex at the junction of the Orinoco and Caroní rivers in S.E. Venezuela—Ciudad Guayana—is planned to become the largest new city in Latin America (see also p. 252). Older planned new cities founded earlier this century include Belo

Horizonte, a major industrial city in Minas Gerais in Brazil, and Londrina in the state of Paraná, founded in an area of expanding agriculture in the 1930s and now the centre of the new coffee zone with important agricultural processing industries. The planning and growth of such new cities is important because it represents an effort to develop new urban foci but the success of such enterprises is limited. In neither Brasília nor Ciudad Guayana was it possible to prevent the rapid growth of squatter settlements while the houses for the middle sectors were built. Although such informal solutions to the seeming inability of governments and international experts to provide low cost housing for the working class were successful at an individual level, the workers' housing was often far from places of employment (Brasília) and difficult to incorporate into the urban plan of the growing cities. The growth of such centres has proved so far to be an ineffective way to divert migrants from their usual destinations in the big cities. Thus the number of migrants to Brasília has not diminished the even greater number that head for São Paulo and Rio. In Venezuela migration is still largely towards Caracas and those going to Guayana form only a very small part of the total migrant population.

The importance of the development of such new cities is that it reflects a willingness of planners and governments in Latin America to realize that the development of new areas is necessarily linked with the development of new urban centres to serve them. The problems posed to planners by both Ciudad Guayana and Brasília are complex and stimulating and Brasília represents a new development in capital city planning. If a unity of plan were a major characteristic of the towns founded during the colonial period, so a search for new ideas and forms may characterize the new cities of Latin America.

Bibliography

SCHURZ, W. L., *This New World*, Dutton paperback, New York, 1964.
An extremely useful and interesting account of a wide variety of features of Latin American landscapes in both town and country with a wealth of bibliographic references.
SCHNORE, L. F., 'On the spatial structure of cities in the two Americas', in P. M. Hauser and L. F. Schnore (Eds.), *The Study of Urbanization*, Wiley, New York, 1965, pp. 347–99.
A valuable analytical study of city structure in Latin America compared with widely used models of urban spatial organization. An extensive bibliography.
HOUSTON, J. M., 'The foundation of colonial towns in Hispanic America' in R. P. Beckinsale and J. M. Houston (Eds.), *Essays in Honour of E. W. Gilbert: Urbanization and its problems*, Blackwell, Oxford, 1968, pp. 352–390.
An important analysis of the problems faced by city founders in the early colonial period in the New World.
SCOBIE, J., *Argentina: A city and a nation*, Oxford University Press, New York, 1971.
In the context of Argentinian historical development selected chapters include an account of the development of Buenos Aires up to the middle of the present century.

Lewis, O., *Children of Sánchez*, Penguin Books, Harmondsworth, 1964.
Life in Mexico City for the poor as told by the members of one family to a North American anthropologist. Enthralling, impressive and exhaustive.

Whiteford, A. H., *Two Cities of Latin America (Queretaro and Popayán)*, Doubleday paperback, New York, 1964.
An account of the class structure and associated characteristics of the inhabitants of two cities, one of which retains many of the characteristics of colonial towns.

Sargent, C. S., *The Spatial Evolution of Greater Buenos Aires, Argentina, 1870–1930*, Arizona State University Press, Tempe, 1974.
A valuable additive to Scobie's work seen through more spatially-oriented eyes, emphasizing the forces which moulded the urban pattern of the metropolis.

Epstein, D., *Brasília: Plan and Reality. A Study of Planned and Spontaneous Settlement*, University of California Press, Berkeley, 1973.
A valuable and thorough study of the city and the peripheral settlements.

Reina, R. E., *Paraná. Social Boundaries in a Latin American City*, Center for Latin American Studies, Tempe, Arizona, 1974.
Useful as a study of a major city in the hinterland of Buenos Aires with an excellent treatment of the social geography of the city.

CHAPTER 5

Land Reform and Colonization

A major reason for discontent in Latin America is the wide gap between the income and way of life of the rich and the poor. Every country, not least the U.S.A. or the United Kingdom, has people who are extremely poor and whose poverty is in part a result of the failure of society to provide for them. In the countries of Latin America (and indeed throughout the Third World) the proportion of the population who are poor according to any one of a variety of criteria is very much greater than in the advanced industrialized countries and in some regions, such as rural Haiti, maybe as many as half of the inhabitants are poverty-stricken. The reasons for this poverty are various but include the monopoly of political power, wealth and ownership of land by a very small segment of the population. Where extreme poverty exists alongside obvious exploitation of many by a few then discontent exists which may erupt into revolution.

The aspect of this problem which is of concern to geographers is the uneven distribution of land and resources and the systems of farming the land which are associated with this maldistribution. Of particular note to social geographers is the pattern of conditions that gives rise to attempts to change the exploitive system. The lack of opportunities for rural people either to maintain or improve their living standards gives rise, on the one hand, to the demand for measures to reallocate land more equitably and, on the other, to a movement by rural people away from their birthplaces to newly-developing colonization zones, often in tropical lowlands, and to the rapidly-developing urban centres.

In this chapter some of these movements will be examined in order to understand something of the new settlement patterns that are emerging. Even land reform in densely populated areas results in changes in both agricultural systems and the spatial organizations of settlements as well as in the legal ownership of land. Settlement in new lands is an ancient process but it has become more rapid and widespread in the past twenty years. Latin America is fortunate in having so much land available for future settlement, even if the agricultural potential of much of it remains to be investigated and proved. In addition, in some desert areas, particularly in Mexico and Peru, new irrigation schemes are bringing fresh land under cultivation and making an even greater contribution to the national economies than do the colonization projects in humid tropical lands.

LAND REFORM IN PROGRESS

One purpose of land reform may be assumed to be to effect a modification of the relations between man and the land he uses and thereby to solve some of the grave problems that affect life in rural areas. It is unrealistic to criticize the results of some land reforms by referring to such abstract matters as a balance of payments crisis that seems incomprehensible to rural workers, whose concern is a lack of title to land that they and their forefathers have cultivated, as well as the excessive demands that the landowner makes upon their time without any form of payment. Indeed, it may be said that the most far-reaching Latin American land reform programmes that have been carried out, those in Mexico, Bolivia, Cuba and pre-1973 Chile, were directed more at achieving a wider measure of social justice for rural people than at increasing the value of agricultural output. Because of this, in this chapter, we shall be concerned with the ways in which man–land relationships have been altered: the new forms of land holding that have emerged, the changes in land utilization, the pattern of cropping or grazing that has resulted, and the degree to which the quality of rural living has been changed by increased income from various sources.

Land reforms can be divided into two categories according to the land holdings that result. On the one hand there are those reform programmes that are *redistributive*, where estates or vacant land is sub-divided and allocated to individual families, and on the other there are those that are *collectivist*, where the ownership of the land is retained in the hands of a corporate body such as the community or even ultimately the state. A sub-division is also desirable between collectivist reforms where ownership is in the hands of the community, however that may be defined, and those where ownership rests with the state. This is an essential difference for example between the Mexican collective *ejido* and the Cuban State Farm or *granja del pueblo* (which in turn are roughly parallel to the *sovkhoz* and *kolkhoz* in the U.S.S.R.).

There are a number of theoretical advantages to collectivist reforms. They retain large land ownership units and are thus in a better position to engage in large-scale farming and to avoid the sub-division of the land as a result of inheritance. A degree of stability in the land-holding pattern is also assured since illegal sale of the land is virtually impossible when ownership is vested in a community rather than an individual. In practice, collective ownership often means a splitting-up of the land into small parcels of land farmed on an individual basis and decisions about farming methods and crops rest with individuals. Often, indeed, the only collective action in which individuals may engage is litigation whilst collective purchases of equipment, seeds, or fertilizer and sales of produce are as difficult to stimulate as in rural freeholding communities. The main disadvantages of reforms that permit this sub-division of land are largely economic. Individualization of productive units, even though in collective ownership, often leads to traditional methods of peasant farming continuing to predominate and overall productivity remaining static. Furthermore, the process of individualization erodes any will that community members may have to co-operate, rendering later development of collective organization much more difficult.

State farms operate in a completely different organizational framework and with distinct man–land relations. The rural workers in this system are paid employees of the State and are paid by the State in proportion to their work contribution. The management of the farm is in the hands of an individual appointed by the State, not by the workers, and although workers may have opportunities for criticizing the management, the production goals are set by a central planning agency. The advantages of this system are obvious. Cropping systems can be precisely determined in the light of national and regional needs, economies of scale can be gained, especially where expensive machinery can be used and where a single crop can be grown over a wide area. The labour force need be no larger and no smaller than is neccessary and theoretically the barriers to a high degree of efficiency are minimized. The disadvantages are various but chief among them in Latin America is the unwillingness of rural workers in many areas to accept a wage-labourer status without any land of their own. Thus the development of state farms in the Andean highlands is impossible to achieve because, despite the degree to which they are grossly exploited, rural families have the use of small plots of land which in practice, in the short term at least, are theirs to do what they like with and their prime goal is to obtain security of tenure for their house and land. But if state farms are as unthinkable in highland Peru as they are in highland Guatemala, on the coastlands the situation is different, for labourers are accustomed to working for wages without having the use of any land. It is this sort of situation in which state farms are a possible alternative form of tenure.

Whatever form of revision of land tenure institutions takes place, or is proposed, there is a large body of intellectual opinion in favour of some sort of land reform. Frequently agencies whose business is land reform are remarkable for the high degree of dedication and personal commitment that their personnel display. Why then are land reforms so few in Latin America?

Firstly it should be recognized that on paper most Latin American countries have at some time passed a Land Reform Law, but that such laws have seldom had any effect, notwithstanding the heady enthusiasm: 'the land will become for the man who works it' shown by Latin American governments in the 1961 Declaration of Punta del Este. The reasons why land reforms have not been carried out lie primarily in the simple fact that most Latin American countries are controlled by a small sector of society which, in addition to having political power, also owns much of the best farmland. It is unrealistic to expect thoroughgoing reforms from the very people who stand to lose most by them. In addition, those who would gain most from agrarian reform, the rural workers, are often ill-organized and without adequate political representation. In many countries only the literate may vote and if 80 per cent of the rural population is illiterate, as is common, then a sizeable sector of the adult population is thus disenfranchized.

To Marxists the simple answer to this problem is that an agrarian reform can only come about through a broadly-based revolution, and an impressively large number of non-Marxist students of Latin American affairs believe this to be the most effective way of bringing about reform. It is hardly surprising that Anglo-Americans, not least the U.S. Government, have developed an alternative view. This is that *integral reform* is to be achieved by the establishment of family-sized farms supported by a comprehensive programme which includes agricultural extension work, supervised credit, and organized marketing. This is, as one very experienced observer said, 'a partial and very narrow projection of Anglo-American institutions' and presupposes the redistribution of land.

Few Latin American countries have either the manpower, in the form of trained rural extension agents, or the money to invest in an expensive social reform whose economic results are hard to forecast and in many cases include a period of static levels of production. Thus the actual experiences in effective land reform in Latin America have been restricted either to countries whose governments, at least for a time, felt a deep political and ideological commitment to help the rural people, or to those who had the money to engage in a type of reform which would help the toiling masses without causing too much inconvenience to the rich and powerful landowners. Other reforms have been scarcely worthy of the name, employing large numbers of bureaucrats and generally carrying out land redistribution in one small area to which foreign visitors can be taken in order to be impressed with what has been achieved.

LAND REFORM IN ACTION

Three countries will be looked at in greater detail: Bolivia because the 1953 agrarian reform was singularly effective and essentially redistributive; Cuba as an important example of socialist-inspired agrarian reform in the Continent, and lastly Colombia as an example of ineffective non-reform.

Bolivia

The high plateau, the Altiplano, at 3800 m above sea level is one of the most desolate and barren highland areas in the New World but almost all of the most fertile areas were part of large estates. In 1950, 70 per cent of farm units were smaller than 10 hectares but occupied only 0.4 per cent of the farmland, while 8 per cent of the farm holdings, over 500 hectares in size, occupied 95 per cent of farmland. These data refer to the whole country and it is possible that an even greater proportion of large estates existed in the northern Altiplano and the fertile valleys in the vicinity of Cochabamba. Apart from the concentration of agricultural land in the large estates, pressure for land reform resulted even more from the semi-feudal conditions under which the estates were farmed. The workers, who seldom received any wages, were obliged to work between two and six days a week for the estate and in addition to provide labour, services or goods for other tasks. In return they received a houseplot and adjacent land (usually known as a *sayaña*), additional crop-land further away, as well as grazing rights for a limited number of livestock.

Although large estates were common in most parts of Bolivia, except for the northern forestlands and the desert central and southern Altiplano, where rainfall was generally less than 200 mm, it was in the highlands of Cochabamba and La Paz departments where the servile ties of the workers to the estates were most onerous. It was in these regions that the agrarian reform of 1953 had the greatest social impact. The great domains of the Suárez family in the humid tropical north-east were broken up, as were other estates in the Santa Cruz region, but in general it was political pressure directed against individuals rather than the normal process of reform which brought changes here.

The agrarian reform decree established three categories of holding. Properties were declared *latifundios*, which were subject to total expropriation, where the workers had been abused, the landowner had seldom resided and where the forms of agriculture practised by the landowner were archaic. *Medianas propiedades* (medium-sized properties) were declared where the landowner had resided and had used some more modern farming methods. These holdings were subject to expropriation in part only if their size exceeded the maximum laid down for its ecological zone (varying, for example, from 6 ha in the irrigated vineyard valleys of Tarija to 350 ha in the cold desert of the southern Altiplano). Small properties *(pequeñas propiedades)* were inalienable so long as they did not exceed the local maximum (3 ha in the vineyard valleys to 35 ha in the southern Altiplano) and those few estates employing modern methods, the agricultural enterprises *(empresas agrícolas)*, were subject to the maximum appropriation of half their land and were permitted to retain 80 ha in the vineyard valleys and 800 ha in the southern Altiplano. The procedure for expropriation was complex, tedious and expensive. But whether or not individuals and communities received titles is irrelevant, for within two years of the reform most of the peasants had of their own accord taken over the estate and sub-divided the land amongst themselves. The work of the agrarian reform service was thus primarily one of legalizing existing situations, arbitrating disputes, surveying properties and issuing titles. Up to the end of 1974 they had distributed 476,964 titles covering 18.2 million hectares of land. Probably only 60 per cent of those who should benefit from the reform have so far received titles. The effect of the land reform was often more far reaching than was initially intended, and although the freeholding communities of peasants were not directly affected by the legislation, many of them had lost land to neighbouring estates. So long as they had lost land later than 1 January 1900 they could sue for repossession. They were thus able to demarcate at least a part of the boundary of the community which was previously ill-defined and, in some cases, to obtain more land. Peasant freeholding communities were also affected by the changes that were taking place in the nearby former estates. Many formed their own peasant unions and others adopted some of the changes in way of life or agriculture that some former estate workers were engaging in. From 1969 onwards freeholding communities have increasingly benefited from agrarian reform procedures and not only have their boundaries been surveyed and legally determined but in some cases, increasingly in 1970 and subsequently, individual holdings have been demarcated and individual as well as communal titles have been awarded.

The most noticeable change in the spatial organization of rural communities that has resulted from the land reform is the development, in several areas, of new nucleated settlements, often in association with new weekly markets. In the area between Oruro, La Paz and Lake Titicaca (see Figure 5–1), as well as in several places in the Yungas of La Paz, rural people have built new towns around a square, often on a highway, thus forming a tiny new village that in time grows to become a small town with 150–250 houses. The houses are two-storey structures, with windows and a corrugated iron roof quite unlike the traditional houses of the countryside. Many remain empty because their owners prefer to live in the coun-tryside, near to their flocks and fields. On market day the square becomes thronged with people and the previously empty houses are full of life. These new

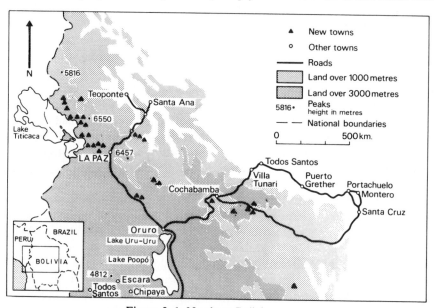

Figure 5–1. Northern Bolivia

towns result from the desire of many rural people to have some sort of urban centre with a wider range of services than they previously had available; from the encouragement given by the peasant union organization to the formation of such towns to stimulate progress; from the need of some members of the community to have a central site where shops can be established and where minor businesses (such as tailoring) can thrive; and finally because the development of new periodic markets following the 1952 Revolution itself encouraged urban growth associated with the market place.

The new markets established since 1952 are a result of the need for a process of exchange to link the peasants as the sole rural producers with the urban centres as markets for their produce. Goods which previously the landlord had sold were now disposed of by the peasants. Many lacked adequate means of bringing produce to cities like Oruro or La Paz and so the urban-based merchants came out to buy the produce.

The changes in agriculture that have resulted from the land reform are variable: while in several regions there has been a transformation of agriculture, in others there has been relatively little change that can be directly attributed to the reform. The income of many farm families has risen since sizeable areas of cultivated land which were previously producing goods for the landowner now produce at least the same volume of goods for the rural workers. Although remarkable changes in the land-use system are uncommon, it must be noted that the potential for change is low. Over much of the Altiplano and the mountain areas rainfall is deficient and frosts common. Where water is available accumulations of soluble salts may make crop growing virtually impossible. Changes in land use that have occurred may be divided into (1) increasing the area of cropland by clearing scrub or ploughing up pasture and (2) intensifying agriculture by planting vegetables or fruit and engaging in what is virtual market gardening. The former changes can be observed in many areas of the Altiplano and in places in the Yungas of La Paz. In one estate on the edge of Lake Titicaca, the pasture next to the estate house, which was in an area of good soil with water readily available, was sub-divided amongst the workers in 1966. It was planted to barley by most people in the following year, and yields were more than double what they were normally. The most spectacular increases in production have been noted in the irrigated lower valley of Cochabamba, in parts of the Yungas of La Paz and in the irrigated valley below the city of La Paz. In each of these areas the intensification of agriculture has been associated with the cultivation of vegetables (in the La Paz valley and the lower valley of Cochabamba), flowers and fruit (La Paz valley), and the cultivation of coffee and extension of the area of coca planting (part of the Yungas). It has been estimated that the value of agricultural production in the lower valley of Cochabamba has increased *tenfold* as a result of these changes in land use. Thus, although in many areas there have been comparatively few changes that are attributable to the land reform, in some areas, each with a relatively high population density, there have been changes and in some of these very remarkable increases in production have occurred. However, the long-term effect of the reform on Bolivian agricultural production as a whole has been negligible. The most important increases in production are those resulting from the extension and intensification of farming in the tropical lowlands, particularly in the Santa Cruz zone, rather than from changes in the highlands.

The effect of the reform has been of much less importance in those areas where feudal labour relations did not exist and where a good deal of land remained that was not intensively farmed. In the eastern parts of Chuquisaca important changes in ownership patterns have occurred with a large number of immigrants in the post-revolution period establishing themselves on scarcely-used land by purchase or just squatting, but landlords had certainly lost their former importance. In Eastern Bolivia the reform has largely affected changes in titling procedures, and restrictions on the acquisition of large areas of land for cattle ranches are frequently circumvented. Where communications are poor, mapping inadequate, and political bosses as powerful as in the 1940s, agrarian reform officials are unable to check the size of livestock herds or of ranches. New ranches, often modern cattle enterprises, are being created and existing properties are incorporating adjacent public, and even private, land rapidly. The maximum size of modern cattle enterprises of 50,000 ha (for 10,000 head) is frequently exceeded but the commercial meat production of the eastern lowlands is increasing—although more in spite of the agrarian reform than because of it.

The Bolivian agrarian reform is only a qualified success. Its objectives were broad and included the transformation of the feudal labour relations on the estates, the incorporation of the indigenous population into national life, the achievement of a fairer distribution of the land among those who work it, and the improvement of agricultural productivity. Although the landlords were effectively banished in most of the areas where feudalism reigned and the status of the Indians has improved, agricultural productivity has not increased, on the whole, in those areas affected by the expropriation of estates nor have glaring inequalities among the rural poor been eradicated. The allocation of land to former serfs *de jure* associated with the prevailing system of equal share of property inherited has led to the widespread creation of minifundia. The failure of the reform to reinforce the role of the community as opposed to the individual as a regulatory landholding mechanism has discouraged the development of co-operatives and any other organization that could help the rural population improve their bargaining power with urban merchants.

Cuba

The pre-revolutionary situation in Cuba was quite distinct from that in almost any other Latin American country. The rural labour force was far from being an impoverished peasantry: the income per head in Cuba was higher than in most Latin American countries and Cuba was one of the more literate nations in Latin

America. Nor was the concentration of large estates so remarkable as in Bolivia. In 1946 57 per cent of the farm area was owned by 3 per cent of the farmers. A more hurried and incomplete census in 1961 suggested that among the estates to be affected by reform 73 per cent of the land was owned by 9 per cent of the farmers.

The need for land reform in Cuba arose less from the concentration of valuable land in large holdings than from the fact that the national economy was dominated by the role of sugar, which was produced in a large part by North American companies. Immediately prior to the Revolution in 1959, 22 of the most important sugar companies occupied 1.8 million hectares of land and 13 of them, all North American, accounted for 1.2 million hectares and had an average size of 90 thousand hectares. In addition to this domination by foreign companies of production of the most important crop, the rhythm of work associated with sugar production was highly irregular. The Cuba Agricultural Census for 1946 revealed that 400,000 people were temporary, paid workers and comprised one-half of the employed agricultural labour force; more than half of them had worked for only four months or less in the year and only 6 per cent of them had been employed for nine months or longer. Data from 1956–57 suggest that the unemployed seldom comprised less than 9 per cent of the labour force but that during the slack season from May to November unemployment could rise to include over 20 per cent of the labour force. Thus seasonal unemployment and attendant poverty were common despite the high levels of *average* income that Cuba enjoyed compared with, for example, Haiti.

A firm commitment to effect a land reform, as part of a revolutionary programme, was made by Fidel Castro in his famous 'History will Absolve Me' speech at his trial in 1953 and a provisional agrarian reform law was prepared three months before the overthrow of the Bastista regime. When this law was put into effect in May 1959 all estates larger than 402 hectares were to be expropriated with compensation; tenancy was abolished (tenants were to become owners); 27 hectares of land was to be distributed to each small tenant farmer, including squatters, free of charge but on condition that it was not mortgaged, sold or sub-divided on inheritance; properties owned by foreigners and land companies were expropriated and co-operatives were to be formed to farm this land. Later, the maximum permitted size of estates was reduced to 67 hectares. The whole process of reform and much control of agricultural production was guided by the National Institute of Agrarian Reform (I.N.R.A.) which was a land reform organization and Ministry of Agriculture rolled into one.

The most important aspect of the reform has naturally been the reorganization of the sugar estates. At first the large estates were run either as State farms *(granjas del pueblo)* or as co-operatives (that is collective farms), and the latter predominated in the sugar cane areas. In 1962 the collectives were abolished and became state farms. In the words of the head of I.N.R.A. they had become 'dead organisms with hundreds and hundreds of members who wanted to have nothing to do with them.' While workers in state farms were paid a guaranteed wage and had a variety of benefits such as new houses and schools, the collective workers were less well treated by the State and conditions of life for them were greatly inferior to those on state farms, even though many collective farmers were able to get good prices for some of their goods on the black market. The remaining small farmers, who farm some 2.8 million hectares, are incorporated into State planning in that they sell their surplus production to official buying agencies although an unknown part of their production 'leaks' onto the market through informal channels. The position of the small farm sector is important with regard to some crops although in 1975 they only accounted for 15 per cent of agricultural production; they account for 80–90 per cent of the production of coffee, tobacco and cacao, for example and one-third of sugar production. Private farms enjoy various advantages: they have far more of their land on the best soils than State farms and are able to attract wage labour more easily, which is of particular importance given the shortage of labour at critical times.

The spatial organization of agriculture has been transformed by central planning but the size of the farm units that have been created has been often so large (some as big as 130,000 hectares) that efficiency has not been achieved. Increased regionalization of agriculture is forecast for the early 1970s with some areas least suited to sugar being turned over to other crops. Attempts are being made to make each province self-sufficient in foodstuffs to decrease crop specialization. This is in part to improve the use of the labour force and should avoid the necessity of moving large numbers of people from one province to another, which consumes valuable transport facilities and necessitates the provision of expensive accommodation for temporary workers. In 1968 the province of Havana for the first time imported less food than it exported.

The main crop under the reorganized agriculture is still sugar cane. Sugar production remains variable and hurricanes have seriously damaged cane-fields so that production in the 1970s has not managed to surpass the 10 million ton target set long ago by Fidel Castro. Mechanization proceeds slowly and the rural labour force is frequently insufficient to obtain the fullest possible harvests. Diversification, after a disastrous period in which a large number of experiments at developing new crops failed, has been moderately successful. Tobacco production has climbed steadily, reaching 29,000 tons in 1969, citrus fruit has greatly increased in importance, production having doubled during 1962–69 but a further increase in production is not expected, owing to labour shortages. An improvement in cattle herds is under way, including improvement of stock, use of artificial insemination, and an increase in the number of livestock. Politically disinterested observers are impressed by the emphasis not only on improved rural social conditions, among which the expansion of education is the most striking, but also the amount of investment in research into new crops and livestock.

The Cuban land reform is directed within an ideological framework even though the ideology is sometimes subject to drastic revisions. But it is not based on individual land ownership. Fidel Castro observed in a speech in August 1962 that no further land redistribution would take place because 'after one piece of land the peasant would want another.' In the particular case of Cuba there is little doubt that this was practical as well as based upon sound socialist doctrine.

The most impressive aspect of the Cuban land reform, according to many non-Cuban observers, is the degree to which social welfare in rural areas has been improved, even at the expense of depriving Havana of resources that its population might expect. Thus, the rural population, which amounts to over half that of the island, is perceptibly better off than before 1959 and a wide range of regional development programmes will benefit rural areas and also the towns and cities elsewhere than in Havana province. As a result, life in Havana appears rather less attractive than it might in a different country which, together with administrative difficulties that prevent would-be migrants getting a job in the capital, has resulted in a low level of capital-directed migration. Why, one may ask, has this been possible in Cuba and not in other Latin American countries? The answer lies in large measure in the nature of the Cuban revolution which has fundamentally changed the organization of development and planning, and the state apparatus is capable of drafting the population to support national development by leaving offices to cut cane, spending weekends in the army, or discussing with superiors and inferiors ways in which performance may be improved. This demands personal sacrifice which many were not prepared to accept but those who did not leave for Miami are those in whose interest a socialist Cuba seeks growth and further independence.

For the Cubans, as for the Bolivians, their land reform has been a social success and carried out at a grass roots level. Most Latin American land reforms are little more than hesitant steps in the wrong direction made by people lacking either conviction of the feasibility of the procedure or the will to act: Colombia's land reform is such as this.

Colombia

In common with a number of Latin American countries Colombia had a land reform law on the statute book long before the present law came into being. In 1936 a land reform law was passed which attempted to regularize the question of squatters' rights and which also contained the provision that land left uncultivated for ten years could be expropriated. By 1946 however the government of the time was disinclined to enforce a clause that would alienate precisely that sector of the population from which it drew its support: the large landowners.

Although Colombia's main export crop, coffee, is grown on small and medium-sized holdings, the best land in the most populated areas is held in large estates. Recent data suggest that almost one-quarter of farm families own no land, while another 47 per cent live on holdings too small to support a family: 70.2 per cent of farm families thus have inadequate land resources. The 1960 Census showed that in the Departments of Colombia (roughly the effectively occupied parts of the country) half the holdings were less than 3 hectares in size and in Antioquia and Boyacá over 60 per cent of the cultivated land was in farms larger than 500 hectares and 20 per cent larger than 2500 hectares.

The case for agrarian reform is undeniable. On economic grounds even the World Bank has criticized a land tenure system whereby cattle graze on the rich plains on big estates, while smallholders over-exploit the surrounding steep hillsides. But the political situation in Colombia has made a thorough-going reform impossible. Traditional hostility between the two major political parties flared into a civil war from 1948–58, known as *la Violencia*, and minor guerilla skirmishes continue in several parts of the country. La Violencia caused disruption in rural areas, and encouraged many to flee to the wilderness of new colonization zones; this resulted in a number of estates being abandoned and subsequently taken over by land-hungry squatters. In 1958 a pact was established between the Liberals and Conservatives which has resulted in the country being ruled for alternate periods by each party for thirty years.

In 1961, in the wake of the Punta del Este Agreement whereby Latin American countries pledged themselves to tackle, among other things, land reform, Colombia passed her Social Agrarian Reform Law. This established a piecemeal approach to reform coupled with adequate compensation for land expropriated. There were no flamboyant phrases to proclaim the universal rights of all to land and the main task of the land reform institute that was founded (I.N.C.O.R.A.) was to promote the settlement of independent cultivators on family farms. The land necessary for this was to come, in order of priority, from public lands, lands farmed by tenants or sharecroppers, and only lastly lands deemed to be inadequately cultivated by their owner. Compensation varied from long-term bonds carrying a low interest rate for uncultivated lands, to short-term, high-interest bonds and a proportion of the value in cash for the more highly valued land: that is, land adequately cultivated by the owner, sharecroppers or tenants.

Work of I.N.C.O.R.A. has been concentrated on giving titles to squatters, as was the aim of the 1936 law, on expropriating unused land and on irrigation projects aimed at settling large numbers of people in situations where highly productive agriculture would be possible. Projects were started in all departments but local opposition from large landowners was fierce and organized. In 1963 in Valle department, for example, a plan to develop a large irrigation project covering 30,000 hectares, only 8000 hectares of which would be expropriated to be allocated to new settlers, was blocked by local estate owners who planned instead to build a sugar mill which would use sugar from the whole 30,000 hectares. Although the agrarian reform land might have been effective had it been possible to implement it in a more realistic way, it contained several important flaws. For example, there was no adequate way of treating absentee ownership or only partially used land, and it was not made possible for I.N.C.O.R.A. to buy land on the open market for subsequent sub-division and settlement. A measure of the effect of the land reform implementation is in the very minor changes in land distribution between 1960–1970 which are revealed in a national survey. Since I.N.C.O.R.A. was established in 1962 until late 1974 only about 20,000 ha of land had been expropriated and land ownership granted to 12,500 families. Even so opposition from the landowners has not abated and the recent introduction of a land revenue tax has demonstrated that some efforts may be made to bring the large landowners more effectively under the control of national legislation.

Other Land Reforms

Land reform experience in three very different situations has been presented, but it should not be imagined that this exhausts the experiences of land reform in the continent. The intention of this chapter has been to provide a demonstration of a range of features of land reforms in order to show how they may alter man–land relations and how they may change the features of the cultural landscape. In conclusion it is necessary to mention something of the nature of three other land reforms that are of considerable importance, in Mexico, Peru and Chile.

The Mexican land reform is the oldest in Latin America and is one that was eagerly watched during the 1930s in order to see to what extent a feudal rural situation could be transformed by the break-up of large estates and by the creation of community collectives *(ejidos)*. By the 1970s the majority of the land that can be expropriated has been distributed, but a large number of landless peasants remain who will never be able to benefit from the land reform programme. The Mexican land reform has been only moderately successful in providing rural social justice. Many of the ejidos were located on poor land while middle-sized private farms on good quality land nearby were a constant reminder to the beneficiaries of their inferiority. The middle-sized farms received finance and technical assistance and increased productivity markedly, and it is this sector which has contributed most to Mexico's agricultural growth. Large livestock farms in the arid north of Mexico were only occasionally affected by the reform and some were even created or consolidated subsequent to the 1917 Revolution. The existence of inequalities and the ineffectiveness of official stimulus to development in the ejidos and the small-farm sector has caused resentment and unrest in several parts of Mexico. Although Indian and non-Indian alike have benefited from the land reform it has not contributed in the same way to the economic and social enfranchisement of the Indians as has Bolivian reform.

The land reform programme in Peru is one of the most recent in Latin America, dating only from the summer of 1969, and yet it has proved important in changing the means of production both in the rich irrigated coastlands and also in many parts of the highlands. In two ways the Peruvian example is striking and may possibly mark a turning point in Latin American rural reforms: the government that initiated it was military and militantly nationalist; and the basis of the land reform was not the breakup of estates into private farms and eventually minifundia but the creation of collective farms on the basis of former estates and also of super-collectives which could unite, in the same region, highly productive estates and subsistence-oriented Indian communities for mutual benefit but primarily in order that smaller and more economically marginal producers could benefit from the example, experience and physical equipment of the former estates.

The recent experience of the Chilean land reform leaves one less enthusiastic about the long-term future for the military in power. While the Peruvian military have become much less dedicated to the social welfare of the rural majority in Chile the democratic government of Allende which had continued and amplified the existing land reform programme started under his predecessor was overthrown by force and wholesale repression was necessary in order to dismantle much of the socialist state structure created by Allende. The land reform programme which had concentrated on the expropriation of large estates and which had created collective farms (asentamientos) in their stead had, by 9 November 1973, affected almost 40 per cent of the usable area of the country (on the basis of Basic Irrigated Hectares, which is a measure of relative area which takes into account the different fertility of the various regions of Chile). The military Junta has been mainly concerned with dismantling the collective structure of the new asentamientos and issuing individual titles on the largely ideological ground that farmers will produce more when working directly for themselves. In addition, the Junta has returned to its former owners land which was thought to have been illegally expropriated which, to the end of 1975, amounted to 23 per cent of the land expropriated, particularly in the South and Centre of Chile. This land includes whole estates that were returned to their former owners and, in about two-thirds of the cases, the return of part of the expropriated land. It will be at least a decade before it is possible to assess the effect of the reforms and now counter-reforms on the rural Chilean population and on agricultural production.

The varied experience of Latin America with regard to land reform reflects a wide variety of approaches to rural problems and the assessment of the effects of such reforms is often clouded by the values of those making the analysis.

The most frequent criticism of land reform programmes is that they lead to a decline in agricultural production. There is plentiful evidence of changes in production patterns following agrarian reform but these may, as in the case of Mexico, be associated with civil strife. The principal aim of any land reform is, however, social rather than economic and it is unfair and largely irrelevant to judge a socially motivated change by its economic results. Land reform does usually bring important improvements to rural areas—schools, roads and expanding towns—and the rural population is thus drawn more effectively into the life of the country. Rural people become consumers even if only in a small way and the market for goods is increased, thus providing more impetus for the growth of industries. Those who suffer most from agrarian reform are the landowners whose estates were so badly tended that they were entirely expropriated. Many had substantial alternative means of financial support; a few had nothing and now live in penury. This seems a small price to pay for an improvement in education, living standards and social progress in rural areas.

A more serious criticism of distributive land reforms is that they create a multiplicity of small plots which can be divided upon inheritance, and thereby the problem of large estates is solved only by the creation of small uneconomic holdings. Collectivist reforms avoid this pitfall and, more often, as was seen in the case of Cuba, have problems resulting from holdings that are too large to be easily managed. One move to combat the growth of small holdings *(minifundia)* has been legislation to prevent the splitting-up of holdings awarded by agrarian reform, but where this runs contrary to the established practice of inheritance it is likely to be ignored. In areas where large estates were absent *minifundismo* is a frequent problem. Many land reform programmes in Mediterranean Europe for example have been aimed more at consolidating small holdings into family farms than dividing up land on large estates. As yet relatively little has been done in Latin America to combat this problem.

COLONIZATION

Land reform is concerned with solving some of the problems of rural areas where there are too many people and too little land available for them. An obvious solution to land shortage is to encourage people to move to other areas where land is available for farming. Latin America has more land potentially available for settlement than many other continents, for the population is highly concentrated in a small number of areas. Almost every Latin American country has extensive areas that are virtually uninhabited and only El Salvador and Uruguay have nowhere for new colonization to take place.

If we seek to identify a common pattern in those areas where high population densities occur and where there is an acute shortage of land, it will emerge that each has been settled a long time, has a good system of communications and often a sufficient degree of physical homogeneity to make it markedly different from surrounding areas. Thus, for example, in Costa Rica settlement is concentrated in the central valley between 500–1000 metres in elevation and nowhere else in the country has a comparable density of population. The area moreover is hemmed in by mountains on two sides and the most accessible areas, towards the Caribbean and the Pacific, have different climates and vegetation and thus present very different agricultural problems from the central valley.

Shortage of land is of course only relative. An area which is unable to provide a living for its inhabitants can be transformed by sowing crops which produce more or which ripen sufficiently fast to permit two crops a year. The provision of water for irrigation can increase productivity enormously. Thus for shortage of land to be linked with a demand for new areas for colonization, there must also be only limited possibilities for improvements in existing farming systems or the soil must be sufficiently exhausted for its fertility to be seriously impaired. The rate of agricultural change in many of the areas with land shortage is so slow that a livelihood can only be provided for all if some people migrate elsewhere. Colonists however are by no means all would-be farmers from the overcrowded rural areas. Investigations in various parts of Latin America have shown that a sizeable proportion of colonists, even a majority in places, are townsfolk, frustrated by the social straitjacket of small-town life, who seek their fortune as farmers even if they have scarcely handled a machete before.

The zones of Latin America that are potentially suitable for settlement include parts of the Amazon basin, in particular the lower foothills of the Andes; the margins of the Llanos of Venezuela and the Gran Chaco; parts of the Pacific and Caribbean coastal slopes of southern Mexico and Central America; and the western parts of Goias and of the southern states of Brazil. Irrigation is a possibility in many arid zones. The recently uplifted mountains of the western side of the continent have been deeply incised by streams whose gorges offer many sites for storage reservoirs or hydro-electric power installations. The long stretch of coastal desert in western South America from Peru to Chile has a number of areas whose highly productive agriculture is based on irrigation. Further areas are expected to be irrigated in the future and the barrier to the extension of irrigation is largely the financial one of the high cost of bringing water to new areas and of the subsequent administration of settlement.

Although considerable differences occur in the problems and needs of colonists in different areas it is possible and useful at this stage to outline some important prerequisites for successful colonization.

1. *Roads.* Without adequate means of communication colonists cannot easily enter a colonization zone nor can they send out their produce to be sold. Railways are inflexible because travellers have to rely on a single entity (the railway company) for transport and only one means of transport, trains, can be used; rivers are apt to flood, to be rendered dangerous by rapids and, only too often in South America, flow in the opposite direction to that in which people want to go. The development of new roads in coastal Ecuador heralded a boom in land, new farms were established, and poor farmers who lived in isolated parts of the forests found a road on their doorstep by which their produce could be transported to the main seaport, Guayaquil, in a few hours. Similarly a valuable study in Central Peru has shown how the fortunes of small isolated settlements in the mountains have fluctuated with changes in accessibility. A recipe for simple colonization is really: 'Build a Road' or for the cynical: 'Plan to Build a Road'.

2. *Adequate soils.* A heartbreaking characteristic of many tropical soils is that their fertility is easily impaired and high crop yields of the first years after clearing the forest give way rapidly to poor yields as the soil fertility declines and erosion progresses. In some areas currently colonized in Bolivia competent soil studies

have suggested that the land cannot sustain cropping for more than 5–10 years and that it would best be suited to properly managed afforestation. Methods of clearing forests and the nature of rainfall should be studied in relation to soil fertility in order that not only should the soil be maintained in as good a state as possible but also that systems of agriculture should be established that have the best possibility of long-term benefit to both farmer and land. To achieve this an efficient extension service is needed.

3. *Education.* People coming to colonization areas seldom have much agricultural experience that is relevant to the new area. They often are not even accustomed to living in tropical lowland areas and are unaware of the dangers and advantages of different ways of living. Working during the midday period when the sun is most powerful is commonplace in the mountains but exhausting and even dangerous in humid tropical lowlands. Personal hygiene assumes a greater importance in a humid lowland environment where bacteria multiply rapidly. The means of telling people about the ways in which the old-established inhabitants overcome these problems is by education. Schools can not only educate the young but people of all ages and thus enable them to make the most of their opportunities. Schools can also inculcate principles of good farming and so help farmers produce more with the greatest benefit to themselves.

The above issues imply a need for previous planning and exploration which is often slow and costly. Governments, subject to political pressures, want quick results. A plan initiated by President X is of little value to him if it comes to fruition during the term of office of President Y, who will naturally claim as much credit as possible for himself. The aims of colonization in many parts of Latin America have been to settle a limited number of families as quickly as possible and to be able to show some positive results within say five years. International agencies, such as the United Nations, the World Bank or the United States Agency for International Development, have a similar need to show results quickly, which often conflicts with a scientifically formulated policy designed to give optimum social and economic benefits. The colonist who is fortunate enough to obtain a plot of decent land not far from a road is still faced with a host of problems which suggests a third important prerequisite for colonization.

Planned and Spontaneous Colonization

A large part of what has been written about colonization has been concerned with areas where colonization has been centrally planned and closely supervised from start to finish. Thus, for example, we know more in Ecuador about the Santo Domingo de los Colorados colonization project which involved only a small number of people than we do about colonization elsewhere in the Guayas lowlands, the Esmeraldas region and the east Andean foothills.

Planned colonization implies the organized movement of selected individuals and families to areas of new settlement where supervision of agriculture and marketing is maintained and even controlled. In some schemes houses are built for the new settlers and feeder roads link their lands to the national markets. Such colonization is expensive: it may cost between U.S. $ 1200–4000 to settle a single family, but only those most likely to be successful are chosen, they receive advice on what to grow, and are helped in a variety of ways to establish themselves. Despite this by no means all planned colonization schemes are successful.

Spontaneous colonization is the result of small groups of pioneers travelling on foot to isolated areas where land is unused and there establishing themselves. As their production of surplus goods increases then they send them on muleback or by canoe to the nearest road. In many cases spontaneous settlement is associated with the building of a new road and new colonists settle beside or within easy reach of the highway. Thus they are able to retain contact with the rest of the country and with the market for their saleable surplus. The essence of spontaneous colonization is that there is no selection of colonists, that nothing is provided for individual settlers save the opportunity to establish individual title to a piece of land, and the main investment that national governments make is the provision of highways. Clearly in some cases there is not even a highway and in others a wide range of services are available: feeder roads, schools, agricultural extension agents and machinery pools to help clear the land for cultivation.

There are manifold advantages to planned colonization. If all goes well your selected colonists are eager, industrious and ready to accept new ideas. Social workers and teachers ensure that people get over initial difficulties, adapt to a new life in a changed environment, and are able to devote all their energies to farming. Economists like planned colonization too. Cost accounting enables a flow of data on how much everything is costing the government. Farmers can be directed to plant crops for which there is a ready market and which give them a satisfactory return. Co-operatives can more easily be established since people are ready and even eager to take advice and thus, notwithstanding the high cost per family established, great benefits can accrue both to the settlers and to the national economy. These advantages have a habit of evaporating when actual cases are studied. Pre-colonization surveys of land suitability are not always accurate; successful colonists are not easily identified from among the scores of would-be migrants; trained extension workers are scarce and often unwilling to forsake a civilized city for the steamy jungle; costs of every stage of the project escalate as a result of poor planning, corruption and unforeseen difficulties; the crops selected by experts do not always grow as well as expected away from the experimental station, they may require elaborate processing, or the selected progressive colonist may prefer to grow bananas for which he knows there is a market rather than cacao which he believes to be harder to grow and whose price he knows nothing about. Every colonization project has tales of ghastly mistakes and costly errors although success is invariably more common than failure for individual settlers. But the overriding consideration in comparing the success of planned and spontaneous colonization is cost. Even where a large proportion of settlers on a planned colonization scheme have made a success of their farms the unit cost of this to the government is high and the number of people who have benefited is low.

There are a multitude of disadvantages to spontaneous colonization. It is difficult to prevent colonists settling in areas where agriculture is likely to give rise to rapid soil erosion on steep slopes. The crops that the new colonist plants are often those already widely available and overproduction may lead to a fall in price which is crippling to the small producer. Colonists establish themselves at different times and there is seldom any organized nuclear settlement. The later establishment of central services, such as electric power, school, infirmary, municipal buildings, is thereby rendered more difficult. Despite these disadvantages there is no lack of potential settlers. Some work first as labourers for others and gain thereby a knowledge of the zone before obtaining land. Colonists grow a variety of crops although there is a tendency to rely on one major cash crop. Although some colonists become discouraged and abandon their land there is always another person ready to take it over. Difficulties do arise when a plot is abandoned and someone wanting to take over the site cannot discover the original owner in order to take over his land legally. A major advantage of spontaneous colonization is that, in spite of the lack of formal urban centres, settlers do organize themselves into coherent social groups and they elect committees to plan improvements and to petition the national government for new schools, or for a bulldozer to clear an area for a small settlement nucleus, or for the establishment of an experimental farm. On planned colonization settlements many facilities are provided and thus the settlers tend to complain about the inadequacy of what they have rather than about what they lack.

There is clearly no solution to the dispute over the merits of planned and spontaneous colonization since they are not easy to compare and both have very different advantages. It is most useful to look at several well-tried projects in different areas to see what sorts of changes have been effected and the extent to which the colonists have adopted modern farming systems.

1. The Fuerte Valley, Mexico: Irrigation, Modernization and Land Reform

The Sonora Desert on the N.W. coast of Mexico renders agriculture impossible except in places where there is irrigation. The area was little settled during the colonial period and it was not until the nineteenth century that irrigation was extended sufficiently for a few estates to be established whose chief activities were cattle raising and sugar cane growing. The Fuerte valley was the site of a brief attempt to establish an advanced socialist colony when it was hoped that an east–west transcontinental railway would be built to terminate at Topolobampo, a fine port site. A new sugar mill built at Los Mochis dominated the economy of the valley until the large estates were expropriated in 1938.

The Fuerte was chosen as the site of a massive and integrated river basin development in 1951. The River Fuerte, together with the Sinaloa, is capable of irrigating a huge area and the Miguel Hidalgo dam built in 1952–56 will be able to provide water to irrigate 230,000 hectares of land. In 1961 the long-dreamed-of transcontinental railway from Chihuahua was completed, thereby opening markets in the centre and east of the U.S.A. to early vegetables for the Fuerte valley (see Figure 5–2).

The new and expanded agricultural possibilities in the Fuerte have given rise to cotton, sugar and rice becoming important crops, with tomatoes of secondary importance. Agricultural reorganization following the agrarian reform and the later increase in area under cultivation has allowed not only improved possibilities for the existing rural workers but also a variety of opportunities in the newly irrigated lands and in the rapidly growing regional trade centres for immigrants from other parts of Mexico. The Fuerte valley is not only a colonization project but rather an integrated regional development plan (like those of Papaloapan in Southern Mexico, the Cauca valley project in Colombia and the Guayana project in Venezuela) which seeks not only to improve existing agriculture, but also to help new farmers get started and to develop new urban centres.

A complex system of land tenure has resulted. In the Fuerte valley in 1960, 110 thousand hectares were in *ejidos* (with 13,800 members) while 75.3 thousand hectares were farmed by 2700 private farmers. The latter are members of a new, increasingly affluent middle class who are progressive commercial farmers and live in the new towns rather than in isolated farmsteads. Many *ejidatarios* rent out their land (illegally) to the private farmers, share-crop land and even work as labourers on their own rented land, but others are successful farmers. The central *ejido* villages have some basic amenities but lack the activity and commercial vigour of the new towns such as Guasave. Furthermore, through historical accident they often have some of the least desirable land. Incomes have risen markedly for many in this area; the increasing dynamism of the regional society and economy has encouraged young people to stay and has provided a new range of opportunities for all the inhabitants.

Colonization over a much more varied and larger area has occurred in the lowlands of the Gulf coast where a valuable recent analysis by Revel Mouroz has enabled colonization to be clearly seen in the perspective of national demographic trends. He demonstrated that colonization is not, at the moment, a viable way of diverting migrants who now head for the cities. The existing underutilized areas of the Gulf Coast could absorb half a million settlers or even 1.4 million with the provision of irrigation systems, but the surplus population needing land by 1980 will exceed 2 million. In the decade 1950–60, 180–200,000 settlers came to the Gulf Coast area but during the same period one state, Oaxaca, lost 150,000 migrants. In 1950–60 while Mexico City grew by 757,000 the Gulf Coast colonization areas received only 145,000 settlers. Furthermore, government investment in the expensive infrastructure needed in a colonization area provides a much lower return in production than similar investment in industry. The govern-

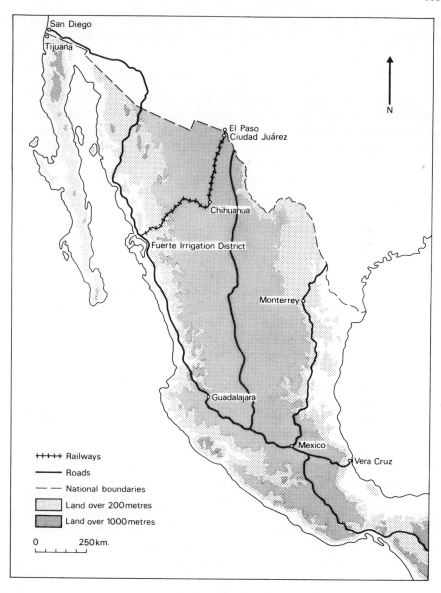

Figure 5–2. Mexico: Fuerte Valley irrigation area

ment is thus faced with a dilemma: colonization is both more expensive and a less adequate creator of employment than urban industrial development.

2. *The Puyo Area, Ecuador: Haphazard Roadside Colonization*

Colonization in Ecuador has traditionally been left to would-be colonists rather than organized by the national government. The only major highway into the eastern lowlands in the early 1960s was that from Baños to Shell Mera and Puyo, and colonization was concentrated in this area. (Plates XI and XII.) More recently the Loja–Zamora–Gualaquiza road has stimulated colonization in the foothills of the southern Andes (see Figure 5–3) and in the 1970s new roads to the northern oilfields have given access to a vast area now being colonized by small-scale farmers.

In Ecuador unused land belongs to the state and can be obtained by petitioners who pay a price varying between 10 p and 50 p a hectare according to the desirability and accessibility of the land. The plots are surveyed for the title to be registered and the purchaser has full ownership of the land only when he has paid the price in full. In addition he is required to clear at least one-quarter of the land within five years. People who in 1962 had settled along the newest part of the road, north from Puyo towards Tena, were predominantly folk from the small sierra towns, people such as small shopkeepers and market stallholders. It was they who had some spare money and the necessary individual enterprise to hack out a clearing in the jungle for their own farm. Puyo, which was reached by road in 1947, was the centre of the colonization zone and had something of the air of a frontier town in the American West. Colonists were growing crops predominantly for sale rather than for subsistence and they had money enough to stimulate retail trade in Puyo and to encourage shops to spring up along the new road north. The school-houses built every 6 or so kilometres sometimes became new settlement nuclei and hamlets, such as Fátima, 7 kilometres from Puyo, which had 22 houses in 1962 and a number of shops. Many colonists had two houses, one on their land, which was often away from the road, and the other at points such as Fátima where social centres developed. Although sugar cane, from whose juice cane brandy *(aguardiente)* was distilled, was the most important crop, a new commercial crop was the *naranjilla* (a yellow, sweet, tomato-like fruit) the juice of which is highly esteemed throughout Ecuador. Smallholdings do not predominate in the new agricultural zone and a number of small estates have been created, with absentee owners, run by a manager and employing labourers who earn several times the equivalent daily wage of the *sierra*.

The Puyo area has many of the characteristics typical of a zone of spontaneous settlement. The highway has been the prime motivator of settlement and the majority of new farms are within 5–10 kilometres of the road. All the new farmers are producing cash crops, although only a limited range. The majority of services are provided largely by the colonists themselves and Puyo and smaller centres

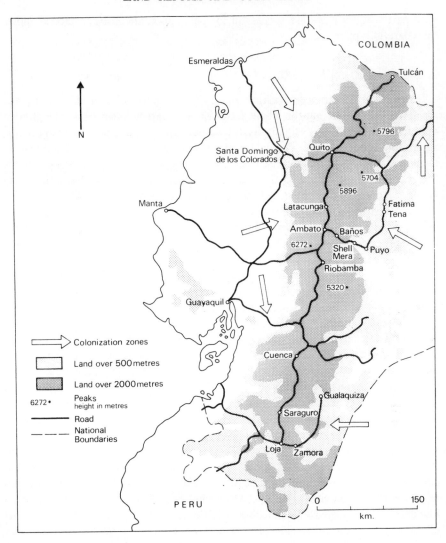

Figure 5–3. Ecuador's lowland colonization zones

such as Fátima are no less successful for being spontaneously developed rather than carefully planned.

3. Brazil's Amazon basin: Grandiose Objectives but a Limited Success

Settlement of the more accessible parts of the Amazon basin has taken place for several centuries, but the whole area has been bathed in the light rosy glow of optimism tempered only slightly by the actual experience of colonists and major agricultural undertakings. The colonization was planned by the Brazilian government associated with the construction of a 16,000 km network of new roads traversing the basin from north to south and from east to west. No other Latin American country has attempted the opening of a major area on this scale and it provides a striking opportunity to discover whether the opening up of a new area can re-direct existing streams of internal migration and achieve greater success than smaller projects.

As it was originally conceived, the social content of the government's Amazon colonization programme was high and, in particular, many of the colonists were hoped to be from the North-East which suffered from severe droughts in 1970. The 1970s programme has been specifically intended to benefit people from that one geographical area but, seemingly, with little success. Efforts at stimulating industrialization had previously been of only limited success and the use of the large areas of forest for settlement was seen to be attractive to farmers from poorer parts of Brazil and economically valuable in also providing surplus production for consumption in Eastern Brazil.

The network of roads established in the 1960s and 1970s (Figure 5–4) are impressive in their length and the speed of their construction. They are less impressive on account of the proportion of national investment that was spent on them and when the number and nature of those who benefited most from their construction is analysed. The agricultural settlement that it was intended to encourage was to be based on the allocation of 100 hectare blocks of land to a depth of 10 kilometres on either side of the main highway with side roads built every 5 kilometres. This controlled colonization was particularly characteristic of the part of the highway on either side of Altamira which was completed in September 1972. It was also planned to found a whole network of new settlements in a programme of disarming simplicity that would surely appeal to any theoretically-minded geographer, where small settlements *(agrovilas)* every 5 kilometres are the fundamental settlement unit among which are located every 50 kilometres or so middle-sized settlements *(agropolis)* and larger centres *(metropolis)* every 140–280 kilometres. Existing settlements were to be incorporated into this framework, but more important problems have stemmed from the variability of the soils which meant that plots of land with unequal fertility were assigned the same value and funds did not stretch to the construction of so many new towns. Although the Altamira region is supposedly one with good terra roxa soils, a re-

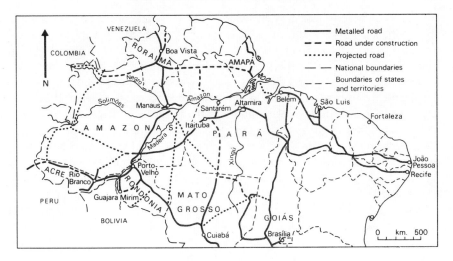

Figure 5–4. Brazilian Amazonia, 1977

cent survey showed that such fertile soils, in fact, only occurred on 6.7 per cent of the 1180 kilometre stretch of road studied, and was interspersed with very poor latosols and podzols.

The experience of settlement in Rondônia is interesting to compare with that of the Altamira zone since voluntary migration has played a more important role, and spontaneous settlement is much more characteristic of this region although five projects along the two main highways had settled over 9000 colonists by the end of 1976.

In both areas farmers had suffered from a range of problems similar to those encountered throughout Latin America, very much attributable to the gap between government promises and reality. In areas of planned settlement the distance from the agrovila to the farms of the settlers was found by many to be irksome and some built shacks on their land to enable them to stay overnight. Eventually the shack was improved and the agrovila house occupied only occasionally. The quality of the housing provided is criticized as being poor even though expansion and the feeder roads that are intended to give access to all the plots are likewise bad and often impassable in the wet season. The services that are supposed to be provided in the different order centres are frequently less than promised and only the larger settlements have an adequate variety of services. Credit is particularly important, especially as colonists wait for their first cash crops, and its supply to medium and small farmers is organized by government agencies. Although small farmers receive loans they are usually small, short-term loans and the whole procedure is complicated by the laborious and slow procedure by which land titles are issued by the government agency.

A feature of colonization in Rondônia, although by no means confined to that area, is the dubious practices by which land is acquired and any inhabitants driven off, known generally as *grilagem*. Land is acquired in various nefarious ways by individuals and companies who wield such power that police, government officials and local authorities are powerless to control their activities. The companies, having acquired the land, then sub-divide it and sell it off to prospective farmers who have waited in vain for the government to allocate them land. Thus the tricksters make a profit and it is the farmer who later realizes that he bought land from a dishonest source. Such activities are only possible if land titling procedures are slow and the government unwilling to react to crooks taking over the role that should be played by the colonization agencies. A large part of the land near the older penetration road from Brasilia to Manaos has also been acquired in this way.

Colonization in the Brazilian Amazon has a strong sense of being encouraged for reasons of national security and it is no coincidence that roads go close to or across existing international frontiers. More recent policies seem to have favoured large companies, and private enterprise has been conceived as having a much more important role to play. Plots of land 3000 hectares in extent, half of which should remain in forest, are available for sale and cattle farmers or companies from central southern Brazil have acquired land. Nestlé, Goodyear and Volkswagen, for example, have bought large cattle ranches and the banks and other business houses find cattle a profitable investment. It is now possible to buy up to 66,000 hectares and the government has set aside some 6 million hectares for this type of enterprise.

Mineral exploitation too is important and has attracted investment from a sufficiently large number of foreign, multi-national corporations such that fears are being expressed about the growing role of foreign companies in such an isolated part of the country.

Three major causes for disquiet emerge from a consideration of the development of the Brazilian Amazon in the 1970s:

1. The lack of effective support for small or medium-sized farmers;

2. The increasing importance of large and multi-national enterprises; and

3. The rapid growth of livestock raising at the expense of the forest cover.

The lack of support for small farmers means that they find it difficult to get established, so the number who acquire land is less than it would otherwise be, and their level of living seldom rises above a low level. They produce only a small marketable surplus and thus the inter-regional flows of foodstuffs or agricultural produce as industrial raw materials are not increased. The growth in the importance of large companies means the employment of extra-regional skill and manpower primarily for the ultimate benefit of the Centre South of Brazil—internal colonist development. That foreign companies are important means that a proportion of the profits do not even accrue to Centre South Brazil and that social criteria have little importance among those considered when alternative investment strategies are being assessed. The rapid growth of livestock is partly a reflection of the difficulty in developing alternative land use systems where labour is scarce but it uses large areas of land, employs few people (only 2.3 jobs per 1000 hectares in development projects accepted by the Amazon Development Agency (S.U.D.A.M.)), and removes a large part of the vegetation cover substituting grasses in its place. If the range is not overstocked, and if a legume component is included in the sward, soils may be maintained or even improved in quality although the long term macro-environmental effects of large-scale forest clearance are uncertain.

Bibliography

Land Reform

BARRACLOUGH, S. (ED.), *Agrarian Structure in Latin America*, Lexington Books, Lexington, 1973.
A summary of the seven country studies carried out by C.I.D.A. to examine the nature of land tenure and its links with agricultural development. A fundamental document.
WARRINER, D., *Land Reform in Principle and in Practice*, Oxford University Press, London, 1969.
A stimulating, informative, critical and intelligent analysis of the meanings and purposes of land reforms in different situations by a scholar with a huge breadth of experience of land reform. Studies of land reform in Latin American countries are included.
SEERS, D. (ED.), *Cuba: the Economic and Social Revolution*, University of North Carolina Press, Chapel Hill, 1964.
A valuable and well-documented study of aspects of post-Castro Cuba by a group of economists.
PEARSE, A., *The Latin American Peasant*, Frank Cass, London, 1975.
A series of thoughtful essays on problems affecting peasants in Latin America as observed in the field and containing an authoritative account of the Bolivian land reform experience.
GRIFFIN, K., *Land Concentration and Rural Poverty*, Macmillan, London, 1976.
An economist's view of land problems on a world scale with essays on rural problems associated with archaic tenure in Ecuador, Colombia and Guatemala.
PATCH, R. W., 'Bolivia: U.S. assistance in a revolutionary setting', in Council on Foreign Relations, *Social Change in Latin America Today*, Vintage Books paperback, New York, 1960, pp. 108–176.
An excellent general account of the events associated with the 1952 Revolution and associated land reform in Bolivia.
PRESTON, D. A., 'The revolutionary landscape of highland Bolivia', *Geographical Journal*, **155**, 1–16 (1969).
An account of the changes in land use, settlement pattern and land tenure in highland Bolivia.

Colonization

DREWES, W. U., *Economic Development of the Western Montaña of Peru*, Peruvian Times, Lima, 1958.

An important contribution to knowledge about the importance of communications in the effective settlement and development of remote areas.

DOZIER, C. L., *Land Development and Colonization in Latin America: Case Studies of Peru, Bolivia and Mexico*, Praeger, New York, 1969.
Useful although superficial studies of colonization schemes in the three named countries.

DOZIER, C. L., 'Mexico's transformed north-west: the Yaqui, Mayo and Puerte examples', *Geographical Review*, **53**, 548–571 (1963).
An interesting and revealing comparative analysis of three different colonization areas in western Mexico.

CASAGRANDE, J. B. and others, 'Colonization as a research frontier: the Ecuadorean case', in R. A. Manners (Ed.), *Process and Pattern in Culture*, Aldine Press, Chicago, 1964, pp. 281–325.
An account of social phenomena associated with settlement in the Puyo-Tena zone of Ecuador of considerable interest to those concerned with how the colonists subsist.

BROMLEY, R. J., 'Agricultural colonization in the upper Amazon Basin: the impact of oil discoveries', *Tijdschrift voor Economische en Sociale Geografie*, **63**, 278–94 (1973).
Account of colonization in N.E. Ecuador following roadbuilding for oil exploration.

ALLERDICE, W. H., *The Expansion of Agriculture along the Belem–Brasilia Road in Northern Goiás, Brazil*, Ph.D. Thesis, Columbia University, 1972.

KLEINPENNING, J. M. G., 'An evaluation of the Brazilian policy for the integration of the Amazon basin', *Tijdschrift voor Economische en Sociale Geografie*, **5**, 297–311 (1977).

KIRBY, J. M., 'Agricultural land use and the settlement of Amazonia', *Pacific Viewpoint*, **17**, 105–132 (1976).

REVEL MOUROZ, J., *Méxique: amenagement et colonisation du tropique humide*, Travaux et Mémoires de l'Institut des Hautes Etudes de l'Amérique Latine, Paris, 1971.
An intelligent evaluation of Mexican colonization experience, with special reference to the Gulf Coast referred to in the text.

CHAPTER 6

Human Mobility: Migration and its Consequences

Changes in the number and distribution of people in Latin America have been important in influencing the development of different parts of the continent. The generally low population densities at the time of Spanish conquest influenced the conquerors to concentrate their activities where the natives were most numerous. The dramatic decline in Indian numbers during the sixteenth and seventeenth centuries resulted in important modifications in the Spanish methods of land exploitation in order to make do without formerly abundant labour. The demographic phenomenon of comparable importance during the twentieth century has been the combination of rapid population increase and a shift of people from the countryside to the town. Now there are more people living in urban centres than in rural areas, in marked contrast to almost the whole of the remainder of the Third World. This characteristic has become more accentuated and the rate of urban growth has increased rapidly during the past two decades. This shift in the human geography of Latin American population is important, not only because of its singularity but also because it reflects major currents in the socio-economic development of the continent. People move from one part of a country to another not just blindly and as a result of poverty but because of a change in their perception of alternative environments and their perception of the values held by decision makers, people of power in the community and their government.

Human mobility is ceaseless and only demands attention when it accelerates or changes direction. The urbanward movement in Latin America's population is a response to the growth of population in environments whose use by man cannot easily be modified to support more people. The growth in population is a result, at least in part, of better medical care and consequently a decrease in the rate of mortality, particularly of the youngest part of the population. Families that have been accustomed for thousands of years to the need for a certain number of births in order to ensure that their family is of an acceptable size now find that the same number of births results in a larger family, there are more mouths to be fed by methods of production that do not seem to produce more each year, and the patterns of conception developed in the past are hard to change. New technology that has dramatically decreased births in industrialized countries is either not available, not attractive or just plain expensive for the poorer two-thirds of humanity and for nine-tenths of rural populations.

The increase in population is not the only reason for the migration of population: people move because they want to go somewhere and they choose predominantly to go to urban places. In some recent work in Andean Ecuador we found that while the family heads that we interviewed had previous migration experience largely in rural areas, and from parish registers we could also determine a predominant rural–rural flow of migrants, their children, however, have gone to and now live predominantly in urban areas. Research in other areas has confirmed this and while most migrants are bound for urban places older migrants will frequently head for nearer regional capitals and younger people migrate to the major metropoli. The movement in this direction is always from areas where monetary incomes are low towards those where incomes are high and it is tempting but not necessarily correct to suggest that the strength of migration currents is proportional to the difference in income. Migration can, at one level, be seen as a reaction to inequalities in income or earning opportunities in different areas. This is a very simple explanation and one which needs to be qualified. The existence of differences does not assume universal knowledge of such differences, for a person may only be described as poor by reference to others who are rich. Likewise, demands for a different life come only as a result of knowledge that such differences exist and perception that such changes are personally available. Finally, these differences have to be valued in themselves, which implies a judgement of the inadequacy of the present way of living. After considering this sort of analysis of the framework in which migration develops it will be apparent that some part of the migration decision is a function of the value system of the individual potential migrant. This value system is, in turn, the result of education in the broadest sense by those around him/her and by information received from a variety of sources, including visual observation, listening to radio and talking with outsiders.

Two factors combine to influence people to migrate citywards as a result of contact with others. Cities have grown enormously and present a wide range of products of industry, to some extent irrespective of where the city is located. The difference between the goods possessed by a farmer and what he sees displayed while on a visit to a big city is mind-boggling; the range of novelties increases each year much faster than the range of goods in his home and this heightens his consciousness of relative deprivation. He feels actually deprived when he sees kinsfolk now living in the city with a style of life far different from that which they used to have in the village. The continually growing flow of migrants increases the ease with which non-migrants hear about the way of life of the successful ones in the city whose example may ultimately lure them away. They hear comparatively little about the problems and failures and so a rosy view develops of what awaits one who moves away from his community to a city full of immigrants.

Population movement on a large scale has traditionally been important in Latin America since the middle of the nineteenth century. The effective settlement of large areas in Brazil and the three southernmost countries of the continent has been undertaken only as a consequence of the immigration of large numbers of Italian and Spanish people as well as others from a variety of countries. A heterogeneous urban and, in places, rural population is therefore by no means unusual. Migration, both national and international, was largely responsible for the growth of two of the largest cities in the southern hemisphere: São Paulo and Buenos Aires. This migration often included a sizeable flow of discontented migrants who had tasted life on the rural frontier and preferred the slums of La Boca in Buenos Aires. Since the Second World War this migration stream has become of much less importance save in news stories of Nazi refugees or escaped train robbers hiding in broad-minded Latin American countries. The quality and comparative success of selected groups of international migrants such as the Mennonites in Paraguay or the Japanese in various countries command attention but are numerically insignificant.

The patterns of human mobility that have had greatest impact on Latin American landscapes are those that involve changes of residence. The overwhelming proportion of migratory movements involving middle and long-term change of residence are towards the large cities, either from rural areas or from smaller urban centres. A basic principle of human geography is that the larger the population centre the more migrants it attracts and this is as true of Latin America as it is of the rest of the developed and developing world. Several recent detailed studies have demonstrated the importance of local and intra-regional migration and even suggest that such movements approach in number those to the metropoli. The attraction exerted by metropoli is also exerted by urban centres on those who live in smaller settlements and there is even perceptible movement from the countryside into villages of only 50–100 houses, which at least replaces the movement from the villages to the towns. A third movement of note is that from rural and urban places to new areas of settlement on the fringes of the densely settled parts of the continent, referred to previously in the consideration of colonization. Such movement is noteworthy because it involves the creation of new settlements and of a new rural as well as urban land use but the numbers of people involved are very small.

It is not sufficient to examine just the origin and destination of migrants because the effect of such migration upon sending and receiving communities varies in relation to the social and economic characteristics of migrants. Since migration affects so many people and is such a universal phenomenon a number of widely accepted generalizations may be made and some of their inadequacies indicated. Among the social characteristics of migrants it is generally agreed that young adults are the most mobile, as are their small children since they must move with their parents. Sex selectivity among migrants is highly variable but different destinations are involved: while young men go to rural colonization areas and to cities, very few women travel to colonization areas except with their husbands. Job selection between sexes is also striking with urban-bound women from rural areas often being most frequently employed in domestic service, at least initially, while men are employed in a variety of jobs particularly in construction. In socio-geographical terms however the movement is usually to socially superior places, as evaluated by urban people, with colonization areas having the considerable attraction of freedom from social and even political restriction common in established settlements. Finally migrants are held to be remarkable because of their openness, willingness to accept new ideas, or to take a risk in order to obtain a possible substantial benefit. This is frequently established and often quoted but is also translated to mean that migrants are the more able and intelligent members of their community or that their migration constitutes a 'brain drain'. There is little evidence which supports this and much is the result of the deprecation by migrants of the non-migrants or the comparison of the educational or other attainment of migrants to whom a wide range of services are available with that of non-migrants who lack such access.

The economic characteristics of migrants before and after migration are complex. It is clear that, in many situations, migrants include people from a wide variety of economic conditions and are by no means from the poorest section of society. In rural areas they include middle peasants as well as smallholders, but few of those too poor to even move away. In some areas, though, they do include the poorest, driven by economic circumstances to leave their village. They migrate to seek casual work in service industries, the booming tertiary sector of Latin America, or to engage in trading, sometimes as itinerant traders of matches and individual cigarettes, or as wholesalers, using their savings to establish themselves in more lucrative business especially in urban centres.

In an attempt to convey some idea of the importance and the effects of migration we shall examine just two parts of the migrant universe: squatter settlements and slums in metropolitan centres and the rural areas deserted by the migrants. It is necessary to remember that migrants are involved in a wide range of experience and that there are undoubtedly many differences between the areas from which migrants come, but we hope to offer a framework of reference which the interested reader can test as he reads more deeply about the characteristics of these areas.

MIGRANTS IN THE CITY

The nature of urban growth is referred to in various parts of this book by both authors since an understanding is valuable of why it is currently so important in Latin America; the characteristics of the pattern and shape of such growing cities are distinctive and are a result of both the excessive concentration of capital, industry, and government in one place and the rapid growth of population as a result, predominantly, of internal migration. Urban growth in Latin America is by no means a new phenomenon. It is axiomatic that the colonial society under Spanish rule was strongly urban-oriented and that life, for the Spanish middle and upper class in Latin America, was certainly barely worth living unless some sort of urban existence was possible. During the Republican period little happened to change that although, in western Latin America, maybe as many powerful families established rural estates at the expense of the native population as during the colonial period. After mid-century however the flow of population from western Europe to the New World encouraged the development of a less urban-centred view of life as previously underutilized rural areas became more productive and supplied the basis of wealth for merchants and landowners and a meagre existence for myriads of rural workers. The fortunes of worker and capitalist alike were made in the city however and many of those migrants who had gone to work in agriculture returned to the port city through which they had passed on arrival and there became established in petty commerce or as wage labourers. Even at the end of the nineteenth century many cities were growing so fast that a proportion of their population was housed in cramped conditions on sites that had been rejected as suitable for permanent settlement and in tenements and squalid rent-yards much as similar populations were housed in industrial centres in Europe.

What is so different in urbanization at the present time is the scale of the process and the numbers of people involved. A further feature of contemporary urbanization in Latin America is the scale on which people have sought their own solution to their housing problems by occupying unused land and creating squatter settlements. Mexico City by 1970 was estimated to have almost 40 per cent of its population in low-income, frequently squatter, settlements and in Caracas 34 per cent of the population in 1970 was also housed in this way. Such areas have been growing annually at about twice the rate of growth for the cities as a whole.

This rate of growth is not characteristic of all cities, nor do all cities have squatter settlements around and within the metropolitan area. Quito, for example, has very few areas where informal or illegal low income settlement can be seen, possibly as a result of the capacity of the urban fabric, particularly in the colonial centre, to absorb a large number of people in the large rooms, passages and courtyards of old buildings. With few such exceptions the main cities of Latin America are characterized by high rates of growth and large areas of squatter settlements or neighbourhoods that have evolved out of squatter settlements, but the main cities of the smaller countries such as Nicaragua or Costa Rica do not experience such growth or such intense immigration as São Paulo, Mexico City or Buenos Aires. Similarly poor, predominantly rural countries such as Paraguay or Bolivia have a similar experience of urban growth to the small countries without major urban centres.

By no means all of the population of the low-income or squatter housing areas has migrated to urban centres but such settlements are those most likely to house the recent and medium term migrants. In addition a proportion of recent migrants, as well as many temporary migrants, are housed in inner city slums, where cheap and low quality housing is available as well as where work opportunities are concentrated.

The reason for the rapid growth of these cities and of their attraction to migrants lies in the gross inadequacy of opportunities for employment in other cities or other parts of the country and of the influence of communications on national value systems which leads to the widespread acceptance of the belief that the solution of the problems of much of the population lies in coming to live in the metropolis such that even people in Guatemala, who may have only a hazy idea of where the capital is, wish to send their children there, or even to move themselves. As more people migrate to the cities so the news of the opportunities that the cities afford spreads, encouraging still more people to move and so the momentum increases. As the dominance of central cities grows the possibility of improving opportunities for work and the quality of life in rural areas and small towns diminishes, for the creation of such opportunities must be at the expense of the major cities, many of whose industries depend on a fluid labour force of migrants to keep wages down and to ensure high profits. Decision makers motivated by self-interest and influenced by urban interests—for that is where they live, after all—find it increasingly difficult to adopt measures that *really* benefit non-metropolitan areas, in addition because they might have to leave the metropolis in order to implement a new development policy in the province.

A consequence of the high levels of internal migration has been a rapid physical expansion of cities, a change in their physical fabric, and in their social geography. The singularity of Latin American large cities is the extent to which their inhabitants have been able to solve some of their problems themselves by invading unused or partly used land and establishing their right to a roof of their own. Other consequences of rapid city growth—the increase in run-down, slum areas, inadequacy of social and physical service etc.—are important but far from unique to either Latin America, or indeed the Third World. The impressive lateral expansion of the cities as a result of planned and unplanned growth on the periphery of the urban area has made arrival by air to such a city a revealing experience as the approach flight path crosses miles of tiny homes, arranged chequer-board fashion on stilts across swamps or on steep hillsides or, near Lima-Callao, across vast dusty wastes. A visitor to such a city may otherwise forget that beyond the colonial city core, the new skyscrapers of the Central Business District or the middle class suburbs and the expressways lined with petrol stations and second-hand car lots lies another half of the city which scarcely existed 30 years ago.

The New Urban Habitats

The new urban environments are not created either for or by migrants alone—they are the result of pressure of many social populations on available space. Just as squatting in large British cities is not a prerogative solely of the poor but includes desperate middle-class young professional people, in Latin American cities those who settle in peripheral squatter settlements include middle-term city residents and people in white-collar employment and liberal professions as well as migrants and a majority of working class people.

The variety of forms of settlement within rapidly-growing cities in Latin America is considerable but a useful, although rather crude, division is between slums, associated with grossly inadequate and static or deteriorating living environments, and squatter settlements once located on the edge of cities where variable, often inadequate, living conditions are gradually being improved. A wide variety of names are used in Latin America to describe the squatter settlements: *callampas* (mushrooms) in Chile, *villas miserias* in Buenos Aires, *favelas* in Brazil, *barriadas* in Peru, *ranchos* in Venezuela, *tugurios* in Colombia and *colonias proletarias* in Mexico City.

The slums are strikingly similar to urban dwelling places that developed during the Industrial Revolution in Britain where the infamous rent-yards housed a proportion of the poorest of the urban population with one or more families, often with many children, in one or two-room apartments with few amenities and extortionate rents. In Latin American cities such areas develop in those parts of the city where there is a heavy demand for living space and where buildings exist which can be modified to house many people very cheaply. The courtyards of old houses are particularly suitable for conversion and offer a high rate of return to people willing to invest capital in buying or renting and converting suitable property. Around the bus and railway stations such places abound, for it is there that a large and transient population needs housing. Slums also develop where there is space available that is not put to other use and in relatively central locations where land values are rising; plots may not be built on as land investors wait for the value of their property to rise sufficiently to sell to borrow money for the construction of offices or high-rise apartments. In the meantime the plot is occupied and shacks built to be rented (for as much as 25 per cent of the family income) until such time as the site is required for further development. The case of Mexico City, recently examined by Peter Ward, illustrates something of the real-life complexity and the distribution of slums *(ciudades perdidas)* shows clearly that they are located throughout the city although well within its built-up area (Figure 6–1).

Major distinguishing features of the slum areas, apart from high densities of people where family-occupied lots may seldom exceed 100 square metres, is that they are frequently rented, seldom the result of squatting and their inhabitants are rarely organized in any recognizable way. The rental from such intensively occupied locations is considerable and can in a year yield a gross income equal to the value of the land. Often lots are sub-let and the profit from the rentals is thus diffused through a complex system of landlords, tenants and sub-tenants. In one case in Lima 158 people lived in 30 rooms in an area the size of a North American houseplot. In Mexico City only 13 per cent of the slums are recorded as having started life with the invasion of land, thus emphasizing the difference with squatter settlements. The lack of social organization in the slums is a vital

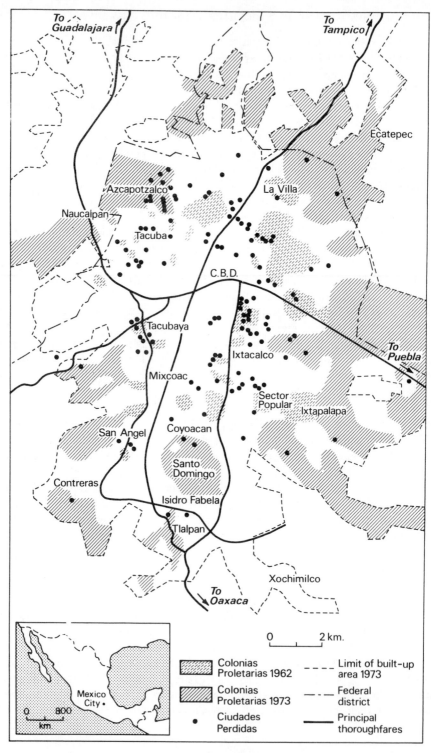

Figure 6–1. Squatter settlements, Mexico City, 1973

difference with the squatter settlements although in many cases individuals organizing an invasion will come together from different slum neighbourhoods within which no comparable organization exists. The lack of organization is particularly associated with the insecurity of tenure and the urgent need for such security, and this insecurity makes any threat to the landlords, such as the formation of an association, also a threat to the continued residence in the slum of the potential members. The persistence of slums in growing cities is also the result of a continuing high demand for very cheap accommodation and the very high returns that such rents can allow encourage entrepreneurs to continue to create or maintain such slums, many of which have existed since the 1940s.

Squatting is a common device used by desperate people seeking a solution, however temporary, to the problem of a space to live. In Latin America, since the Second World War, such settlements have developed as a result of the incapacity of the existing dwelling market system in large cities to provide lodging for them at a level that the inhabitants felt was adequate. The physical problem posed by large numbers of new families arriving in the big cities could not be solved by city governments. Only in Cuba has such growth been checked by tight state control on human mobility, the creation of a wide range of employment opportunities in rural areas and small urban centres, and deliberate lack of provision of further facilities to the metropolis. Squatter settlements were created peripheral to the built-up area of the city but as the city expands laterally so early squatter settlements become more firmly embedded in the spatial structure of the city. The inhabitants of such settlements, usually with young families, were initially highly organized in order to affect a rapid and effective invasion of land. Some invasions involve the establishment of over a thousand families overnight and such organization is subsequently crucial in the legalization of the squat and the eventual provision of services. Homes have more space than in slums (in Mexico 150–250 square metres) and a continuous process of improvement takes place from a cardboard and matting shack on the night of the squat to maybe a concrete two-storey home with bedrooms, bathroom and kitchen a decade or so later. Renting does occur, especially as the squatter settlement develops and time passes, but seldom of individual rooms by an absentee landlord and owner-occupation predominates in most cases.

It is the relative success of the squatter settlements to settle large numbers of people and to legalize their occupation of land that encourages more squatting and a further influx of migrants to the cities. They are further encouraged by the cohesive nature of the families in the new neighbourhoods and by the range of services that are gradually provided.

MIGRATION FROM THE COUNTRYSIDE

The universality of rural emigration in the western world is at once impressive and depressing. It represents the total dominance of urban-based values throughout national society and the maintenance of the countryside as a pleasure park for city dwellers and as a place for large capital-intensive farms owned by city dwellers and managed by technocrats. If this is a pronounced view it is not difficult to sustain it through the personal history of many of the readers who will be city bred folk but descended from rural families within a couple of generations. The degree to which 'western' values permeate Latin America, as well as elsewhere in the developing world, is demonstrated by the underlying features of rural emigration in Latin America. First hand experience of rural emigration in highland Ecuador in 1975–76 and a number of recent studies of Mexican communities testify to the importance of external factors as the motor of rural emigration.

Emigration appears to be concentrated in those areas where least farmland is available since rural non-agricultural employment is on the wane. Local handicrafts, such as weaving and carving, seem to be unable to provide either adequate income or employment for the growing rural population. In addition, those areas where agriculture is dependent on rain, and crops may be lost by an absence or excess of rainfall, are particularly prone to have high rates of emigration when sheer poverty is exacerbated by climatic accidents (which seem to have increased in the past 20 years). Areas where emigration has become important tend to lose a large proportion of the population as a result of migratory inertia. The more people have left a community the greater the rate of emigration even though some of the original causes of emigration may have disappeared. In some West Indian islands a labour shortage that results from overseas migration stunts economic growth even though it was the lack of employment opportunities that drove away the early migrants.

The size of migration and its importance to the rural population is difficult to measure. Our work in Ecuador suggested that as many as two-thirds of children attending the village school in 1960–61 in one of our sample villages no longer lived there and over 70 per cent of them now lived in urban areas. By contrast only 10 per cent of their parents no longer lived in the parish. Leaving aside the lack of comparability of the two population samples, one may still conclude that well over half the children born in some rural areas are likely to live a part of their lives elsewhere. In many areas the migration is temporary: in many north and central Mexican rural areas temporary migration to the U.S.A. is widespread despite the huge cultural gap between a highland village and the working class districts of San Diego or Los Angeles. In other areas, migration to sugar milling areas or commercial coffee plantations in response to relatively high wages is widespread and common and has become a part of the customary pattern of human mobility. For some migrants a temporary job becomes permanent or an increasing awareness of the range of opportunities available often leads to long-term migration. Among those migrants who are itinerant traders, too, a proportion stay in an area where they have business contacts, establish themselves with a shop and maybe some wholesaling, and there live for 20–30 years only returning to their native village in their old age. Thus the idea of permanent migration is relative and a measure of migration by the absence of a part of the population at a particular moment or of the migration experience of normally-resident population is an alternative way of measuring mobility. In a Zapotec village in southern Mexico a recent study identified that only 45 per cent of the villagers, men and women, had never spent more than a few days outside the village.

The Impact of Migration on Rural Communities

Since migration is in response to an individual perception of local inadequacies and strongly related to shortage of land it might be imagined that, to some extent, migration will alleviate some local problems. Three areas of interest may be defined in order to examine ways in which emigration affects the communities left behind: the distribution and tenure of agricultural land, the land use system and the changes to which the residual population are subject as a direct and indirect result of migration.

Several studies in different parts of the developing world have suggested that migrants include a broad range of the population, and, although in some areas the very poor make up an important part of the population, in others they are excluded because of the cost of migration. In many cases, therefore, the migrants will possess land which they will not be able to cultivate if they are absent from the community for long periods. Their migration thus releases land that will be farmed by others who thereby benefit directly from migration. In other cases migrants sell their land and thus the land stock of the community is available to more people than it would have been otherwise. Crucial questions that must be asked if the results of migration are to be understood are who has access to more land and does this result in a more or less even distribution of land in the community? Very few of the various studies on emigration from rural areas have considered the changes in land distribution that result from migration, but our own work in Ecuador suggests that much of the land belonging to migrants is rented (for cash or a share of the produce) and only sold as a last resort or when a migrant needs all possible capital to establish himself in his new home. The increase in availability of land is thus much reduced. In some cases it is difficult to find anyone willing to share-crop or rent land if it is in poor condition and the land is abandoned or planted with trees. When land is sold there was no evidence, save in one case, to suggest that it was enabling any individual to accumulate property or that very few, better-off people were the only possible purchasers. In one case, in southern highland Ecuador, severe drought in the late 1960s caused emigration, depressed land prices and several individuals did acquire over 100 hectares of farmland which, when the drought broke, enabled them to greatly improve their position in the community. This was an unusual situation and clearly in these circumstances it is possible that a few people will be able and willing to take advantage of emigration to improve their social and economic position.

The land use system should logically change in areas of high emigration. Population decreases, labour becomes scarce and under-employment gives way to over-employment, wages rise, productivity per man increases as it does per unit area. Migrants can provide a flow of new ideas to improve farming and their savings may make necessary new investments and thereby cause a resurgence of agriculture. In fact, evidence from a range of places suggests that this rarely happens and we must therefore ask why. In the first place the actual extent of labour shortage is difficult to discover. There is evidence in Ecuador and Mexico to show that wages in such areas rise no higher than in other rural areas where wage labour prevails, although this is associated with a decline in the use of exchange labour. A variety of other factors also make middle-scale farmers economize in the use of labour, not least the relatively low returns from agriculture.

The experience that migrants have while away is of little benefit for agriculture at home for two reasons. On the one hand, a majority of migrants go to urban areas which cuts them off from farming and they can only derive positive benefit if they listen to farming programmes on the radio or visit farm stores in the city; on the other hand, even those who do go to rural areas find themselves engaged in tropical agriculture in a quite different ecological area from home with new crops, soil conditions and weather.

Our own experience confirms what has been found elsewhere, that although there are some instances of migrants being initiators of important and far-reaching agricultural changes this is not common and in many cases the introduction of change has proceeded without any relation to migration. Frequent absence of menfolk in areas of temporary migration may also reduce the chances of innovations being adopted. It also seems probable that urban migration experience, but also possibly any migration experience, results in a desire for a different level of living the cost of which absorbs migrant savings and leaves little for investment in farming.

If so far we can suggest that migration affects rural communities very little a body of literature suggests that emigration may constitute a rural brain drain, robbing the country districts of their most able people. Although empirical evidence suggests, not surprisingly, that migrants include the more open, inquisitive members of the community there is little to substantiate the idea that it is the inherently more able and intelligent who migrate. Migrants receive more schooling than non-migrants but this is more a result than a cause of migration. On the other hand, it seems likely that children with most schooling are more likely to migrate than those with only some schooling. Migration is highly age-selective, it being mainly men and women in their late teens and twenties who leave, but this is not surprising and strictly as in accordance with findings on mobility and age made in Sweden thirty years ago. For many young people, however, migration is characteristic of and confined to a brief exploratory experience around the age 18–20 often described as being 'to take a look' even though it may not lead to lengthy or permanent migration. A limited amount of return migration takes place and some long-term migrants return only in their declining years although many appear in their home town each year at festival time in order to show off their affluence and to demonstrate the particular success of their migration.

An important consequence of migration experience and of hearing the experience of others is the widespread acceptance of urban values, both cultural and economic, which results in greater expenditure on consumable items and the increasing importance of cash in the domestic economy. This has been reported in both Mexico and Ecuador as well as in a study in Senegal in Africa. Agriculture is not necessarily seen as a way to provide the necessary cash because urban values decree that agriculture is demeaning and it is relegated, or rather maintained, as a subsistence operation while cash is earned in some other way to buy the required goods. This is a further reason for the lack of investment of migrant savings in agriculture and which condemns farming to a secondary role which might impede increased production.

In summary, then, the principal consequences of migration for sending areas are a change in their age structure, a loss of manpower and a series of interlocking changes that obstruct the introduction and acceptance of agricultural change but which do not prevent it in all circumstances. A most optimistic summary of our conclusions would be that change is not more widespread in areas of emigration than in other rural areas.

Future Migration Patterns

The flight from the countryside in Latin America has reached such proportions that it is necessary to look ahead and attempt to see if this is likely to change in the future. I believe that no change is in sight save possibly in Cuba where the check on Havana's growth may in future diminish in effectiveness. No nonsocialist government in Latin America (and possibly elsewhere) has managed to overcome urban bias in decision-making and thus rural people will continue to move elsewhere. The growth of a capital intensive commercial farming sector, such as in Mexico and Brazil, seems likely to continue and may help rural incomes to rise more noticeably than in the past although the difference between rural and urban incomes will widen. In major cities the future is less clear as many grow to such a size as to seriously threaten regional development by the demands upon water and power resources that they make and as pollution and a decaying modern urban fabric become more important problems. The solution to housing found by squatters seems likely to continue to be important and to be Latin America's most dramatic contribution to contemporary urban experience.

Bibliography

Migrants in the City

PATCH, R. W., 'Life in a *callejón*', *American Universities Field Staff Report*, **8**, No. 6 (1961).
Absorbing semi-fictional account of what happens to rural folk who arrive in the big city, in this case Lima.

DE JESUS, C. M., *Beyond All Pity*, Panther Books, London, 1970.
The account of her life by a decidedly bitchy Rio slum dweller. Great literary success in Brazil and useful as an account of how people get by in the slums.

TURNER, J. C., 'Dwelling resources in Latin America', *Architectural Design*, **33**, 360–393 (1963).
Stimulating article on the housing problems of shanty town dwellers largely based on the author's experience as a consulting architect to the Peruvian Government in Lima. The same issue contains many photographs as well as other articles of interest.

MANGIN, W., 'Latin America's squatter settlements', *Latin American Research Review*, **2**, 65–98 (1967).
An important summary statement of present knowledge about squatter settlements in Latin American countries. Contains a valuable bibliography.

MANGIN, W., 'The role of regional associations in the adaptation of the rural population of Peru', *Sociologus*, **9**, 21–36 (1959).
An account of the work of the regional organizations in a rapidly growing city.

LEEDS, A., 'The significant variables determining the character of squatter settlements', *América Latina*, **22**, 44–86 (1969).
An analysis of why squatter settlements grow the way they do with reference especially to Rio de Janeiro.

WARD, P. M., 'The squatter settlement as slum or housing solution: the evidence from Mexico City', *Land Economics*, **52**, 330–46 (1976).

Emigration's Impact on the Countryside

CONNELL, J. et al., *Migration from Rural Areas: the Evidence from Village Studies*, Oxford University Press, New Delhi, 1976.
A broad survey of the findings from research throughout the world but especially in Africa and Asia. A valuable background.

ARIZPE, L., *Migration and Ethnicity: the Mazahua Indians of Mexico*, Ph.D. Thesis, University of London, 1976.

BUTTERWORTH, D. S., *Factors in Out-Migration from a Rural Mexican Community*, Ph.D. Thesis, University of Illinois, 1969.

YOUNG, C. M., *The Social Setting of Migration: Factors affecting Migration from a Sierra Zapotec village in Oaxaca, Mexico*, Ph.D. Thesis, University of London, 1976.

PRESTON, D. A., TAVERAS, G. A., and PRESTON, R. A., *Rural Emigration and Agricultural Development in Highland Ecuador*, School of Geography, University of Leeds, Final Report to O.D.M., 1978.

PART II

Major Themes in the Economic Geography of Latin America

by

PETER R. ODELL

CHAPTER 7

Antecedents to the Contemporary Geography of Economic Activity

The geographical patterns of any contemporary economy are only in part a function of the economic, social, political and other forces currently at work in shaping decisions on the location of new economic activities. Major constraints on any locational decision, whether taken by an individual, an entrepreneur, a corporation or a government, include, first, the influences of the historical patterns of development and, second, the behavioural characteristics of the decision takers.

The way in which the first constraint operates can be seen, for example, in decision making on the location of new steel-making capacity. Any contemporary evaluation of a maximum profit location for such capacity which took into account only transport charges on raw materials and finished products together with land and labour costs in different locations would invariably produce a recommendation for a coastal site with access to deep water and with plenty of flat land on which to build a modern, extensively-designed plant. But such clear-cut advice based on current spatial variations in factor costs can often be undermined when the alternative of providing the new capacity by extending an existing plant is considered. Though the existing location may mean higher costs in terms of transport, land and labour, the unfavourable effects of these on the location decision can be more than offset by the savings possible through the economies of scale and other economies (in administration, energy consumption etc.) related to a decision to expand *in situ*. In other words, past decisions on location affect the new decision.

Similarly, location decision takers in all societies build up a set of traits which become entrenched in their geographical behaviour and which thus influence every new locational decision. In the United Kingdom, for example, the 'north' is traditionally considered to be the 'industrial part' of the country. Though it has, in fact, lost most if not all of the late eighteenth and nineteenth century advantages it enjoyed in respect of industrial development, the continuing impact of this traditional view remains powerful enough to continue to persuade governments that they should pursue regional policies designed to ensure that industry locates in the 'north', rather than in areas further south which most of the industrialists themselves seem to prefer in light of contemporary location factors which give much more emphasis to the geography of the market.

Thus, any attempt to understand the location of existing patterns of economic activities or any effort to predict the evolution of the geography of economies can only be achieved in the light of knowledge as to what has gone before. This, of course, applies universally, but one can argue that it applies particularly strongly in Latin America where most societies are so well-structured and so conservative that they lack the dynamism of more open societies such as those of the U.S. and Western Europe. Such societal structures in Latin America are reflected geographically in the inertia which inhibits change in the use of the land and in the reshaping of the geographical patterns of development. Thus an understanding of Latin America's contemporary economic geography demands some knowledge of the evolution of the settlement and development patterns.

Pre-Columbian America

Present spatial patterns of economic activity can, to some degree, even be correlated with the 'economic geography' of the continent in the pre-Columbian period. It has been shown by Steward and Faron in their study, *Native Peoples of South America* (see Bibliography at the end of the chapter for the full reference), that in the period before the Conquest there were significant spatial variations in the relative intensity of the use of the land. These arose not only out of major contrasts in the physical environmental conditions of different areas, but also from the existence of contrasting groups of people variously equipped to make use of the development opportunities offered. These contrasts produced an uneven distribution of the population. Estimates of the size of the population at the time of the Conquest have ranged from 8.4 to over 100 million and even now, after much research and scholarship in recent years, 'it is a subject that is still much in dispute' (Sanchez-Albornoz, 1974). It is in respect of the population of South America that there is the greatest remaining uncertainty. In this larger part of Latin America it is, however, generally agreed that there was well under half of the total population and that it was, moreover, heavily concentrated in the valleys of the Andes stretching from present day Ecuador southwards to Bolivia. Indeed, at least 60 per cent of the South American total was, it is estimated, located in this very limited part of the continent such that the densities there were far above the average. The numbers of people in this region may, however, have been as few as 5 million or as many as 30 million. As we shall see later, this relatively large number of indigenous inhabitants was, in any case, a very powerful attraction to the Spanish conquerors.

Figure 7–1, partly based on estimates made by Steward and Faron, shows the geographical distribution of the population in South America at the time of the

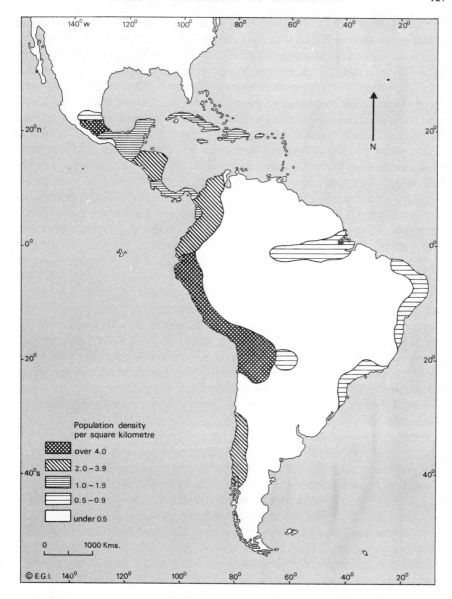

Figure 7–1. South and Central America: indigenous population densities at the Conquest

Spanish Conquest. Several reasons have been suggested for the heavy concentration of population in this Andean region indicated on the map. First, the existence there of a wide range of altitudes and of climates which offered favourable conditions for a broadly based pattern of food production. Second, the existence of soils less subject to destructive leaching than those of the tropical rain forest. Third, the availability of adequate water and of organizational expertise and ability to make irrigation works possible. Fourth, there was the possibility of access to the offshore guano deposits (used for fertilizers). These resources, on various islands along the Pacific coastline, were imperially controlled by the Incas whose empire at the time of the Conquest included all the region of densest population. This region was not, moreover, still entirely rural. Ceremonial centres had developed into towns and cities fulfilling not only religious but also military and strategic functions. Their evolution eliminated some at least of the marginality of life and of living and thus enabled the local populations to grow significantly larger. A little farther north, the somewhat lesser densities of population reflected the use of environments similar in many respects to those of the central Andes but in an area without access to the guano deposits and with societies less well organized and less 'urbanized' than the Incas. The societies, however, were able to produce an economic surplus sufficient to keep their populations above subsistence levels and they were, therefore, able to expand. Throughout most of the rest of South America, however, the population was made up of scattered tribal groups. These generally simply survived in environments over which they exercised little or no control and they produced little or nothing beyond subsistence requirement. And over most of the continent there was, as shown by the map, a virtual absence of population except for transient shifting pastoralists and hunters etc.

These general elements in the spatial pattern of population distribution and contrasting economic activities were repeated in Middle America. In this region the total population at the time of the Conquest almost certainly exceeded 40 million, of which more than half, over 25 million it has been estimated (Denevan, 1976), lived in what is now Central Mexico within the region of the Aztec kingdom. This area had a density of population somewhat higher than that in the central Andes. It was also dependent on a successful system of irrigated agriculture and it contained the largest city by far of pre-Columbian America (viz. Teotihuacán, with a population at the time of the Conquest—according to the chronicles—of several hundreds of thousands). The Mayan civilization of Yucatan and present-day Guatemala was numerically and economically much less important though these areas had the second highest population densities in Latin America. Still smaller societies with early post-subsistence economies formed small population nuclei in certain upland areas of Central America. Elsewhere in Middle America population was in scattered groups of subsistence peoples. Some were sedentary and relatively numerous, as with the Arawaks of the Caribbean islands; whilst others practised shifting cultivation at best, or nomadic hunting, collecting and fishing at the other end of the scale. They thinly peopled the arid areas to the north of central Mexico as well as the tropical fringes of the Middle American land area.

The Geography of the European Colonization

All this discussion of the indigenous peoples of the continent would be of interest primarily to historical geographers, however, were it not for the effects that the geographical pattern of population distribution and associated land use characteristics had upon the development of the Spanish Conquest and Spain's occupation of the continent. The Spanish expansion into the continent is described somewhat inaccurately as a 'conquest of Latin America'. It can be described rather more accurately as a conquest of the peoples of Latin America. The distinction is important for it has implications for the determination of the main areas of Spanish interest within the continent. Initially Spanish interests lay essentially in the Caribbean, but the relative lack there both of a large enough indigenous population and of precious metals made it mainly an area of short-lived interest only, except in terms of the need for bases within the region through which trade between Spain and the more important colonies could pass and from which the defence of the gold carrying and other merchant ships could be organized.

It was the two pre-existing civilizations of the Aztecs and the Incas that so enthused the Conquistadores and their successors. In Central Mexico and the Central Andes respectively, these two civilizations offered not only the labour that the Spanish wanted in large quantities to exploit the areas within which they settled, but also wealth in the form of precious metals and workable and worked land, the productivity of which had been greatly enhanced by effective irrigation systems. The indigenous peoples' knowledge of both mining and agriculture enabled the Spanish to build up their level of economic activities in their newly-won colonies very quickly. The Indian population was decimated in the process (as a result of the harshness of the labour system, epidemics of newly introduced diseases and the loss of land which made it impossible for Indian communities to survive), but this was of concern to the new civilization mainly because it threatened to denude the continent of the labour essential to the success of the Spanish colonial enterprise. However, in the main areas in which the Spanish took an interest, sufficient of the Indians survived (Sanchez-Albornoz, 1974) to enable the economic system to work effectively enough for a considerable period. Indeed this availability of Indians as a labour force became almost a *sine qua non* for the development of different parts of the continent. When and where the Indians failed to survive in sufficient numbers, slaves were introduced from areas controlled by the Spanish (and Portuguese) in Africa and, later, the Far East.

Thus, under Spanish colonial rule, the spatial pattern of economic development depended very largely upon the pre-existing situation of human occupation of Latin America. Use was made of only a few parts of the vast extent of the continent nominally under Spanish control but within which there were too few Indians to provide an adequate work-force. The centres of government of the Spanish Vice-royalties were established at Mexico City and Lima and were essentially successor capitals to those of the Aztec and Inca civilizations respectively. Mexico City was built on exactly the same site as the Aztec capital which it replaced, whilst Lima was established on the coastal plain to the west of the Central Andes where the Rimac river and its valley provided a water supply, a harbour and a means of access to the mountain region in which the Inca capital had been located. Moreover, in this new location Spanish experience with low-altitude irrigation agriculture could be put to good use and from it the offshore guano deposits were even more accessible. Elsewhere, Spanish towns were established where Indians were thickest on the ground and where, in many cases, there was already some pre-existing form of urban settlement. Bogotá, Guatemala City and Quito are good examples of this type of development. Around such cities the Spanish settlers, administrators and military personnel participated in or supervised the development of agriculture and they continued the search for precious and semi-precious metals.

The Spanish systems of government, of land tenure and of control over the Indians were basically functions of the economic motivations for their settlements, the development of which represented the major feature of the geography of Spanish economic activities in the continent. This had its corollary, of course, in the virtual absence of any significant early Spanish development in areas of less important or non-existent Indian activities. The most outstanding example of an area of very little early Spanish influence was that of the whole of the southern part of South America where, as we saw earlier in Figure 7–1, there was little pre-Columbian development of the temperate grasslands and of areas even further south. This pre-Columbian emptiness was mirrored in a general lack of Spanish attention to what is now Uruguay, Paraguay and Argentina. Only at a later stage in their colonial history when the Spanish were obliged to defend the small outposts of Empire they had created, at places like Buenos Aires and Asunción, from the dangers of Portuguese expansionism from bases further north along the east coast of the continent, was their level of interest in such areas increased. Even then little effort was made to exploit the resources of the vast region which remained dependent on Lima even for its contacts with Spain. Spanish interests also largely failed to seek out opportunities east of the Andean divide in areas further north for there, too, there were few Indians and no readily usable land. Thus, throughout this region at a later period in its development, Brazil was able to expand its national frontiers to take in territory that had been made nominally Spanish by the Treaty of Tordesillas. In Central America neither the resources of Indians nor those of metals were sufficient to justify other than a limited development of the area and Spanish activities there remained, as in the Caribbean islands to an even greater extent, at a relatively low level. This close spatial correlation between the regions most heavily populated by Indians and the areas of greatest Spanish development is illustrated in Figure 7–2.

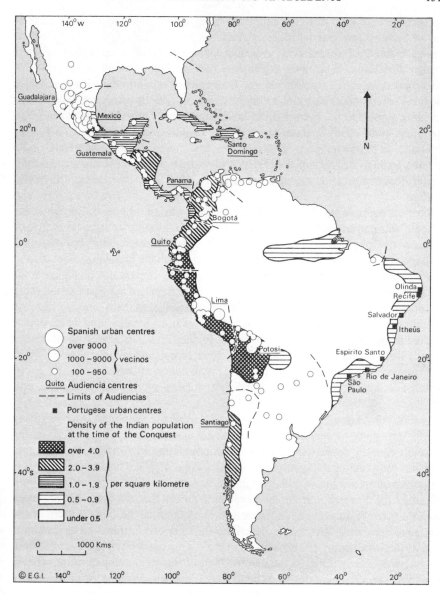

Figure 7–2. Spanish/Portuguese Colonization and the Indian Population

There were, of course, a few important exceptions to this geographical correlation of Spanish interests with pre-existing Indian activities. The most important was undoubtedly Panama City, the most influential Spanish settlement between Mexico and Lima, in an area which had been virtually devoid of Indians. But Panama was essentially a strategic and trading city responsible, until a much later stage in the colonial history of Latin America, for the transhipment of goods—including slaves, which provided the local labour force required—between Lima and Spain (and other Spanish possessions). In its rapid emergence to a role of economic importance, as a result of the first political and commercial links between Latin America and the Old World, lies a first hint of the later, and even greater, economic and strategic importance of this 'crossroads-of-the-world' location.

Another example was Santiago de Chile. This was an outpost of Empire as far as Spain was concerned and was one which rose to importance in part because of the attractive physical environment in which it was located. The region around Santiago consisted mainly of the type of land on which the Spanish system of land tenure could most effectively be established. It had a climate not dissimilar from that of Southern Spain from where well over 50 per cent of the Spanish migrants to Latin America originated (especially from Andalusia), thus making familiar agricultural practices possible. In part, too, however, its location and development resulted from the military function which it fulfilled in a frontier region where the Indians were the only ones never to be conquered by the Spanish in the whole of their area of interest in the continent. The combination of these two factors led to Santiago being developed as an important nucleus of Spanish settlement and activity.

Spanish migration to Latin America following the Conquest was relatively limited averaging, it has been estimated, no more than 2000 per year in the sixteenth century so that the total Spanish population in America by 1574 was probably only about 150,000 (Sanchez-Albornoz, 1974). This limited growth of the population, together with the continued dominance of the motivations already described for Spanish rule in the continent, meant that succeeding decades in Spanish America produced few fundamental changes in the basic pattern of the continent's economic geography. The Spanish American Empire had its economic base in the production of high-value minerals with the limited local profits from this being mainly invested in the development of the main administrative centres, especially the Vice-royalties of Mexico and Lima and also the Audiencia cities (see Figure 7–2). The mining activities themselves produced the growth of resource-based and significant urbanization including such important 'silver' towns as Potosí, in present-day Bolivia, and Taxco, some 120 kilometres to the south-west of Mexico City. Indeed, the former grew to be the third city of the continent, surpassed only by Mexico City and Lima.

The cities of course, produced an intensive local demand for commercial agricultural products but such influences were felt only within a small radius of the main centres of population. Outside these limited zones of more intensive agricultural development around the cities, 'agriculture' was organized, in general, on the basis of the hacienda system within which the non-economic motivations were often stronger than those of an economic character. Thus the *hacendados* often saw ownership of land principally as a means of establishing their prestige and their position in the hierarchy. Indian and slave labour ensured that even inadequate husbandry produced a more than adequate income to the land owners. As a result, commercial agriculture failed to develop to any large extent in response to economic opportunities presented by external markets. There were, of course, some minor exceptions to this, and locally they produced significant developments. One good example was the commercial production of indigo in favourable (viz. near coastal) locations in Middle America and another was cotton grown in irrigated areas along the coast of northern Peru. Another example, on a somewhat larger scale, was expansion in the production of sugar—again mainly in the Caribbean area—for sale in the expanding markets in Western Europe. But this first of the great plantation crops of Latin America was, in fact, more effectively developed in those parts of the continent outside Spanish control.

The Portuguese settlement of Brazil was always more basically economically motivated than the Spanish conquest of the rest of Latin America. In particular, the way in which the Portuguese colonies were organized did at least encourage individuals to make effective economic use of the territory which they were awarded by the Crown. Moreover, Brazil did not have too much of the mineral wealth which was financing development elsewhere in the continent. This, coupled with a much less urban-oriented outlook on the part of the Portuguese settlers, in contrast with their Spanish counterparts, produced a need and a desire on the part of the colonists to use their lands for agricultural products which could be exported back to Western Europe. Thus, the coastal fringe of Brazil was developed as an area of relatively intensive land use given over largely to the production of tropical crops for export to the markets of Europe. For such crops, especially sugar which was introduced in 1552, the favourable environmental conditions of the region together with its closer location vis à vis the main consuming areas in Western Europe gave it a comparative advantage over competing areas.

But an even greater response to the growth of European markets for sugar and other tropical products emerged in the case of those limited parts of Latin America which fell to the domination of other European powers. The most important example of this arose from the agricultural enterprise of the Dutch in the coastal fringes of the north-east corner of South America. Here the economic motivation provided by the rapidly growing European markets for sugar lay behind the Dutch expansionist ventures into territory which was nominally Portuguese. Having extended their area of influence from the region of the present-day Guianas to coastal areas well to the south of the mouth of the Amazon, they set about the exploitation of the suitable climatic and soil characteristics of the region for large-scale sugar production (by Latin American colonial standards). In the Caribbean itself they were rivalled by the enterprise of the British whose military and political successes there in securing territory were quickly followed by the commercial exploitation of islands such as Jamaica and Barbados for plantation crops.

At a much later period (from the mid-nineteenth century onwards), with the development of large-scale markets for tropical foodstuffs and raw materials in North America as well as Western Europe, plantation agriculture was to become an important element in the land-use patterns and economic systems of Latin America. The antecedents to this development can be seen in these early colonial efforts to exploit the agricultural export potential of appropriate coastal areas of the continent and its convenient offshore islands. The fact that Britain and Holland, and the British and Dutch colonies, thrived as a result of this activity was, however, as much a function of the Spanish lack of interest in such matters as it was of the particular abilities of the nations concerned. Had Spain really been interested in developing the use of the land for commercial purposes, and had the organization of its colonial system made this possible, then Britain and Holland would have had a much harder fight to secure the positions they achieved. The plantations in their colonies might well have been much less effectively developed and much less profitable than they were, as a result of competition from the same crops which could have been produced from the extensive areas of Spanish America which were environmentally well suited to such developments.

Thus, by the time the colonial period came to an end in Latin America (that is, by the mid-nineteenth century if we ignore the small remnants of the Spanish Empire in the Caribbean and also the relatively unimportant non-Iberian colonies in the Caribbean), there had been relatively little extension geographically of the areas of economic significance compared with the pre-colonial situation. Economic activities were, in the main, still concentrated around those areas which had enjoyed relatively high levels of development at the earlier period: Central Mexico and the Northern and Central Andean region. Though mining activities for gold, silver and other high-value minerals had been intensified, it is possible to argue, on the other hand, that the establishment of the Spanish hacienda system had had the opposite effect on the level of agricultural activities except in the zones of more intensive cultivation around the cities. The great decline in the numbers of Indians as a result of Spanish rule and European diseases had relieved population pressure on the land in areas which had previously had to provide sustenance for much larger numbers. Moverover, as shown previously, this pre-Columbian motivation for as intensive a land use as possible had not been substituted by any strong motivation for high agricultural productivity on the part of the Spanish landowners. Their holdings were sufficiently large to enable most of them to achieve an entirely satisfactory and acceptable standard of living without needing to put their land to anything like its fullest possible use. Nor were they under any effective obligation to Spain to produce agricultural exports.

Overall, therefore, the use of land in the Spanish Latin American Empire was a function of other than economic forces. Indeed, it was only in three quite small areas of Spanish rule that there was a significant degree of colonization. The most important was the development—with the help of a considerable inflow of African slaves—of the island of Cuba based on plantation agriculture: that is, the Spanish response to similar sorts of economic development by other European powers elsewhere in the Caribbean. Second in importance was the agriculturally-based expansion in Central Chile where the Indians were gradually absorbed or pushed south (towards the forest zone)—though never conquered—so as to allow the growth of traditional Mediterranean-style agriculture over a gradually increasing area. And third was the colonization of the Antioquia–Cauca region of Colombia—an isolated and hitherto declining region which, for reasons not yet fully understood, achieved the sort of growth and development reminiscent of the colonizers of the east coast of North America.

Apart from these changes it was only elsewhere in the continent where other colonial regimes were established that economic motivations produced large new areas of agriculture. These were largely coastally located developments of tropical plantations the products of which were orientated to the export markets. In addition, it was during this period that the first effective colonization of non-coastal areas of Brazil took place—based essentially on the rush for gold and other high value minerals on the plateau of Minas Gerais. As a result, a hitherto little known and sparsely populated part of Brazil became the continent's most important growth region—for a short time. Ouro Prêto—the centre of the mineralized region—grew within two decades to a city of up to 100,000 inhabitants so that it briefly enjoyed the status of the third city of America (after Mexico City and Lima) in terms of population. Its status was, however, short-lived—and much of the wealth of the region ended up with the Paulistas (the people of São Paulo) who had all along tried to control the development in their own interests.

The economic geographical effects of the colonial period had another facet arising from the fact that the continent's political system depended on the external relationships of the Latin American territories with their respective metropolitan powers. This necessitated locational developments which were orientated to this political situation. Hence the economies in most parts of the continent were organized, in spatial terms, around a coastally-located most-important point of contact between the metropolitan power and the local administration. Thus one can argue that what would today be termed tertiary economic activities became, in most cases, concentrated in the main point of seagoing contact with the metropolitan power. When this point did not also happen to be the capital of a colony, these linking functions enabled it eventually to emerge as a rival centre to the capital city of no little importance. One example, on a relatively small scale, is the establishment and development of Guayaquil as the port through which the audiencia city of Quito maintained its contacts with Spain. On a much larger scale, and much grander, was the role of Veracruz, which served as the port for Mexico City, and which therefore began to rise to a high position of administrative and commercial importance. Panama City has already been mentioned in this respect and it, of course, had continental rather than just local importance with its contacts extending along the whole length of the western coast of Latin America.

In cases where the capital city was near-coastal, the point of external contact was established at the nearest suitable coastal site. In these circumstances the port settlement functioned very much as a 'satellite' town of the capital and specialized only in those activities which demanded a port location. The most outstanding example of this was Callao in its relationship with Lima and, to a lesser degree, because of the greater distance between them, Valparaiso and Santiago de Chile. Maracay, the colonial capital of Venezuela, was also near enough to the coast to enable it to inhibit the growth of a port which could rival it in status. Later, however, one factor which enabled Caracas gradually to assert its dominance over the original colonial capital might well have been its greater degree of accessibility to the main coastal point of contact with Spain and the outside world, viz. La Guaira.

Elsewhere in South America, however, one notes two strongly contrasting spatial responses to the need for contact between colonies and the metropolitan power. The Colombian capital, Bogotá, was just about as isolated from the outside world as it was possible to get: a journey of well over a week by river and land transport from the Caribbean ports of entry. In spite of this situation, however, Bogatá maintained its absolute supremacy in the economic, as well as the political and social, life of the country. Thus the ports provided only the essential maritime services in much the same way as Callao did in Peru and Valparaiso in Chile. The ability of Bogotá to maintain its leading role in Colombia in this way is one of the still unexplained problems of the economic geography of the colonial period.

At the other extreme lies the great reversal in the geographical pattern of development in what now constitutes Argentina. As already pointed out, early Spanish interest in the lower River Plate region was very limited and though Buenos Aires was established in the sixteenth century, it languished at the end of a very long supply route coming over the Andes from Lima and down through a series of relatively fertile intermontane basins in what is now North-Western Argentina where cities such as Salta, Mendoza and Córdoba were founded and which for much of the colonial period far exceeded Buenos Aires in importance. The relative status of the inland cities, on the one hand, and of Buenos Aires, on the other, changed, however, with the Spanish need to protect their claim to Argentina from the expansionist tendencies of the Portuguese in the direction of the River Plate estuary. As a result of this, Spanish interest in Buenos Aires was heightened and initial military interest soon widened into other interests. Eventually permission was given for the city to trade across the continent via Lima and, indeed, during the period between 1713 and 1750 when the British South Sea Company gained the monopoly right (by the Treaty of Utrecht) to provide slaves to Spanish America, Buenos Aires was designated as the point of entry for the southern part of the continent, so reversing the previous trading relationship with Lima. However, the continuing absence of much Spanish interest in the effective use of the grassland areas behind Buenos Aires limited its potential for growth but, nevertheless, it was made an Audiencia city and it did become a transhipping point for goods, apart from slaves, for the southernmost parts of the Spanish empire. These developments were sufficient to enable it to become the single most important settlement in the south of the continent and by the last half-century of the colonial period it had risen in importance and status beyond those of the previously more important inland Argentine cities, the development of which was related to locally intensive agriculture in inter-montane basins and to their location on the routes between Buenos Aires and Santiago, Lima and other towns in the mining region of the central Andes. Figure 7–3 attempts to summarize the main elements in the economic geography of Latin America as the colonial period drew to a close at the beginning of the nineteenth century.

Independence and the Geography of Economic Activities

Thus during the colonial period in Latin America economic development was geographically rather limited. It was based on such limited areas of development that the newly independent Latin America states of the nineteenth century had to build their own national economies. As it turned out, however, the fundamental political change from colony to independent nation had, in most cases, only limited social, economic and geographical effects. The new rulers were almost invariably imbued with Spanish traditions and their essential interests lay in maintaining the structure of society as it had developed. In these structures they usually occupied a privileged position. Thus ownership of land remained primarily as a mark of social standing and not as a means of making money. Moreover, its ownership was so concentrated in a few hands that those that had land could make more than enough profits—still utilizing the low-cost labour which was part and parcel of the system— by a far less than optimum use of the resources. Thus, even into the independence period, one of the main reasons for the underutilization of the continent's land resources contined to apply.

In one respect, however, independence did make one important difference even in this sector. As they became sovereign states each country had to make a choice as to which economic strategy to follow. Each newly independent country had to decide either to associate itself economically with a nineteenth-century world in which trading and other commercial interests were then expanding rapidly, or instead be content merely with what it could produce nationally, for, of course, Spain would no longer accept responsibility for providing imports within the framework of its own currency and exchange system. In fact, given a situation in which the national leaders of the newly independent countries were already well used to the wealth and variety of an exchange economy and were unlikely,

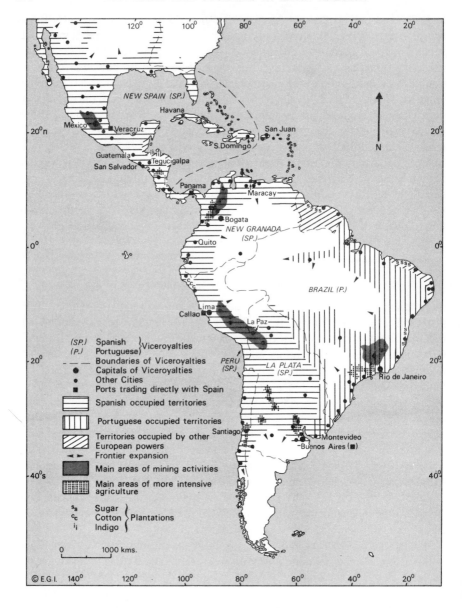

Figure 7–3. Latin America: Economic Geography at end of Colonial Period

therefore, to be prepared to forgo the advantages stemming from such a system, a choice in favour of participation in the international economic system was fairly self-evident. Moreover, to hasten along this choice of strategy there were outside interests very anxious to get footholds in the economic systems of the newly independent states. Thus, the Independence period is marked by the beginning of large-scale investment by foreign non-Spanish entrepreneurs and by companies anxious to make money out of exploiting the continent's resources for which the industrializing nations of North America and Western Europe provided ready markets. In doing so they thereby provided the Latin American nations with foreign exchange and domestic revenues so that the imports of consumer goods needed by the 'aristocracies' could be financed and, more important from the standpoint of the continent's economic geography, they also financed the development of elements of a modern, nineteenth-century economic infrastructure, such as railways, public utilities and other aids to city life.

We shall return to examine, in more detail, the structure and geographical effects of this exploitative economy in the next chapter, rather than dealing with it here, for one can argue that this pattern of development does not form an antecedent to the contemporary patterns of economic life but is, in fact, in many respects, still part of the economic pattern on which the existing economic geography of the continent is based! Here it will suffice to point out that amongst the phenomena involved in bringing about major changes in the geography of the continent were activities such as the development of plantations, the building of railways, the construction of ports and the effects of the migration of large numbers of Europeans to Latin America (particularly to the southern part) so as to provide, in the main, the labour supply for the economic activities arising in the exploitative economy.

In the next chapter, moreover, we shall also try to differentiate between migration and settlement which was an integral part of the process of exploitation as defined, and the migration and settlement which was more closely related to pushing back the frontiers of the occupied territory as a strategy in its own right on the part of some of the new nation-states. In respect of the latter sort of development one thinks in terms of the attempt to extend the occupied area of Chile into the forested south, using both domestically available manpower resources and foreign immigrants; or the expansion and intensification of the settlement of Antioquia in Colombia; or agricultural expansion from the core area of San José in Costa Rica. Overall, however, we shall see that these developments had a relatively minor impact on the geography of the continent when compared with the much greater impact of resource exploitation for foreign trade purposes. Even this in its turn, however, with the exception of the development of the Pampas of Argentina and Uruguay for agriculture, still affected only relatively limited areas of the countries of the continent. Even by the middle of the twentieth century the situation, as far as most countries were concerned, was still one in which most of them had the larger parts of their national territories either unused or underused: in marked contrast with the effects of exploitation and settlement in North America over the same period.

Finally, as an antecedent to contemporary patterns in the continent's economic geography, one must also note the effect of the emergence of the system of sovereign states. The political geography of this development is not our objective, but what does need to be emphasized here is the economic-geographical effects of such nationalism. As successor states to the Spanish Empire, almost all the new Latin American nations were bequeathed a highly centralized form of administration and a tradition of capital city living by the élite groups. Thus tertiary economic activities were usually concentrated almost exclusively on the capital city, or, at best, and in a few cases, on one or more cities in addition. This spatial concentration of non-agricultural activities within nations established the prior conditions necessary for the emergence of the modern imbalance between regions in the Latin American nations. In this respect, therefore, the historical accidents of the emergence of states and the choice of their capitals have been important economic geographical antecedents.

One or two examples will demonstrate the validity of this argument. With the overthrow of Spanish control, which had administered Central America as a single political unit with authority being exercised only through Guatemala City and Panama City, the Central American isthmus soon broke up into a set of separate sovereign states. Guatemala City was left with only a small national territory (like Vienna after the fall of the Hapsburg empire). Panama suffered an even more ignominious fate: it became a province of Colombia and was, therefore, ruled from Bogotá which cared little for its welfare. But, on the othar hand, what had been small provincial towns in the Central American Vice-royalty (e.g. San José, San Salvador) now became capital cities of new sovereign states, with all the attendant advantages which such status gave in terms of the possibilities of attracting a range of secondary and tertiary economic activities.

Further south, post-independence rivalry between Argentina and Brazil had ultimately led to the formation of a separate sovereign state of Uruguay whose territory was, in most other respects, in the same relationship to Buenos Aires as that of half-a-dozen other Argentinian provinces. Had Uruguay remained an Argentine province, then Montevideo would have been just another provincial capital like Rosario or Córdoba. Instead it became a national capital and ultimately one of Latin America's 'million' cities. Away at the other end of the continent one has evidence by which to judge what might have happened to Montevideo if Uruguay had not become a separate sovereign state. If Guadalajara, an audiencia city since 1548, had succeeded in its efforts to secure its independence of Mexico City, it would have become the capital of another successor nation. Instead it continued in its subordinate status to Mexico City. Only recently, after a period of more than 100 years of Independence, has it managed to develop into anything much more than a sleepy, provincial, colonial town. This could well have been Montevideo's fate as well, given a different political solution to the Uruguayan problem. Thus, in the capital cities of the successor states to colonial rule, we see the main antecedents to the establishment of these selected cities' 'initial advantage' for development and on the basis of which emerged the 'core regions' in the contemporary economic geography of Latin America.

Bibliography

There have been few studies of the historical geography of Latin America. However the following books and articles are most useful in achieving an understanding of the historical background to the exploitation of Latin America.

SAUER, C. O., 'A geographical sketch of early man in America', *American Geographical Review*, **24** (1934).
This provides a background to the initial human occupation of the Americas—in part on South and Middle America. See also Professor Sauer's much later work, *The Early Spanish Main*, University of California Press, Berkeley, 1966, for a fuller treatment of Middle America.
STEWARD, J. H. and FARON, L. C., *Native peoples of South America*, McGraw-Hill, New York, 1959.
This contains very useful sections on the distribution and organization of different societies in South America in the pre-Columbian period.
HARDOY, J. E., *Pre-Columbian Cities*, Allen and Unwin, London, 1973.
KELLY, K., 'Land Use Regions of the Central and Northern Portions of the Empire', *Annals of the Association of American Geographers*, **55**, 327–338 (1965).
KOSOK, P., *Life, Land and Water in Ancient Peru*, Long Island U.P., New York, 1965.
SIMPSON, L. B., 'Exploitation of the Land in Central Mexico in the 16th Century', *Ibero-Americana*, no. 36, Univ. of California, 1952.
WILEY, G. R., *Prehistoric Settlement Patterns in the New World*, Johnson Reprint Corp., New York, 1956.
The above five publications are concerned with interpreting the patterns of economic activities in various parts of the continent prior to colonization and are amongst the most geographical of the studies of the pre-Columbian period.
DENEVAN, W. M., *The Native Population of the Americas in 1492*, University of Wisconsin Press, Madison, 1976.
This book draws together in a series of essays, by scholars involved in the research on the problem, the controversies and opinions on the size and distribution of the pre-Columbian populations of the Americas. Almost 80 per cent of it is devoted to Central and South America and the Caribbean.
WOLF, E., *Sons of the Shaking Earth*, Chicago Press, Chicago, 1959.
An anthropological interpretation of the indigenous cultures of Middle America which is very helpful in explaining their relationships with the colonial system.
SANCHEZ-ALBORNOZ, N., *The Population of Latin America: A History*, University of California Press, Berkeley, 1974.
This population history of Latin America from pre-Columbian times to the present is devoted mainly to the pre-Independence periods. It is more geographical than demographic in its approach and conveys clearly the main elements in the changing geography of Latin America's population.
HERRING, H., *A History of Latin America*, 3rd Edition, Cape, London, 1968.

PENDLE, G. A., *A History of Latin America*, Penguin Books, Harmondsworth, 1963. These two general texts, the first one long and the second one short, on the history of the continent are more geographically orientated than alternatives.

BOXER, C. R., *The Portuguese Seaborne Empire, 1415–1825*, Hutchinson, London, 1969.

HARING, C. H., *The Spanish Empire in America*, Oxford University Press, Oxford, 1947. The two standard texts on the history of the empires in Latin America.

WHITTLESEY, E. A., *The Earth and the State*, Holt, New York, 1944. Chapters 13 and 14 present a political geographical interpretation of the colonization of Latin America and of the development of the independent states of the continent.

CHAPTER 8

The Economic Geography of the Exploitative Economy

As shown in the previous chapter, the achievement of political independence by most countries of Latin America in the first half of the nineteenth century coincided with the increasing interest of the industrializing nations of North America and Western Europe and their entrepreneurs in exploiting the resources of the continent. Their interest was, of course, a response to the rising demand for imported foodstuffs by their rapidly growing and urbanizing populations and the demands for industrial raw materials, both vegetable and mineral, by the growing number and variety of factories in Western Europe and North America. This chapter is concerned with a description and evaluation of the economic geographical effects in Latin America of this development, the main aspect of which is the commercial exploitation of the land and its resources. Our hypothesis is that the geography of Latin America's economic development in the second part of the nineteenth century and up to at least the First World War (much later in some areas) can largely be explained in terms of such exploitation and its secondary effects.

The Acceptance of Foreign Capital

We have already pointed out that, given the circumstances of independence and of the interests and the motivations of the groups that achieved political control in the newly independent countries, acceptance of the idea of 'development' by foreign capital was never really in doubt for most of the newly independent countries. Moreover, at the time the Latin American countries had brotherly feelings towards the United States on account of its successful late eighteenth century anti-colonial fight, and this persuaded them of two things.

Firstly, that U.S. capital for development purposes was welcome. This was because it was felt that the U.S., with its fifty years of post-independence experience behind it, would surely know exactly what it was that the Latin

143

American countries wanted and needed in order to achieve a successful transition from colonial status. The United States would, moreover, surely be prepared to show its sister republics in the Americas just how to achieve the same mighty economic progress that it had made in the period since Independence. Latin American governments had, therefore, little difficulty in persuading themselves that by welcoming U.S. capital to their countries they were taking the right kind of action to ensure that their countries would follow the U.S. example and pattern of expansion.

Secondly, the Latin American governments were also aware that capital originating from the newly industrialized nations in the north-west of Europe had helped the U.S. to achieve economic growth. During the time that this had been happening they, on the other hand, had been languishing under the handicap of being part of the economic system of Spain which, as they saw, had suffered a serious relative decline in its status amongst the European nations. Spanish rule had also severely circumscribed investment in Latin America by other European countries. This barrier was now out of the way and the United States offered an example of what could be done by making use of investment capital from Britain, Prussia and other European powers.

From the point of view of the capital surplus nations, particularly Britain and the United States, the opportunity to invest in Latin America was welcome. Such investment opportunities lay either directly in resource development or indirectly in infrastructure, such as railways, which would then facilitate resource development and which, of course, could also be highly profitable in its own right given the monopoly conditions which could often be negotiated. Large-scale investment in resource development was thought likely to offer the promise of high returns, for the 'el Dorado' attitude towards the continent persisted in spite of Spain's earlier inability to maintain its wealth from the mining of high value commodities. Moreover, Latin America also presented a range of types of physical environment from which many of the growing requirements of industry and of industrial, urbanized populations could be met. Thus, North American and European capitalists were prepared, and indeed anxious, to go out to seek investment opportunities in Latin America.

In both political and economic terms, Latin America was 'ripe' for commercial exploitation and both individuals and companies went to it with enthusiasm. The varied fortunes of those involved do not concern us here except to note that a lack of familiarity with some of the difficulties of working in Latin American environments was responsible for the loss of not a few fortunes. We shall, however, return later to consider the phenomenon of the failure of the exploitative economy to affect other than a small part of the continent. As we shall then see, there were important social and institutional, as well as physical environmental, factors which caused this geographically limited impact of resource development.

Space considerations alone, apart from other factors, make it impossible to present a systematic and chronological account of the changes in the continent's economic geography arising from the impact of the forces of exploitative capitalism. Instead we shall pick out a few of the outstanding examples of the changes that were brought about, and in discussing three cases in particular we shall also become aware of some of the main issues involved in this process of economic geographical change. The most important single development was the commercial exploitation of the pampas of Argentina and Uruguay. Another significant development was the massive expansion of the plantation system involving both new crops and new areas. And a third resulted from the impact of the search for mineral wealth in Latin America.

The Economic Development of the Pampas

In the previous chapter we saw how Spanish interests in the temperate grasslands of the southern part of the continent to the east of the Andes remained largely unaroused except, at first, in response to a political/strategic threat from the Portuguese pushing down from the north and, later, after 1776, in the Spanish decision to permit the development of Buenos Aires as a new and more convenient coastal point of contact between Spain and the southern part of its Latin American empire which, at the same time, was detached from the Vice-royalty of Peru. As a result of this, present-day Argentina, Uruguay, Paraguay and Bolivia became the Vice-royalty of the (River) Plate. However, in spite of the political change, Spanish interests in the region remained limited and the pattern of the economic geography of the River Plate region at the time of independence consisted of the relatively new main urban and trading centre of Buenos Aires surrounded by an area of agricultural development concerned principally with raising food for the city. Other settlements in the region—such as Montevideo (founded as recently as 1724 but thereafter benefiting from its official designation as the port of call for all Spanish ships sailing to the Pacific) and the line of towns along the west bank of the River Plate, along the route to the north and west—were much less important. There was also a somewhat more extensive area of pastoral activities—notably for the production of salt beef and of hides and, even more important, for horse and mule raising on the unimproved native grasslands. The latter constituted the main export commodities—they were sent north to meet the transport requirements in the mining areas of highland Peru and Bolivia.

These coastal and near coastal activities were both geographically and structurally separate from the longer-developed economic activities of the interior basins of Argentina. They lay in the foothills of the Andes where the local economies had grown up over a much longer period on the basis of traditional Spanish patterns of agriculture in environments not dissimilar from those of the central parts of Spain. Each basin was organized socially, economically and politically around its central city: Mendoza, San Juan, Tucamán etc. Each region was jealous of its independence and, although collectively they could have offered strong opposition to the dominance which Buenos Aires sought, they were unable to work effectively together in either economic or political terms. As a result, Buenos Aires was eventually able to achieve a dominant role in all spheres of national life and when it finally became the federal capital in 1880 Argentina secured a centralized political system which provided an ideal framework within which the economic revolution, which had already begun a quarter of a century earlier (with the 1853 Confederal Constitution), could be achieved.

By the middle of the nineteenth century, in the early post-independence years, there was already some element of appreciation of the potentiality of the pampas as an area which could supply industrializing Western Europe with part of its growing food and raw material requirements. In respect, for example, of larger supplies of salt-beef and for high quality wool based on improved strains of sheep which were gradually introduced on the pampas. However, it was not until the political domination of the country by the 'porteños' of Buenos Aires after 1850 that there was a political environment within which the potentiality could be realized. As a result, the next half-century proved to be a period in which there was a complete transformation of the pampas under the stimulus of changed geographical values. This transformation has been succinctly described and explained in the following words: 'The transformation . . . was the result of a combination of factors. Some of the more important were the coming of political stability in the new Argentina after the overthrow of the dictator Rosas in 1852; the expanding markets offered by the industrialized nations of Western Europe; the elimination of the nomadic Indian hunters to the south-west; the introduction of agricultural and pastoral techniques such as barbed wire, fences, windmills, and machinery; the influx of capital from a prosperous and expanding British economy; the immigration of Italian labour . . . to till and harvest the new lands; the spread of the railway network over the region; and last, but not least, speedy trans-oceanic transport with refrigerated facilities to bridge the gap of 6000 miles between producer and consumer.' (Butland, G. J., *Latin America*, Longmans, London, 2nd Edition, 1973.)

The significance of each of these elements involved in the transformation has been examined by Crossley (in *Latin America: Geographical Perspectives*, Eds. H. Blakemore and C. T. Smith, Methuen, London, 1973). He also draws attention to an important omission in this brief quotation, viz. the absence of any reference to the impact of the system of land tenure which was evolved following the success of Buenos Aires in achieving control over the country's affairs. Most of the pampas were not, at that time, under formal ownership which thus became vested automatically in the state. But state power was more or less identical with the power of a few score leading families of Buenos Aires. Thus, in spite of legislation which was specifically designed to prevent the lands of the pampas becoming privately owned, these families managed to obtain the right to use the land on terms which, sooner or later, secured them ownership of the title. Once this transfer of ownership to private hands had been achieved, the way was open to the rapid exploitation of the land. This was achieved largely, though not exclusively, within the framework of a system of short-term tenant farming. Immigrants to Argentina, largely from southern Europe, were 'given' the right to use an area of virgin land within one of the large landholdings. In return for their expenditure of labour and expertise in improving the land they shared the crops with the landowners for a few years. Thereafter, the immigrants had to leave (either to find unimproved land elsewhere on which they could again become short-term tenants or to become urban dwellers in a rapidly expanding Buenos Aires). The landowner, of course, was left with an additional hectarage of improved land, generally under alfalfa and thus suitable for a further extension of the pastoral economy dedicated to the production of beef for export to Britain and to other parts of industrial Europe. At the same time as this improvement and intensification of agriculture was taking place in the parts of the pampas already under cultivation, the area in production was being quickly expanded as the increasing flow of immigrants sought land for settlements. Such land was available on the drier margins of the pampas proper and this could be developed given technological developments, especially in respect of water supplies and of rail transport facilities. The network of railways, as shown in Figure 8–1, steadily increased the areas accessible to Buenos Aires, Rosario and Bahia Blanca, the main ports for the export of Argentine agricultural production: this rail network, built primarily by British companies, represents the world's best example of a transport system which was developed to ensure the exploitation of the potential of a region for the production of primary goods destined for use in the world's industrial nations. This export-orientated nature of the motivation for the system is clearly demonstrated in the late (post-1885) inter-connection of Buenos Aires and Rosario—the country's two most important cities, but also the two main ports serving the needs of the country's exporters and thus with their respective rail systems orientated to connections with the outside world rather than to each other and hence to considerations of national integration.

Thus, fundamental land use changes and the expansion of cultivated land and settlement achieved an agricultural revolution. More than this, however, they also produced a region of economic growth and strength, unrivalled in the southern Hemisphere and surpassed only in the northern one by a few important manufacturing regions such as the Ruhr and the North-East United States. Buenos Aires itself developed into one of the world's biggest and richest cities and ports of the period, while the rail transport network of the whole region—and particularly of areas within a 300 km radius of Buenos Aires—achieved a density of route development and of services which matched those of the world's main industrial regions. The continuing strength of the external demand for the wheat, maize, meat and other agricultural products that could be grown so cheaply in the near ideal physical conditions of the pampas, under a system in which the exploitation of the immigrant workers ensured low production costs, produced so much wealth that Argentina as a whole was numbered among the top ten nations in income per

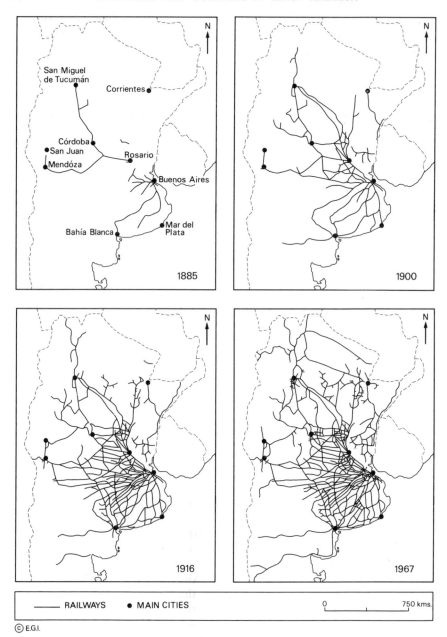

Figure 8–1. Argentina: expansion of the Rail Network

head from the later part of the nineteenth century through to the Great Depression of 1929. In that Argentina outside the Pampas, moreover, remained largely undeveloped and relatively poor, one can judge that the pampas themselves, and Buenos Aires in particular, achieved standards of development well up to those of the world's industrial powers at this time. Thus, the exploitation of the potential of the pampas, arising out of an external demand for its agricultural products and financed largely by foreign capital, produced the most important change in the economic geography of Latin America in this period of economic colonization.

The Expansion of the Plantation Economy

The massive expansion of the plantation system in Latin America, involving both new areas and new crops, is the second aspect of the geographical impact of exploitative capitalism that we must examine. Plantations had, of course, long been part of some colonial systems, most particularly the British, with sugar as the most important plantation crop. But this sort of agricultural land use in Latin America had been restricted by the great geographical extent of Spanish rule. As shown in the previous chapter, Spain's peripheral position in the process of industrialization in Europe, together with its deteriorating economic and financial position in the crucial eighteenth century, meant that it had neither the incentive nor the ability to make use of those of its possessions with suitable environmental conditions for plantation agriculture on a large scale. And, as also shown previously, it was not prepared to allow the exploitation of its colonies by capital and/or entrepreneurs from other countries. Following the establishment of independent nations in former Spanish America, this restraint on the development of plantations disappeared and concessions from the new national governments of environmentally suitable regions were sought and obtained by foreigners in response to the rising demands for tropical products in other parts of the world.

In contrast with the mainly European investment in Argentina and Uruguay, the financing of plantations in tropical or sub-tropical regions of ex-Spanish America was mainly American. Indeed, the major European powers had much less need for plantations in former Spanish possessions since they retained their own colonial territories in Africa and Asia, many of which also enjoyed appropriate tropical climatic conditions for plantation crops. Thus their relative lack of interest in the potential offered by the newly-independent tropical South and Central American republics for the expansion of plantation agriculture left the field open for entrepreneurs from the United States. By this time, moreover, the United States was experiencing sufficient growth in industry, income, and in population to justify foreign investments designed to secure overseas supplies of foodstuffs and of raw materials which could either not be produced at all or not be produced cheaply enough within its national territorial limits. Thus, U.S. capitalists sought land concessions on a large scale for the plantation production of sugar, cocoa, coffee, bananas and, at a later stage, with the growth, in particular, of the automobile industry, of rubber. As a consequence, the traditional stock-raising and the cultivation of indigo and cacao which formed the commercial agriculture corner stones of the economies of the small nations of Central America were substituted by new crops to be grown on a large scale for export. Coffee production in the tropical highlands of Costa Rica was first established in 1832 and from there spread to regions with similar climate and other physical conditions in El Salvador, Nicaragua, and Guatemala. By 1860 its production was important in all four countries and has remained so to date (see Figure 8–2), with a high degree of foreign control and involvement in its production and marketing if not in terms of actual land-ownership.

It was, however, the alienation of large areas of the coastal plains of these small countries of Central America by a few U.S. companies, anxious to produce bananas for the American market, which provides the outstanding example of the impact of the plantation system in newly-independent Latin America (see Figure 8–2). Large-scale American interest in bananas in Central America dates from the 1870s when lands physically suited to banana production on the Caribbean coastlands, generally at altitudes of less than 500 feet, were opened up for cultivation by the development of railways such as that from Puerto Limón to San José, the capital of Costa Rica. In fact, for this railway (as with others in Central America, such as the line from Puerto Barrios to Guatemala City) the need for a basic income from freight traffic provided the stimulus for the use of the land alongside their tracks as banana plantations.

In other areas it was the rapid success of the banana industry, following its establishment to supply fruit to the American market, that provided the incentive for further railway construction and for the development of port facilities and other items of infrastructure. An example of this is seen in the case of the Caribbean coastlands of northern Honduras, where there had been no earlier incentive for development. The country had, indeed, been orientated towards the Pacific Ocean, mainly because Tegucigalpa, the old, inland capital, had its external connections in that direction and because environmental conditions for both subsistence agriculture and earlier commercial crops has been so much better on the Pacific side of the country. Now, the development of bananas along the Caribbean coast had the effect of reorientating its spatial economy—including the geographical distribution of the population—in a completely different direction. As a result Tegucigalpa was isolated from the new geographical pattern of development of the country.

Thus banana plantations in the period from 1870 through to the second decade of the twentieth century, when expansion was thwarted by the onset of disease which necessitated the progressive abandonment of plantations, provided the means whereby the economic geography of these areas was transformed. The transformation was significant even though the area affected in no case amounted to more than 7 per cent of the total crop land of any one of the countries concerned. The impact was, indeed, sufficient to make bananas one of the mainstays

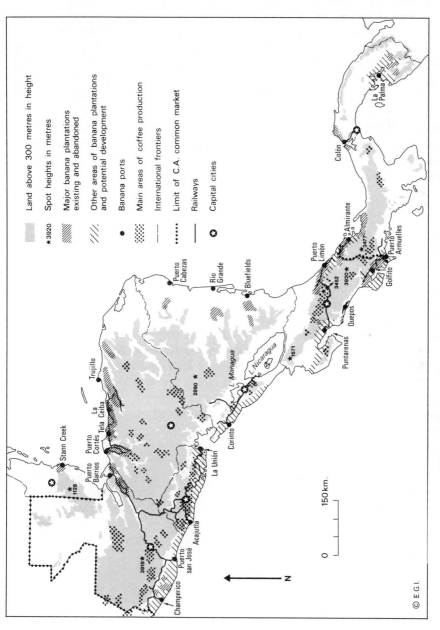

Figure 8–2. Central America: banana and coffee plantations

of the countries' economies and to cause these nations to be dubbed 'the banana republics'. This, however, was not so much a description of the dominant element in the actual land use in the Central American countries, as it was a manner of indicating the apparent potential of the foreign companies concerned to secure first refusal on any and all land which they considered was potentially suitable for the production of bananas. Moreover, the ability of the companies in this respect was one aspect only of their more general ability to mould government action in whatever directions were acceptable to and needed by the companies. Thus, the importance of the development of banana plantations in Central America was a function of the combination of very small countries, lacking the abilities to sustain competent or even adequate governments, with the incidence of one very powerful company, the United Fruit Company, with access to far greater resources of funds and expertise than any one of the Central American countries. Thus wherever it operated in the region it could be certain of securing whatever conditions for exploitation of the land were necessary to ensure its profitability, and so provides a classic example of a region's economic geography emerging from a country's exploitation by foreign capital intent on producing a commodity for consumption in the world's industrialized and wealthy nations.

Much the same line of argument can be used in explaining the conversion of Cuba into a sugar-plantation-based economic colony of the United States, following the end of Spanish rule there after the Spanish–American War of 1898. The excellent physical conditions, both climatic and physiographic, for the production of sugar in Cuba had, as we have already seen, ensured its relative importance in the economy of the island even under Spanish rule. But in the late nineteenth century, after most of the former Spanish colonies in Latin America had gained their independence, Spanish political and economic conditions did not provide much of a stimulus to the continued development of its plantations. Thus, production remained relatively small-scale compared with that from sugar plantations elsewhere in the Caribbean where wealthier and more active colonial powers were encouraging the development of the crop. Production in Cuba was, indeed, largely concentrated in the western part of the island where the economic infrastructure, particularly in essential transport facilities, was sufficiently well developed to enable use to be made of the highly favourable physical conditions. Annual levels of production were also affected by highly unstable political conditions in Cuba from the mid-nineteenth century onwards—conditions which deteriorated into virtual civil war over quite long periods. Thus, whilst in 1860 there were reported to be some 2000 small sugar mills in Cuba, the number had been reduced to 1200 by 1878 and to only just over 200 which were still in operation by 1899 when sugar production was under half-a-million tons.

Thereafter, the 'Pax Americana', with the opportunity it gave to U.S. capital and expertise to seek openings for profitable investment in the island, rapidly changed the situation. Cuba was quickly converted into a land of extensive sugar plantations and its economy became largely dependent upon the greatly expanded sugar mono-culture developed by an estimated $1000 million of U.S. capital investment. Considerations of profit maximization on the part of the U.S. corporations involved, together with similar motivations for those Cuban companies and individuals which managed to survive the modernization of the industry, now emerged as the sole criterion by which decisions on land use in Cuba were taken. Such corporate enterprise (which squeezed out most of the former small landowners and made them into plantation workers) was able to take advantage of the excellence of the physical conditions for sugar cultivation (viz. the large area of level or gently rolling land suitable for easy harvesting and for local transportation to mills and ports, plus the appropriate tropical climate with the dry harvesting period). These, plus the low transport costs involved in getting the sugar away to the U.S. markets from the many ports which could be developed for the sugar trade and most of which were only short distances from the main producing areas (see Figure 8–3), combined to give Cuba a significant comparative advantage in the production of the commodity. Only a quarter of a century after the Americans took over the sugar economy, output had multiplied to nearly 20 times its 1900 level and production had been pushed to all areas of the country where climatic and other physical conditions were suitable: except where, locally, a more highly valued crop, most particularly tobacco, could be produced.

Ultimately, land dedicated to sugar cane came to involve not far short of 50 per cent of the total land area of Cuba (see Figure 8–3). It should be noted, however, that not all this land area would actually be producing sugar at any one time. The actual area in use at any moment depended, firstly, on the rotational requirements of the crop in different areas (soil and climatic conditions affect the length of the period of recuperation required for the land following its use for cane production) and, secondly, on the price level for the commodity on the world and U.S. markets. With high sugar prices, as in the years of World War II, investments in fertilizer could be substituted for fallow periods. Thus in such years the amount of land actually under sugar cultivation could be increased so that advantage could be taken of the high prices to increase revenues and profits.

The introduction of a modern, geographically extensive and capital intensive sugar plantation economy into Cuba quite fundamentally changed the island's land use. The type of development had, moreover, consequential effects on many other aspects of the country's economic geography, most particularly in the incentive which it gave to the expansion of the island's transport system and in generating population changes. As with banana plantations, there was much railway building by the plantation operators to serve their own needs and, indeed, such lines came to account for about two-thirds of the island's total railway mileage. In addition, however, other capital was attracted by the opportunities presented for the construction of lines from the sugar producing areas to the ports which themselves had to be expanded and modernized or even created out of little more than fishing harbours. The plantation-to-port railway lines eventually linked up to form a relatively comprehensive rail system second only in Latin America,

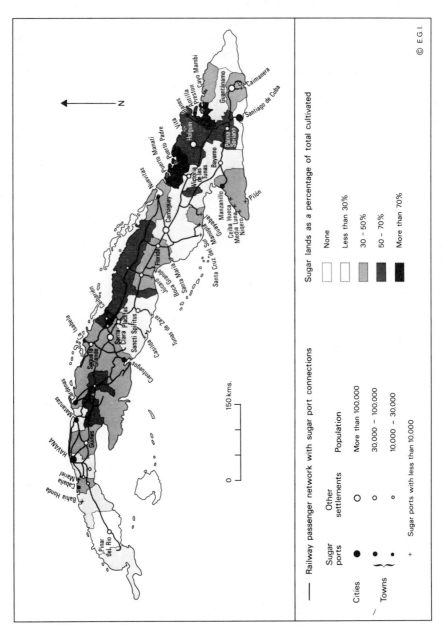

Figure 8–3. Cuba: sugar land and transport facilities

as regards its density and connectivity, to that of the pampas of Argentina (see Figure 8–1). As far as its effect on population was concerned, the American-financed sugar-producing industry stimulated immigration since the demand for labour, both directly in sugar and indirectly in secondary and tertiary activities, increased beyond the abilities of the existing resident population to meet it.

Investment in sugar made it possible, and, indeed, even necessary, to reduce the hitherto too high mortality rates arising from relatively easily-controllable diseases like malaria and yellow fever, thus adding to the propensity for population increase. As the overall result, therefore, population grew from only a little over 1.5 million in 1900 to almost 4 million by 1930. Thereafter, economic difficulties and controls introduced by the government to protect the interests of the existing population had the effect of substantially reducing the rate of immigration and hence of the rate of population increase.

The geographical expansion of the sugar lands, moreover, together with their accompanying 'centrales' for the basic processing of the cane, created a demand for the provision of services and encouraged the growth of transportation facilities. Thus enlarged, or even new, service centres were created, providing another element in the changing geography of the country's economy. Thus, spatial correlation between population increase and the growth of the sugar economy is also recognizable within Cuba. This is also seen in the fact that the greatest proportional population increase in the country occurred in the provinces which enjoyed the greatest expansion in sugar output: most notably the eastern provinces of the country which were brought under sugar plantations for the first time during this period.

Cuba thus demonstrates very clearly the importance of the plantation system in changing the economic geography of an hitherto generally underutilized country. Though it is strictly beyond the scope of this chapter of the book, this opportunity must not be missed for pointing out that sugar plantation development in Cuba—largely financed from the United States and designed to produce a commodity to be consumed largely in the United States—led to social and political problems which contributed greatly to the revolution in Cuba in 1959. Such a high degree of foreign control over the very basis of a country's economy, and thus over its political development too, at least as far as the main strands of policy are concerned, constituted an extension of colonialism which became unacceptable in the modern world. Further attention will be given in the next chapter to the geographical implications of this unacceptability of the plantation system in its traditional form.

Meanwhile, however, it would be incorrect to leave the impression that the plantation system was invariably based on foreign ownership. Plantations were, most frequently, foreign-owned, given that plantation agriculture was, in essence, a geographical extension of the economic systems of the rich industrial nations of the time. Such nations provided the capital, the expertise, the ocean transportation, and the markets and these functions outweighed in importance the land and labour provided, almost incidentally, by the host countries. However, one important Latin American plantation crop did not develop in this way to anything like the same extent. This was coffee, which up until 1945 was provided for world markets almost exclusively by Latin American countries. In the case of this crop the enterprise has often been indigenous and where it has been imported, as in the case of the German cultivators of Guatemala, Costa Rica and other Central American states, the foreign entrepreneurs involved became residents of the countries concerned and so involved themselves in national life, rather than remaining merely the local representatives of foreign-owned companies. The case of Brazil, traditionally responsible for about half the world's total supply of this commodity, illustrates the situation.

As shown in the previous chapter, the agricultural exploitation of Brazil under the Portuguese was concentrated on the northern and north-eastern coastal lands where sugar could be produced with slave labour on the large landholdings of those to whom land grants had been made. The boom in sugar had, however, largely worked itself out before the end of the colonial period as a result of competition from other colonial areas. Thus the main economic interest had gradually moved further south, with particular attention focused on the discovery and extraction of gold and other precious metals and stones from Minas Gerais from the late seventeenth century onwards. Gold production 'financed' a population expansion so that towns and settlements grew up and created a new 'core area' for Brazil. The lands in this new central region of interest were divided into fazendas which provided the foodstuffs required by the still relatively small but growing population and the fazendeiros' income was further supplemented by the sale of cattle and other products to other regions. Needless to say the system generated relatively little wealth (compared with that which had been generated out of the sugar plantations in the north at an earlier period), particularly after 1800 or thereabouts when gold production began to diminish. In spite of this, and also in spite of expanding market opportunities, attempts to expand the production of coffee as a cash crop at this time within the framework of the existing system were not very successful though exports did begin as early as 1779. There was insufficient motivation for basic changes in the production systems on the part of the landowners. Moreover, as the land was already under ownership and some form of use, it was not open to coffee exploitation by foreign enterprise. Thus, the expansion of coffee to the status of Brazil's most important economic activity, and one which successively occupied most of the suitable (and some unsuitable) land in the south and south-eastern parts of the country, had to await the acceptance by the fazendeiros of the idea that their land should be utilized in a new way—and this did not occur until after independence in 1822.

Coffee cultivation necessitated, first, land clearance and then continuing high inputs of labour over a period of several years into the establishment of a plantation. Coffee trees take from four to six years to reach bearing age during which time they must receive constant attention. Such a large demand for labour was initially beyond the capability of Brazil to supply, as population numbers were still small and most of them had interests which lay mainly in the towns and cities. At the same time international pressure and action had by this time eliminated the possibility of the introduction of large additional numbers of slaves to provide the work force required. (Though it should be noted that slaves did provide a limited solution to the opening up of coffee production on a significant scale as slavery was not finally eliminated in Brazil until 1888.) The ultimate solution to this labour problem in the development of really large-scale coffee cultivation did not begin to emerge until the second half of the nineteenth century and, indeed, labour availability only reached the level necessary for the rapid exploitation of the land for coffee plantations after 1885. The solution found lay in the encouragement of European immigration on a similar basis to that which we have already examined in connection with the development of the Pampas in Argentina. Immigrants were offered short-term tenancies on the fazendas during which period they cleared the land and established the coffee plantations in return for the right to grow food and certain other crops between the immature coffee trees, the numbers of which tripled in the 10 years between 1890 and 1900. The immigrants had their tenancies terminated at the beginning of the period in which the trees started to bear fruit and they then had to seek similar opportunities elsewhere—and so the frontier of coffee exploitation expanded.

Utilizing immigrant labour in this way enabled coffee plantations to spread over much of the states of São Paulo, Rio de Janeiro, Minas Gerais and Espirito Santo in response to the rising demand for coffee by the outside world. Though coffee cultivation thus remained almost entirely under national ownership and control, the use of the land remained essentially exploitative in the crudest sense, as there was little effort to conserve the ability of the land to continue to produce the commodity. As land quality became depleted below the level demanded by coffee, so the frontier of coffee exploitation moved on. The speed of advance of the frontier and the abandonment of land for coffee cultivation were functions of the fluctuating price levels for coffee on the international market. These price fluctuations were a phenomenon which were essentially outside the ability of the Brazilians to control, though some half-hearted measures were taken to curb the flow of coffee to the market in time of glut. This generally unsuccessful action depended on governmental purchases of some of the crop either for destruction or for release at a later, less-depressed state of the market. As the first centenary of the large-scale exploitation of coffee in Brazil approaches, one notes that the coffee plantation and its product still remain the key to Brazilian economic well-being though, as we shall see later, even a nationally-owned plantation-type crop has been condemned as an inappropriate base for the agricultural economy of a modern state.

Foreign Exploitation of Latin America's Mineral Wealth

There were few countries in Latin America where the economic geography, in the later nineteenth and first half of the twentieth centuries, was not radically affected by the types of exploitative agricultural development described so far in this chapter. There is, however, another somewhat different aspect of the geography of economic colonialism to which we must give some attention: particularly so because it applies most of all to those countries of Latin America which were least affected by the agricultural developments of the economic colonial system. This is the economic geography of the extractive mineral industries, the development of which in Latin American countries was also to provide for exports of the minerals concerned to the manufacturing nations of Europe and North America. The system closely parallels that of the plantation economy as it also involves the use of national territorial resources at the behest of external forces with, traditionally, the host government having no control over, or even any say in, decisions on developments—or retrenchments. It is, of course, sometimes argued that developments of these activities did, in fact, lie entirely within the control of a host government which had an initial right to decide whether or not a concession should be made to the company seeking to exploit the natural resource. A government can, of course, also lay down the conditions on which the exploitation shall take place. Until quite recently, however, all Latin American governments were unwilling and/or unable to negotiate effectively with the large foreign companies seeking concessionary rights to seek and to work mineral wealth, particularly as, almost always, the companies sought their concessions with the tacit, or even the open, support of either the U.S. or the British governments.

In addition, all too often in the past, many Latin American governments were concerned much too little about the longer-term interests of their countries in such negotiations. This was because the sale of concessionary rights to foreign companies created the possibilities of personal gains on a considerable scale by unscrupulous politicians. Thus, one can hypothesize that the geographical pattern of the development of extractive industry in Latin America has principally and simply reflected the foreign exploiting companies' evaluations of the relative profit-earning ability of the products from different locations when produced for sale on world markets. The pattern of development has not reflected national wishes and needs in respect of resource development.

In that most of the products involved are of great bulk with a low value per ton, a prime consideration determining the profitability of particular deposits has been, and, to a large degree, still remains, their location in relation to points of export. By and large this has created a significant advantage for coastal or near coastal deposits such that even today extractive industry is largely confined to locations within 300 kilometres of tidewater (see Figure 8–4).

The most important nineteenth century development of mineral resources was that of Chilean nitrates, the availability of which was a function of the particular physical conditions of the Atacama Desert. Their large-scale occurrence as a surface phenomenon in the geomorphological and climatic conditions of Northern Chile ensured that they could be worked at low costs and their location, in turn,

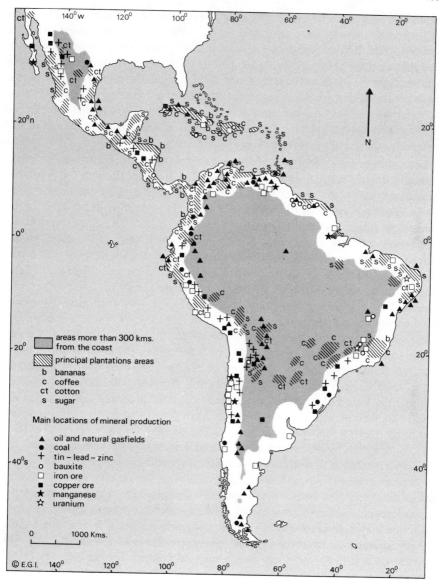

Figure 8–4. Latin America: the location of extractive industries and plantations

meant that they could be transported at low cost to the nearby coast in spite of the harsh, arid and unpopulated environment. Once the territorial boundary problems between Chile, Bolivia and Peru had been settled, albeit only at the cost of a war between the three countries, caused partly by their anxiety to secure some of the benefits likely to arise from the exploitation of the nitrates, then the rapid expansion of the industry could take place in response to the burgeoning industrialized world's demand for nitrates (for both industrial and agricultural use). As a result large parts of the Atacama Desert region of Chile secured a rail-transport infrastructure unmatched in the world's arid regions (see Figure 8–5).

The railways were either built by the nitrate companies themselves or by other, generally British, companies which responded to the opportunities for profitable investment created by the potential traffic to be generated by the nitrate companies. The railways were thus designed essentially to provide the shortest or the lowest-cost route from the 'oficinas' (the locations where the nitrates underwent preliminary primary processing) to the ports, which were constructed at the nearest possible points of access on a coast the physical geography of which was generally unattractive for the building of railways to the interior, given especially the high and steep escarpment immediately behind the coast. This barrier was overcome by the railway engineers and the railways were then generally orientated across the narrow width of Chile. Nevertheless, some parts of their routes could often be incorporated into the northward extending longitudinal railway which Chile was attempting to develop in order to link the north of the country more effectively with the populated central region—based on Santiago—and so consolidate Chilean control over the regions disputed with Peru and Bolivia. Without the local railway developments related to the production of nitrate in the desert this railway would probably never have penetrated north of the northern end of the Central Valley of the country. The demand for rail transport facilities created, however, by the extraction of nitrates, and, somewhat later, of copper, ensured its completion to Antofagasta and even beyond Iquique, though never to the northernmost part of Arica. Nevertheless, from Antofagasta it was then continued across the Andes into Bolivia (see Figure 8–4), so providing a means whereby the Chilean government could exercise its authority over its northern regions. (In contrast, one may note in passing the absence of any commercial incentive to build a railway southwards from the Central region into forest and Atlantic Chile. The absence of a railway there led to a continued concern for the security of the southern provinces.)

Apart from the consequential and not unimportant transport linkages achieved as a result of the development of the nitrate industry, there were, not surprisingly given the nature of the environment, few other local multiplier effects arising out of its expansion. Indeed, for most other intents and purposes, what happened in the desert north of the country remained a matter of indifference in the mainstream of Chilean development, except in as far as the Chilean government was eventually able to collect revenues from the companies concerned and, with

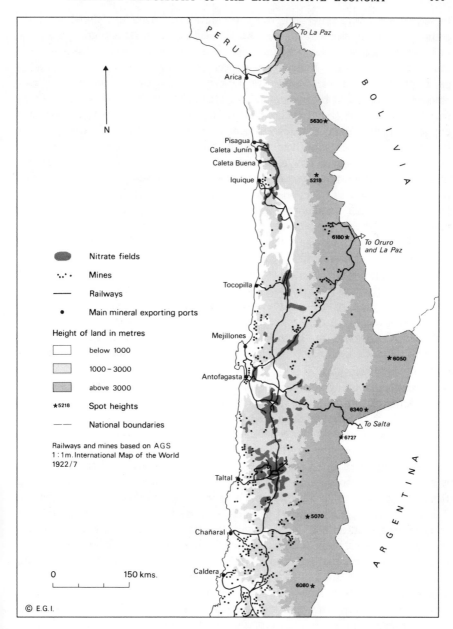

Figure 8–5. Chile: railway development and the location of extractive industry

these available, was better able to pursue development politics elsewhere in the country though bodies such as the state-financed Chilean Development Corporation, whose activities have included oil development as well as investment in manufacturing industry. But this was a result of nitrate development which had its geographical impact elsewhere in the country. Meanwhile northern Chile was in essence run from and by Britain and the United States. It was from these countries that the capital and expertise for the extraction and export of nitrates (and of copper) originated and the development of these extractive industries in Chile produced more benefits for their economies than for that of the producing country itself. This is certainly a view of the impact of the exploitation of Chile's mineral resources which is widely held in Chile where, in recent years, there has been first the 'Chileanization' of the copper industry (under President Frei), and then (under President Allende) its nationalization. However it can be argued that Chile nevertheless gained by having its nitrates and copper exploited by foreign enterprises. Without such foreign-financed development the whole of the northern part of the country would just have remained so much unused, and unusable, land unable to support a population. In as far as Chile would have had to take an interest in it for strategic and political reasons, it would have been a burden rather than an asset to the nation by virtue of the costs which would have been incurred in maintaining contact with it and in keeping out neighbouring powers possibly anxious for territorial expansion. Economic colonialism in Northern Chile made the territory, in fact, irrevocably Chilean and also provided the means whereby it could be defended.

However, in looking at similar developments of extractive industry elsewhere in Latin America, not even this justification for economic colonialism can be advanced. Tin in Bolivia and copper and lead in Peru both provide examples of the geographical, as well as the economic and political, separation of the foreign-controlled extractive industry from the mainstream of national life. But it is the petroleum industry in Latin America which provides not only the most widespread, but also the most blatant, examples of 'enclave' development arising from foreign ownership and control. It is worth noting first, however, that the dangers which were considered as likely to arise from foreign-owned and controlled oil exploration and development were recognized very early in the history of the industry in some Latin American countries. Chile, for example, after allowing foreign oil companies to investigate the geological possibilities of oil occurrence in the extreme south of the country, on the Chilean part of the island of Tierra del Fuego, then decided in 1923 not to grant the companies concessions to exploit the resource. This decision was made on the grounds that such foreign-owned activities in an area so remote from the effective centre of government could lead to a situation in which there was the chance of collusion between the companies and Argentina, whereby the latter might be enabled to take over the region. Chile thus decided to work the deposits through its own national efforts and went on to establish a national, state-owned monopoly for the exploitation of oil and gas. A similar policy towards oil exploration and development was adopted by Argentina at about the same time; by Brazil in 1950; by Peru more recently in 1969; and by Venezuela, the most important oil country in Latin America, as recently as 1976.

In part these and other Latin American nations with state-controlled oil sectors have reflected the earlier Mexican experience with foreign oil companies. There, oil companies from the U.S. and Britain, within the framework of the highly favourable opportunities established for foreign enterprise in the country by the regime of Porfirio Diaz in the last quarter of the nineteenth century, acquired vast land concessions for petroleum exploitation in the Gulf coastal areas of the country. Exploration efforts were successful and the companies concerned began to produce oil not mainly for distribution in Mexico, where demand was still small, but principally for export. These oil concession areas became tantamount to states within the state. In the petroleum enclaves the law which mattered was that made by the company concerned and it was upheld by 'armies' operated by the companies. The exploitation of the oil reserves was, the companies argued, a matter of concern only to them. For this privilege the companies had to pay little more than a nominal sum to the Mexican government and in return they secured the ownership of the country's oil. Even after the Mexican revolution of 1910 which arose in part because of Porfirio Diaz's 'sale' of Mexico to foreign companies, the oil companies were powerful enough not to have to take much cognizance of the fact and, given the market opportunities of the early post-World War I period, took what amounted to anti-Mexican action by deliberately over-producing the fields in search of short-term profits at the cost of the longer-term viability of the reserves.

Neither at the political nor an administrative level were the companies prepared to come to terms with the revolutionary governments which naturally had stronger feelings over such matters than did previous administrations. Finally, by 1938, the government felt strong enough to act, perhaps encouraged by the 'New Deal' Latin American policy of the U.S. Roosevelt administration in which there was recognition of the way American companies were considered to be exploiting the natural resources of Latin America without paying a 'fair' price for the commodities produced and exported to the U.S. In order to re-establish national sovereignty over the oil-industry alienated territory, and also in order to establish conditions in which the petroleum industry could be made an instrument for the development of the Mexican economy, the oil companies were expropriated and the whole of the petroleum industry was placed under national ownership. In a later chapter we shall examine the significance of this step for the economic geography of the country. At this point we need only to emphasize that the country took over several enclaves of development which were very largely unrelated economically, or even politically, to the rest of the national territory.

The expropriation of their producing fields in Mexico was the main cause why the oil companies, anxious to secure control over new supplies and potential supplies, then strengthened their interests in Venezuela, where the petroleum industry, worked entirely by foreign companies, had been slowly but steadily increasing in importance since the mid-1920s. Following Mexican expropriation in 1938, the companies eagerly sought to expand their activities, particularly in the proven prolific areas around Lake Maracaibo. The Venezuelan government of the time raised no objections to this pattern of development and, in spite of events in Mexico, laid down no conditions on the future exploration and development of oil which would prevent a recurrence of the Mexican situation. As it turned out however, wartime opportunities for bringing pressure to bear on the companies, and their countries of origin (the U.S. and the U.K.), and a changing politico-economic environment within which international business has had to be carried out, combined to make oil colonialism in Venezuela less objectionable and unfavourable to the host country. In recent years, in fact, such pressures were sufficient to turn the ventures virtually into company/government partnerships with the bulk of the benefits flowing to Venezuela rather than to the companies. This, and the 1976 nationalization of all foreign oil companies in Venezuela will be discussed in a later chapter.

In the meantime oil development in the period from 1940 through to 1958 had geographical implications arising from the essentially colonialistic nature of the economic relationship between Venezuela and the companies involved in the exploitation of Venezuela's oil. Having secured their concessions from the government for exploration and production rights in extensive areas of the country (see Figure 8–6), the companies' way and speed of working them, together with the development of transport and refineries facilities associated with the production and export of petroleum, were determined solely by reference to the international requirements of the companies and not at all to the needs of the Venezuelan people or economy. For example, exploration and oilfield development facilities and settlements, developed to house and serve the staff and workers of the companies, were established as enclaves of modernization—and even luxury—within a generally very underdeveloped part of the country. The modernization influence of these developments ceased abruptly at the enclaves' fences, only spilling over, at best, into a marginal settlement of occasional workers and the providers of low paid services on the far side of the company road. This was a situation which made for easy visual comparison of the wide gap in living standards between those in the enclave and those outside it. Moreover, petroleum, unlike most other mineral developments, does not even produce a transport infrastructure which is generally available to the public. Except for a limited number of access roads to the developments, it produces only pipelines which are not only useless for anything but the movement of oil but which, of course, are also invariably directly controlled by the companies which build them. Thus, the movement of tens of millions of tons of oil from producing areas around and under Lake Maracaibo over the 300 kilometres to the new export terminals, which were constructed on the Paraguana Peninsula (see Figure 8–6), produced no jobs (other than the short-

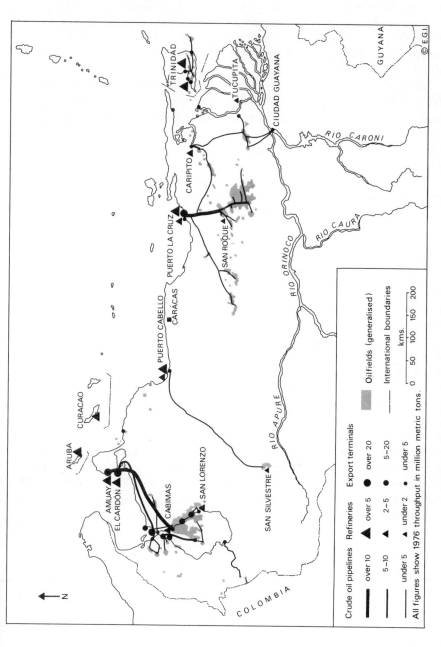

Figure 8–6. Venezuela: the location of oil industry activities

term opportunities involved in laying the line) and no entrepreneural possibilities for the provision of services en route. Petroleum pipelines do not, by their very nature, produce transportation service centres and so the country between production points and export points remained undeveloped and outside the geographical enclaves of modernization created by oil exploration activities and also at exporting/refining locations.

Nor did the growth of the oilfields themselves produce much effect on the development of local services in that the oil company-owned communities were developed so as to be as self-sufficient as possible. They incorporated everything from utilities, such as electricity and water, to social services, such as primary and secondary education and health services up to and including hospitals. Thus, overall, the Venezuelan oil industry's exploration, development and transportation facilities produced a series of isolated islands of economic development in areas where the general level of development was either that of subsistence agriculture or, at best, the commercial cash cropping, on a relatively small scale, of products like cacao from the forests of the Maracaibo basin.

Furthermore, even these separate islands of corporate-sponsored development achieved little by way of functional relationships with each other given their separate ownership by different oil companies, and the fact that more or less the same services were provided independently in each of them. There was, in other words, no element of specialization in service provision nor was there the development of a hierarchy of settlements as there would have been in an open system.

In 1943 the Venezuelan government negotiated a new agreement with the oil companies. Amongst other provisions, this obliged the companies to expand their oil-processing activities in Venezuela and there was a consequent rapid expansion of refining facilities particularly by Shell and Esso, the two most important oil companies operating in Venezuela, on the Paraguana Peninsula (see Figure 8–6). The two refining complexes, with their associated export facilities, came to extend over several square miles of this arid and hitherto little-used part of Venezuela. Inevitably, built alongside them were the company towns to provide living and recreation facilities etc. for their employees. Perhaps one should not be surprised that these, too, became just two more islands of development around which the high perimeter fences marked the geographical extent of their influence to a very high degree. Their location was a function of their anticipated relationships with outside, foreign markets rather than a function of their relationship with other parts of the Venezuelan economy. Their geographical contacts with the latter were essentially no more than accidental. Such a divorce from the domestic economy ensured that there could be no forward or backward linkages into other sectors and the refineries remained almost as isolated for the whole period of company ownership as when they were first built. And again, as with the oilfields themselves, the complexes were self-sufficient for services and offered little traffic, either in or out, on which an enhanced local transport structure could develop.

Thus, partly as a result of the very nature of oil industry operations, in terms of their strong locational ties to the resource itself and of their independence of any public system of transportation, but partly also as a result of their foreign ownership, control and operation, with the effect that this has had on attitudes to the indigenous role and responsibilities of the industry, the geographical pattern of the development of the oil industry in Venezuela has been essentially as described so far in this chapter. But at least a hint must be given at this stage of another side to the picture: even though we shall return to these considerations in more detail in a later chapter. First, one should note that the Venezuelan oil industry did produce a local multiplier effect as far as the city of Maracaibo was concerned. At the beginning of the oil period this long established capital city of the State of Zulia had under 20,000 inhabitants and served as the administrative, marketing and collecting/exporting centre for the west of the country which had remained relatively little developed (see Figure 8–6). Now, by virtue of its location in the main area of oil exploitation, it became the centre from which all the companies co-ordinated their field activities as well as the centre for the required transportation facilities. For example, some of the early export terminals were located in the vicinity of the city. As a result it gained both in population and in functions and rapidly grew to become the second city of the country. For such activities, developments by the individual companies were impossible and Maracaibo enjoyed the stimulus offered by an open system in which both public and private capital were involved, with the latter coming not only from the oil companies but also from other entrepreneurs.

Ironically, in more recent years Maracaibo has suffered a series of setbacks to its development as a result of the 'rationalization' (as seen and as calculated from the point of view of their own internal costs) of their Venezuelan activities by the oil companies. Increasingly effective telecommunication links and the growth of air transport made co-ordination of company activities at a regional level in Maracaibo unnecessary and inappropriate. Fields, company towns, refineries and terminals could now be linked directly into national headquarters at Caracas, thus enabling them to achieve cost reductions largely at the expense of Maracaibo's local economy. In parenthesis one notes here that the retrenchment of activities affected the regional, rather than the national, capital and thus further emphasizes the fact that the single most important geographical effect of oil industry growth in Venezuela lay in its influence in Caracas. Though this has partly arisen from the companies' expenditure and activities there (in head office developments etc.), a much more important aspect has been the influence of government. In the first place, the high degree of centralization of government activities in Venezuela was in large part responsible for the decision of the companies to locate their head office activities in Caracas. In the second place, the expenditure of government revenues arising from oil industry activities, and these rose quickly after the renegotiations of the concessions in 1943, has been heavily skewed in favour of the Caracas area. In this way revenues earned by Venezuela out of the exploitation of the resources of the oil-producing regions have been geographically shifted away from the regions to benefit the centre.

We shall return to consider this theme more closely in the next chapter, for it is a phenomenon that is not restricted to Venezuela, though it is demonstrated there most clearly as a result of the scale of revenues secured by the government from the oil industry. The point that needs to be made here is that the blame for the phenomenon can hardly be laid on the oil companies themselves as a necessary consequence of their neo-colonialist activities in the country. The phenomenon is a result of Venezuelan government's actions. This is one indication that the hypothesis we have examined in this chapter, viz. that the geography of Latin America's economic development can be explained in terms of the effects of the system of economic colonialism, has, throughout the independence period, been only a partial explanation of the geography of the continent's economic development. Moreover, as the twentieth century has progressed and as foreign resource-seeking companies became of decreasing relative importance in most Latin American economies, it has decreasingly explained the geographical pattern of economic activities in Latin America. It is, therefore, now time to turn to describe and examine other phenomena and considerations involved in our study of Latin America's contemporary economic geography.

Bibliography

a) Some of the general texts recommended for chapter 7 also provide background reading for the ideas presented in this chapter. Specific interpretations of the relationship between the world capitalist economic system and the exploitation of Latin American resources can be found in

FRANK, A. G., *Capitalism and Underdevelopment in Latin America*, Monthly Review Press, New York, 1967.

FURTADO, C., *Economic Development of Latin America*, Cambridge University Press, Cambridge, 1970.

URQUIDI, V. (ED.), *Latin America in the International Economy*, Halsted Press, New York, 1973.

b) For a specifically geographical approach to the phenomenon of the capitalist exploitation of the resources of Third World countries, see

SLATER, D., 'Under-Development and Spatial Inequality', *Progress in Planning*, **4**, Part 2, 1975.

An alternative view will be found in

HILHOURST, J. G. M., *Regional Planning: a Systems Approach*, Rotterdam University Press, 1971.

This author's analysis of patterns of geographical development in Third World countries does not consider colonialism or capitalist exploitation as factors involved in the process. In this respect it is firmly in the western technocratic tradition which sees development—including its spatial aspects—as matters of reorganization of the national systems. See

GILBERT, A., *Latin American Development: a Geographical Perspective*, Penguin, London, 1974,

for a study of Latin America which falls in the same tradition.

c) The idea of the economic exploitation of Latin America within the framework of an inequitable world economic system provided much of the motivation for the enthusiastic activities of the U.N. Economic Commission for Latin America in the 1950s and early 1960s and its publications, particularly the annual *Economic Survey*, provide useful reading in this respect. For a critique of E.C.L.A.'s work see

BAER, W., 'The economics of Prebisch and E.C.L.A.', *Economic Development and Cultural Change*, Vol. X, No. 2, 1962.

d) There are several publications which deal with the theme of foreign investment in Latin American agricultural and mineral development. See, for example,

BERNSTEIN, M. D., *Foreign Investment in Latin America*, Knopf, New York, 1966.

GRUNWALD, J., 'Resource Aspects of Latin American Economic Development' in Clawson, M. (Ed.), *National Resources and International Development*, Johns Hopkins Press, Baltimore, 1964.

MAY, S. and PLAZA, G., *The United Fruit Company in Latin America*, National Planning Association, 1958.

ODELL, P. R., 'The Oil Industry in Latin America', in Penrose, E., *The Large International Firm in Developing Countries*, Cass, London, 1968.

PAN AMERICAN UNION, 'Plantation Systems in the New World', *Social Science Research Monograph no. 7*, Washington, 1959.

e) For books which analyse the consequences of exploitation of land and/or mineral resources in particular countries, see

BERNSTEIN, M. D., *The Mexican Mining Industry 1890–1950*, Antioch Press, New York, 1965.

CRIST, R. E., *The Cauca Valley, Colombia: Land Tenure and Land Use*, Waverley Press, New York, 1954.

EIDT, R. C., *Pioneer Settlement in North East Argentina*, University of Wisconsin Press, Madison, 1971.

FERRER, A., *The Argentine Economy*, University of California Press, Berkeley, 1966.

GIRVAN, N., *Copper in Chile*, University of the West Indies, Mona, 1972.

GUERRA Y SANCHEZ, R., *Sugar and Society in the Caribbean*, Yale University Press, New Haven, 1964.

GRUNWALD, J. and MUSGROVE, P., *Natural Resources in Latin American Development*, Johns Hopkins Press, Baltimore, 1970.

JEFFERSON, M., *Peopling the Argentine Pampa*, American Geographical Society, New York, 1926.

LIEUWEN, E., 'Petroleum in Venezuela', *California University Publications in History*, Vol. III, 1954.

McBRIDE, G., *Chile: Land and Society*, American Geographical Society, New York, 1936.

NELSON, M., *The Development of Tropical Lands: Policy Issues in Latin America*, Johns Hopkins Press, Baltimore, 1973.

PARSONS, J. J., *Antioqueño Colonisation in Western Colombia*, University of California Press, Berkeley, Revised Edition 1968.

ROEMER, M., *Fishing for Growth: Export-led Development in Peru*, Harvard University Press, Cambridge, 1970.

Only a few of these publications are specifically geographical in authorship and/or objective but they all provide valid background from which to extract implications for the spatial structure of the economies concerned.

f) Finally, here is a short selection of articles which look in greater detail at particular cases of land and/or mineral exploitation.

DYER, D. R., 'Cuban Sugar Regions', *Revista Geográfica*, **67**, 1967.

GALLOWAY, J. H., 'The Sugar Industry of Pernambuco in the Nineteenth Century', *Annals of the Association of American Geographers*, **58**, 1968.

HUTCHINSON, H. W., 'The Transformation of Brazilian Plantation Society', *Journal of Inter American Studies*, Vol. III, No. 2, 1961.

JAMES, P. E., 'The Coffee Lands of S. W. Brazil', *Geographical Review*, **22**, 1932.

JONES, C. F. and MORRISON, P. C., 'Evolution of the Banana Industry in Costa Rica', *Economic Geography*, **28**, 1952.

PARSONS, J. J., 'Bananas in Ecuador', *Economic Geography*, **33**, 1957.

PORTEOUS, J. D., 'The Company State: a Chilean Case Study', *The Canadian Geographer*, **17**, 113–126 (1973).

PRESTON, D. A., 'Changes in the Economic Geography of Banana Production in Ecuador', *Transactions of the Institute of British Geographers*, 1965.

YOUNG, B. S., 'Jamaica's Bauxite and Alumina Industries', *Annals of the Association of American Geographers*, **55**, 1965.

CHAPTER 9

Regional Imbalance in Economic Development

In the last chapter we examined the geographical significance of a situation in which Latin American governments, most of which were generally economically and politically weak, had to face up to the greatly superior resources and expertise of foreign companies and corporations seeking concessions to exploit the continent's natural resources for export to the industrialized nations. This 'unfair' situation in terms of the relative strengths of the two parties to secure advantages from the economic developments involved, was made even worse for the Latin American countries in that the foreign private entrepreneurs were often backed-up diplomatically, and sometimes in other more questionable ways, in their search for profitable investment opportunities, by the governments of the United States and Britain (and other European nations). As a result, Latin American governments were, until very recently in the case of most countries, either content or obliged to see the speed and patterns of their economic development shaped by the forces of international commerce.

The Geographical Impact of the Exploitative Economy

The main growth sectors of the national economies of the Latin American nations under this system of economic colonialism were generally those which produced primary commodities for export markets. Usually, as we have seen, this created a need for extensive areas of land which could be used for the production of plantation crops or minerals. However, the degree to which the land was used or the mineral resource was developed at any given moment in time was a function of the state of world demand for the product concerned and the relative strength of the competition from other areas of the world supplying the same commodity or a substitute for it. The degree of development was thus not determined by competition for the factors of production from other sectors of the local economy or by demand for the products in the national economy. Given such conditions of the virtual isolation of these export-orientated activities from the rest of the economy in a country, the question of their location within national territories and their intensity of development was a matter over which national governments had, even if they might have wished otherwise, no control. Governments could certainly deny the use of certain lands to such enterprises, perhaps for political or strategic reasons, but, on the other hand, they had no means of forcing the enterprises to develop the resources concerned or of ensuring that they developed them at a rate preferred by the government in light of national needs. Such decisions were taken by the companies concerned in their London or New York headquarters. As the companies almost always operated in more than one country they could choose instead to embark upon a development in some other country, either within or outside Latin America, where similar climatic, soil, or geological conditions also enabled them to produce the commodities they wanted. They thus became used to doing what they wanted, without let or hindrance from awkward governments.

These considerations applied, moreover, not only to the commodities themselves but also to the development of industries concerned with the primary processing of the food-stuffs, agricultural raw materials and minerals. The companies concerned were able to evaluate internationally the lowest cost/maximum profit locations for such secondary economic activities and, if they were not allowed to locate them in their chosen area of a given country, then, as likely as not, they would be in a position to take the investment elsewhere in the world. And this meant a loss of jobs for the national economy concerned and, possibly, even the loss of an opportunity for an industrial growth point through the forward and backward linkages that could be created by such location decisions.

The development of oil refineries by Shell, Esso, and other international oil companies to process the oil they produced in Venezuela is an example of the lack of any national control over the activities of such foreign companies. At first almost all Venezuelan oil was taken out of the country for refining (to installations built on the off-shore islands belonging to the Netherlands: viz. Aruba and Curaçao). Even when refineries were at last built in Venezuela, at a time during the Second World War when the Venezuelan government was able to exercise some influence over the companies, they were located in a region of the country quite eccentric to the pre-existing areas of development in Venezuela, and in a way wholly unrelated to the internal spatial structure of the national economy. This, of course, was because the locations were chosen by the companies to minimize costs at the international, rather than the Venezuelan, level in that the companies concerned sold over 95 per cent of the refineries' production overseas and thus had neither need nor incentive to take note of Venezuelan requirements and wishes. Another example is seen in the locations in Peru and Bolivia of the plants to process the minerals produced in these countries. These were established at places convenient for handling the ores and for exporting the products from the countries concerned rather than in locations which were related to the needs of the countries' spatial-economic development patterns. Given a similar kind of situation throughout most of Latin America, it can be argued that each of the national economies was 'out of control' in respect of its geographical or spatial aspects of development as, indeed, in all other aspects of the economic process affected by this dependence on foreign enterprises. In that locational decisions by such enterprises were based on considerations external to the national economy, they were thus unrelated even to questions of maximizing national income, let alone to considerations of maximizing national welfare or some other less quantifiable objective. Thus the 'bodies' of many Latin American economies were wagged by what should have been the 'tails', and even if national governments might either have wished or have wanted to do anything about the matter, all they were, in fact, able to do was to make little more than the most of a fundamentally adverse situation.

However, as it was, few governments either wished or sought to do much about the economic geographical implications of the foreign controlled developments, except when there were political and strategic issues at stake as a result of their relations with neighbouring countries. In such special circumstances they sought to control or to prevent activities by foreign companies in border areas. Generally, however, their increasing efforts to contain the impact of economic colonialism and the exploitative economy were usually limited, as pointed out in the previous chapter, to concern about the share of the profits which they could secure from the companies concerned. This was not, of course, an unimportant aim for, in achieving a larger share of the profits arising out of exploitative ventures, governments secured revenues which could then be used for other purposes. Those purposes might be the creation of personal fortunes for members of such governments whereby, amongst other results, they could ensure that they continued in office through the power of patronage this conferred on them. On the other hand, profits accruing to the government could mean the availability of funds for possible investment in a country's basic economic and social infrastructure.

In the case of governments which were made up of individuals concerned with securing personal fortunes, increased governmental revenues from foreign companies were likely to have their main geographical expression in the intensification of the small islands of conspicuous consumption which had already been brought into existence by the geographically-concentrated expenditure of the considerable profits which were made in most countries from traditional land holdings. Firm witness to such use of profits are the elegant suburbs and richly endowed avenues and paseos of cities like Buenos Aires, Rio de Janeiro and Santiago and the sophisticated, and almost equally elegant, developments of summer resorts such as Mar del Plata, the Chilean Lake District and resorts of a like kind, but on a smaller scale, in almost every other Latin American country. Needless to say, the conspicuous consumption of the income arising from shared profits or from land ownership which found its expression in the grand tour of Europe, or a season in Paris, or in investment in foreign banks and companies in London, New York or

Zurich did not leave any imprints on the economic maps of Latin American countries!

For governments with some, or even as in a few cases an overriding, interest in using revenues arising out of the exploitative economy for investment in a country's economic or social infrastructure, the geographical results are much more significant. However, an examination of the geographical pattern of investment that emerged from this form of use of these revenues reveals that there was an almost continental-wide propensity to invest the funds at the principal pre-existing national centres of economic and social activities. Such centres were, almost always, the capital city of each country.

The background to this geographical pattern of infrastructure investment by the governments concerned emerges out of the predilection of the Spanish rulers and settlers in Latin America for life in urban centres and for the consequential evolution of highly-urbanized and urban-orientated colonial societies. This was briefly described in Chapter 7. The successor governments, following independence from Spain, were constituted by people who had basically similar attitudes and outlooks. These new rulers were, moreover, in the main able to satisfy their material desires out of the profits from their land holdings and, to an increasing extent in the later part of the nineteenth century, from the concessions which they granted to foreign companies and corporations in 'outlandish' areas. These were generally areas about which they cared very little and of which they often had even less knowledge. When revenues started to flow to the governments from these concessions, so providing an opportunity for investment possibilities in infrastructure developments, what could be more in keeping with their interests and inclinations than to make the investments either in the centres which they knew and from which they worked or, if it was to be investment in transportation facilities, then on roads and railways leading to and from the centres.

In that governmental systems of most of the Latin American countries at that time were highly centralized, such decisions by the national governments took care of most of the revenues which became available from the plantation and mining companies etc. Local government was weak and in many countries it was, moreover, deliberately kept that way so as to avoid any possibility of local independence movements. Local authorities were, therefore, in general not endowed with any rights to collect revenues from any concessionary companies which operated in their province, department or municipality. What money they were permitted to expend was usually made available from the central government, which thus almost invariably acted as an intermediary between the companies which paid the revenues and the local governments which would have welcomed the chance to collect it! As a result of such politico-economic arrangements, as well as of the other factors mentioned, there were significant regional variations in the degree of public investment and a consequential spatial imbalance in the development of the Latin American countries' infrastructure. The geographical emphasis in such infrastructure investment was markedly on expenditure on the needs of the capital city which, as a consequence, achieved an even higher degree of primacy within the nation's space economy.

Nor was this development just a matter of central government decisions on the location of the expenditure of government revenues. Private investment decisions were also locationally related to those of governments—for several reasons. In the first place, most finance available for private investment originated at the centre which was the most likely residence of individuals wealthy enough to have savings available. Even when they made their money out of land holdings or out of agriculture in other parts of the country, this was largely remitted by them or their agents to the capital or central city where banking and financing institutions were developed to a high enough degree to enable those with capital available to participate in the local opportunities for investment. Similarly, capital coming into a country from abroad for investment (to sectors of the economy other than the plantations and the extractive industries for which financing was usually arranged internationally rather than locally) came first into the primate centre, through local branches of European or American-based banks, where it could be merged with the flow of domestic funds. Finally, on the demand side, the opportunities offered for investment in the centre were safe, easy and profitable enough, for both political and economic reasons, effectively to inhibit interest in possible investment opportunities elsewhere in the national territory.

Moreover, many governments were interventionist in national economic affairs, and particularly so as far as the development of industry was concerned. Therefore, in order to secure all the necessary permissions for private development in this field, early and effective liaison with appropriate (often many) government departments and ministers was essential in order that the investor could succeed in ironing out all the continuing difficulties. Geographically to isolate any investment in the private sector from the bureaucracy was a sure means of accentuating the problems of an industrial company. Thus, politically there was much to be said for locating private investment in the geographical centre rather than at the periphery of the national space-economy.

This political motivation for a primate city (or near primate city) location for private enterprise developments in the secondary and tertiary sectors was, moreover, strongly backed up with an economic motivation. Most private investment was in those sectors of a Latin American country's economy concerned with the production and transportation of goods and services for final consumption. Thus, investment was important in sectors such as the construction industry, the servicing of vehicles and machinery and, a little later in the development process, in the production or assembly of goods already being consumed locally but which had hitherto been imported. The bulk of the markets for such goods and services were, again, almost invariably geographically concentrated in the core region. Such regions usually contained the only sizeable group of potential consumers who, of course, could only be found among those sectors of the population which had sufficiently high incomes to place them in the market for such goods. And these were essentially those people whose strong urban orientation has already been mentioned earlier in this chapter. Thus, lowest cost/maximum profit locations for investment in these sectors of the economy was also at the centre. To have located elsewhere in the country would have involved the firm or entrepreneur in the additional costs of transport necessary to get his goods back to the main market area, with very little likelihood that other than a small part of those additional costs would be offset elsewhere by lower costs in other parts of the production processes.

The Core/Periphery Phenomenon in Economic Development

Thus there emerged the so-called core/periphery phenomenon in the economic geographical patterns of development of Latin American countries: a phenomenon which was marked by major contrasts between the degree of economic development achieved in different parts of the national territory. The areas that developed as core areas, moreover, still reflected, in the main, the locational preferences of the Spanish conquistadores in their choice of their most important administrative centres. On the other hand, areas in which the Spanish had been uninterested still remained, even now, outside the main loci of economic activities. However, before going on to look more closely at this fundamentally important component in the contemporary economic geography of Latin America, it is necessary to define rather more precisely what is meant by the 'periphery' of an economy. It must also be related geographically to another important phenomenon in the economic geography of Latin America; that is, the so-called 'empty heart' of the continent.

This must be done because although one can, and should, be very concerned about the low standards of development and the absence of opportunities in large areas and regions of Latin American countries with significant populations, it is difficult, and often inappropriate, to worry in the same way about the mere existence of empty lands where the low levels of economic activities largely reflect the fact that there are very few people living there. If the peripheries of the spatial economic structures of Latin American countries merely coincide with the empty, unpopulated areas, then this is not necessarily a matter for concern or even for attention. Concern and attention in such cases would rather be to evaluate whether or not the empty lands represent 'resource frontiers' capable of potential development. This, however, is a quite distinct issue in the geography of development and must be dealt with separately from the problem of regional imbalance in the levels of development within those parts of the national territories that are already populated.

The Economic Periphery and the 'Empty Heart' of Latin America

As previously shown, the idea of a Latin American 'el Dorado' dies hard. It is, indeed, part and parcel of the concept of the limitless opportunities waiting to be exploited in an 'empty' continent in which man's colonizing activities have barely penetrated beyond the coastal margins! Figure 9–1 shows the relationship between the geographically rather limited areas which have a density of population of at least 10 people per square kilometre and the national territories of the largest Latin American countries. It is an example of the sort of evidence that can be produced to demonstrate the existence and the size of the empty heart of the continent. However, the description of the main elements involved in man's use of Latin America which was presented in the last two chapters will already have indicated that this sort of evidence hardly represents a profound analysis of the reality of the geography of Latin America in respect of the potential for development.

Indeed, empty lands, other than those of the semi-deserts of the northern part of Mexico, rarely exist on a large geographical scale in Middle America. Parts of Honduras and Nicaragua are undoubtedly almost empty but these largely unpopulated lands are in close juxtaposition with the very overcrowded rural areas of El Salvador and Costa Rica. This 'unequal' situation has already given rise to unofficial immigration across the frontiers as well as to political difficulties between the countries concerned. A recent example of this was the so-called 'Football War' between El Salvador and Honduras in 1969 when Honduran concern for boundary transgressions by landless El Salvadorean peasants led to hostilities between the countries. There are similar situations in parts of the Caribbean. The Dominican Republic does, for example, have unused but usable areas within its frontiers, and these are, in many cases, almost within hailing distance of land-hungry Haitians, many of whom, like the landless Salvadoreans, have found their way across political frontiers in search of subsistence-type holdings from which to meet their basic needs. Elsewhere in the Caribbean only Cuba could be described as underpopulated in relation to the known resource base for sustaining primary economic activities and, as a result, it was also a land of immigration for people from over-crowded islands before the communist revolution.

Even in South America, where as Figure 9–1 shows, there are large unpopulated areas, perhaps the single most significant feature of the settlement pattern is not the emptiness of parts of the continent, but rather the continued pressure of population on available land resources in parts of the Andean region. Here even the cumulative effects of a lengthy period of out-migration to lower altitudes and/or to urban centres have not succeeded in reducing the populations of parts of Central Peru and Bolivia to levels at which living standards much above the subsistence level for those remaining are yet possible. On the other side of the continent we have already noted the transformation of the previously empty pampas of Argentina and Uruguay and their settlement by millions of European migrants. This has led to a situation in which the area, in spite of more recent citywards out-migration, still has an average density of rural population almost twice as high as that of the U.S. prairies. This comparison is surely the relevant one to

Figure 9–1. Latin America: national frontiers and populated areas

make as it indicates that increasing living standards in areas of extensive agriculture, producing commodities for export, lead to smaller rather than to larger populations and in this context the pampas are probably over rather than underpopulated.

North-East Brazil, as we shall see in more detail later in the chapter, is also increasingly becoming an area of excessive human demands on its limited resource base. As a result it constitutes a major area of difficulty and of overpopulation, in relation to its potential for development, in present-day South America. Further south in Brazil, the coffee boom described in Chapter 8 took agricultural settlers well into the interior of South-East Brazil far beyond the area which can be described as a 'costal margin'. Although much of the land has long since been effectively worked out as coffee-producing land, it has more recently been utilized for other forms of agriculture. Such agricultural activities have been increasingly stimulated by the increasing food and raw material demands (e.g. sugar, meat and cotton) of Brazil's rapidly expanding cities which are concentrated, of course, largely in the adjacent southern coastal regions of the country. Moreover, further south and south-west than coffee was ever grown in significant quantities (because of the recurrent, rather than occasional, dangers of winter frosts), the 'frontier' of agricultural settlement was gradually pushed inland, away from the original coastal settlements, from the beginning of the twentieth century onwards. This agricultural expansion progressed most effectively in the 1920s and the 1930s as a result of the search by former coffee plantation tenants for more permanent land holdings. This internal migration to new areas of agricultural development was, moreover, accompanied by some of the new migrants to Brazil from both Europe and Japan, in some cases as a result of the deliberate encouragement of immigrant groups for land colonization schemes. This agricultural use of this southernmost part of Brazil brought settlement there up to the frontiers with Uruguay. Almost the whole of Uruguay's territory has, of course, been effectively settled since job opportunities offered by its expanding agricultural sector in the second half of the nineteenth century stimulated the same kind of migration of agricultural workers from Europe as we examined in the case of Argentina.

More recently, however, moves that have already begun towards the rationalization and the modernization of agriculture in parts of south Brazil and Uruguay as well as in the extensive pampas of Argentina seem more likely to lead to a *reduction*, rather than to an increase, in the present level of the rural population. This, of course, is a situation and a prospect which necessarily excludes this vast region from the 'empty heart' of the continent.

Further south, the emptiness of Argentina beyond the pampas appears very obvious on Figure 9–1. This is so in spite of the fact that parts of southern Argentina were also areas of significant immigration in the late nineteenth and early twentieth centuries. Between the 1860s and 1914 various groups of foreign settlers either unwilling to accept the uncertain opportunities offered by the short-term tenant farming, which was all they could secure on the pampas, or else unfamiliar with the climatic conditions and agricultural practices required in those areas, sought opportunities in the more southerly parts of the country. The valleys of Patagonia presented the preferred areas of settlement and were successively occupied by farmers utilizing the locally variable physical environments which thus provided initial opportunities for diversified, largely subsistence, agriculture. Later, when they were firmly established, and following the improvement in transport facilities, they were able to specialize in fruit farming in the more northerly valleys and in the production of wool from areas further south. However, much of the upland area of Southern Argentina between the more fertile and less exposed valleys remained empty because it could not be profitably utilized. It should be noted that this was the case even half a century ago when the farmers' expectation of returns on their labour was at a much more modest level than it is today and at a time when few alternative opportunities existed. More recently, as growing populations in the valleys exerted considerable pressure on the limited agricultural resources of the valley areas, there has been consequential out-migration to the north rather than an extension of agriculture to the unutilized upland areas of Patagonia. The description of these areas today as 'empty areas' is true only in the same sense that the southern uplands or the highlands of Scotland can be described as empty areas. They are basically unsuitable for agricultural development such that any possibilities for resource frontier development in Southern Argentina lie only in the field of mineral exploitation, and even that seems unlikely to produce great possibilities for population expansion except in certain coastal areas in the event of offshore oil and gas exploration on the continental shelf proving to be very successful.

Across the Andes (which are themselves also empty in the south of the continent for very obvious physical reasons of height, climatic conditions and inaccessibility), it is difficult to find areas of Chile which can be considered as 'empty' when viewed in relation to the lack of opportunities offered for the agricultural use of the land by highly adverse conditions of climate, soils and topography which affect two-thirds of the country and within which less than 25 per cent of the population currently lives. The impossibility of agricultural development in the Atacama Desert, covering about the northern third of Chile, has already been demonstrated in our earlier discussion on the establishment and growth of the nitrate industry there. At the other 'end' of the country lie forest and Atlantic Chile. They together constitute another one-third of the area of the country and can also certainly be correctly described as empty in any crude comparison of people with area. But again, given the adverse conditions of the physical geography of these regions which are, in most parts, extreme, even by the standards of the most rugged, wettest, and windiest parts of north-west Europe, it is, perhaps, the extent to which colonization and settlement have been pushed, rather than their absence, which is the more surprising attribute of the human geography of Chile south of Concepción and the River Bió-Bió.

Nineteenth century colonization across the Bió-Bió, south from the Mediterranean heartland of Chile, followed the Treaty in 1883 with the Araucanian Indians. This Indian nation, the only one in Latin America which did not submit to the Spanish, had made its homeland in the forested areas south of this river frontier some 300 years earlier following the tactical retreat in the face of Spanish expansionism from its original region of permanent settlement further north. The late nineteenth century European settlers now brought large areas of forest Chile under a type of peasant farming which had to have a high degree of local self-sufficiency consequent upon the relative isolation of the region from national, let alone world, markets. The colonists were, in part, earlier migrants to central Chile who had become nothing more than landless labourers in that region of haciendas and a Spanish style of agriculture and rural settlement and who, therefore, moved south in order to get away from the absence of economic opportunities on the large estates of Central Chile. Of more importance, however, in settling the south of Chile were the new immigrants from Central Europe who brought with them the traditions and practices of an agriculture more suitable for the forest zone. However, the special difficulties of the Chilean forest environment were such, and the consequences of isolation from markets were so great, that even by the standards of the nineteenth and the earlier parts of the twentieth century, it could not really be said that the colonization thrived. At best, just acceptable standards of life and minimally viable populations were maintained.

Since the first decade or so of the twentieth century, however, such environments and such conditions have given rise to strong out-migration movements on the part of the peoples concerned. This is so throughout the world of European type civilizations and development and as much in Europe itself as well as in the areas of colonization overseas. The fact that it has happened in 'forest' Chile is in line with this general phenomenon and it is this which clearly indicates why this part of Latin America must also be excluded from those parts of the continent where further colonization might well be expected. Thus, future settlement in southern Chile only seems likely to be orientated to the industrial exploitation of its forests for wood products and, more especially, for pulp and paper and, much less likely, to the utilization of its assets for tourism. Neither of these developments is, however, going to fill the region with permanent settlement on a large scale and both of them are, in any case, dependent for their development upon the construction of a high-cost network of transport and communication facilities—investment which seems likely to have a low priority in the development planning of any Chilean government.

Thus, for good and continuing reasons the population of Chile is concentrated in the central one-third of the national territory and here there is little empty land. Much of the upland in this central region is, indeed, overpopulated relative to its agricultural development and potential, and any hopes for increases in living standards in such areas seem likely to require a continuation of existing out-migratory trends. In the lowlands themselves, only the acceptance of a labour-intensive agriculture (to replace the traditional haciendas), of a type that has long been practised in Mediterranean Europe, can create new opportunities for settlement. Even if it were accepted, however, the chances of this approach providing other than a short-term solution to the problems of rural unemployment and underemployment in Central Chile seem remote. For effective longer term development the region will probably have to become increasingly dependent on the sort of mechanized 'Mediterranean-style' agriculture now being utilized in California, Australia, and southern France. This could lead in turn to a continuing need for further rural–urban migration in order to bring down the population densities to a level at which reasonable living standards could be achieved for the remaining highly-productive agricultural population.

Thus, around much of Latin America, the 'empty' lands remain empty for very good reasons. Moreover, in many cases, as we have seen, these good reasons are becoming even better; particularly in light of the rising expectations as to what constitutes a reasonable standard of living in the second half of the twentieth century by a population which is essentially European-orientated in its outlook and philosophy. In other words, the 'emptiness' of much of Latin America is a rational human reaction either to the occurrence of very adverse environments for human occupation or to the possibilities of developing productive agriculture without a locally resident high density of agricultural workers and their families. 'Emptiness' does not, in other words, always indicate the existence of limitless resource frontier regions waiting and asking to be opened up by populations which are being denied their opportunities as a result of political and/or economic factors.

It will not, however, have escaped the reader's attention that in the discussion so far of the concept of Latin America as an empty continent, we have more or less 'skated' around its periphery. By doing this, we have, of course, successfully avoided the need to face the issue of the continental interior of South America which consists essentially of the basin of the Amazon and its numerous tributaries. In all, this massive river system basin covers about 30 per cent of the total area of South America and includes parts of the national territory of every South American country except Argentina, Uruguay, Paraguay and Chile. As in pre-colonial days (see Chapter 7, pages 126 to 128), the basin is still very empty with a total population barely exceeding 10 million: under 6 per cent of South America's total. Moreover, in none of the countries within which part of it is located does the section of Amazonia in that country form part of its developed core area. The Amazonia region is, indeed, always highly peripheral to the central zone of development. In respect of many of these countries, however, it is represented as a resource frontier in which expansion can and should take place. In some cases, it is represented as an area potentially able to provide living space and opportunities for development through which national problems of imbalance between man's growing demand for land and the supply of land can be solved.

This latter attitude is most clearly demonstrated in the cases of Bolivia, Peru, Ecuador and, to a lesser degree, Colombia. In these countries, as we have seen, the Andean highlands are overpopulated such that colonization of the upper areas of Amazonia immediately to the east of the areas of overpopulation will, it is argued, provide the solution to this problem. But the facts of this situation have been so for many decades. Indeed, the arguments for population migration eastwards have already been put forward for almost half a century during which period of time the techniques for effecting colonization have been steadily improved: as, for example, in the steady growth of knowledge as to how tropical soils should be used for productive purposes. During this period also, man's ability to exploit unused regions has increased through the increasing availability of mechanical equipment and of new means of transportation. In spite of these favourable developments, however, there has still been relatively little effective colonization of Amazonia by the west-coast countries of Latin America. Even many officially sponsored, and often relatively well-financed, schemes for the resettlement of people from the Andean regions have, after reaching the stage of implementation, soon foundered in the face of social and economic difficulties.

The social difficulties have emerged from the traumatic experiences of groups which have had to move from a long-established, well-structured society in a familiar, if somewhat inhospitable, environment in the Andes to profoundly different societal and environmental conditions for which none of their accumulated knowledge and experience offered any guidelines for action. Even more significant economic difficulties have arisen not from the inherent unproductiveness of the areas of colonization, but from the fact that most of the colonies could not become economically self-sustaining in a high import cost and low net prices back for exports situation and also because of the high capital cost of creating an effective settlement pattern. In as far as the government or other sponsoring body concerned naturally tries to recover part or all of the capital costs from the settlers, the first reason for the lack of success is, in part, a function of the second. The settlers become too over-burdened with capital debts to permit them to earn enough surplus from their agricultural activities either for investment in improvements in their holdings or even to achieve an acceptable level of consumption. In this context the location of the colonies in relation to the markets for their products and the sources of their needs, leading to low sales prices for the commodities they produce and high delivered prices for their imports respectively, leads to a high propensity for economic defeat for the communities concerned.

So far too little has changed in these general conditions influencing the situation to indicate a greatly increased likelihood that settlements in the Oriente of the countries concerned can become economically self-sustaining in the foreseeable future. The existence of a small number of apparently successful settlements would not appear to negate this general conclusion concerning the overall settlement possibilities for the vast areas involved. Part of the reasoning behind such a conclusion lies in the inability of settler communities themselves adequately to service the capital that must be invested in large quantities in such schemes. Given that there can be neither expectation nor hope that these capital costs could or should be recovered in the short to medium term from the settlers themselves, then expenditure on the necessary roads, communication systems, and the provision of social and other facilities invariably becomes a charge on the funds of the central government. In the absence of any significant income from taxes either from companies or people in the areas which are being opened up, the necessary expenditure on such colonization schemes thus represents a drain on the financial resources provided by other regions of the country concerned. Government revenues in none of these Andean countries, however, have been, or are, noted for their buoyancy and plentitude. Indeed, exactly the opposite is the case at most times, for the demands on government revenues far exceed their availability as the normal state of affairs. Thus, any funds spent on opening up areas of a country for colonization, through the provision of basic infrastructure and social services in the new regions, diminish the money available for investment in the already populated areas of the countries concerned. Yet, in each case, the populated areas of the countries concerned are in desperate need of whatever development funds the government can make available out of revenues or which can be borrowed from abroad.

Thus, the question of opening up the empty areas of the 'East' of the Andean countries has, in every case, become a politico-economic issue. It involves a sort of tug-of-war between those, on the one hand, who would have significant resources devoted to the development of the Oriente, in what they believe to be the long-term interests of the country and of the people concerned, and those, on the other hand, who argue that the shorter term investment needs of the already populated areas of the country are the more pressing. This latter group sometimes also argues that resources put into the populated areas will, in any case, produce a better return on investment particularly because new developments in such areas immediately become heavily and effectively used.

It is as a result of such political attitudes towards the investment of resources in the largely unpopulated areas to the east of the Andes that one finds that investment policies there have often been inconsistent and lacking in continuity. For example, periods when money was available for road building and other infrastructural developments have alternated with periods of the non-availability of funds for continued investment in such projects. Thus, the process of 'opening up' the east has been patchy and irregular. This is a particularly unfortunate way to proceed with such developments for in the physical environment of the selva, where the climate and vegetation characteristics tend to depreciate untended and incompleted man-made projects very quickly, such irregularity in the flow of funds really means the misuse of what capital has been invested. A road that stops in the 'middle of nowhere', or a power or water supply system which has been installed but the distribution facilities of which do not reach the majority of the potential consumers, produce no return on the investment made. Even where particular projects have been successfully completed, their scale has usually been so relatively small as to ensure that the results are almost lost in the immensity of the area involved. Moreover, such schemes produce too little by way of a cash flow, either in the public or the private sector, to make internally generated funds for their continuing expansion possible. Further recourse to external capital sources for ongoing development is still necessary.

Thus, the Oriente of Colombia, Ecuador, Peru, and Bolivia, lying in the upper reaches of the Amazon and its tributaries, still remain almost empty of population and largely unused, except for developmental efforts, mostly still only tentative, in the areas immediately to the east of the Andes. Thus they still lie largely outside the effective national territories of the countries concerned.

In late-twentieth century conditions the effective colonization and settlement of this pioneer fringe appears to demand a massive and continuing capital investment on a scale far beyond the present capabilities of the countries concerned, even if they could all agree on jointly planned, directed, and implemented efforts whereby the economies of scale generated could help towards making the investment worthwhile. Peru has formulated such a plan, orientated around the so-called Andean 'marginal highway', and this will be evaluated in Chapter 10 of this book when we look at the emerging themes in the economic geography of the continent. In the meantime, the individual efforts of the separate countries concerned to develop their eastern regions have had basically no impact on the general patterns of the spatial distribution of economic activities in these west-coast, Andean nations.

To the east is the larger part of the Amazon basin, lying mainly in Brazil. This part of the 'empty heart' is, as a whole, not quite as empty as it was or quite as limited in the degree and extent of economic activities achieved as in the case of Peru and Bolivia etc. However, one must still emphasize that what has been happening in the Brazilian part of the Amazon basin is still relatively small scale, both in terms of the amount of capital involved and of the number of job opportunities created when compared with the results of the development of the Brazilian economy in the growth areas of the country in the south and south-east. Indeed, investment in buildings alone in the city of São Paulo in the last twenty years appears to exceed the total capital invested in the whole of the interior (except for the investment which has gone into Brasília and its road system)!

As described earlier in this chapter, migratory movements in Brazil by the 1920s had already taken settlers well inland in the south and south-centre of the country in search of land to use and to occupy on a permanent basis in preference to an uncertain existence as insecure tenant farmers in the older-established areas of coffee plantations. Recent investigations show that the spontaneous movement of peasants is continuing and is now taking them even into the Amazon basin. Their settlements and landholdings for agricultural development are being carved out of the selva ahead of the developing road system in the far interior of the country. Then, as the road system is expanded and extended, so the degree and effectiveness of this settlement and development pattern increases.

Apart from these peasant-scale, unsponsored and unsupported ventures, the establishment of most of which is still too recent to make possible any effective evaluation of their degree of success, there has also been development of a very different sort in even more remote valleys of the northward-flowing tributaries of the Amazon and in the upper Paraná valley. Here, again, however, the colonization is so recent as to make an evaluation of its long-term significance impossible. Largely as a result of significant tax incentives offered by the Brazilian government to companies and entrepreneurs willing to put money into the interior of the country (capital invested in the Amazon region can offset taxes that would otherwise have to be paid on profits earned in other enterprises), large-scale investors have begun to exploit the possibilities of commercial cattle raising in the selva. The first ventures have involved the clearance of thousands of hectares of forest and the establishment of a grass cover. Such work very obviously involves a high investment in the purchase of heavy machinery and also in its transportation to and within an area basically without roads. This is a development, moreover, which will, at least in the early stages of production, also involve the airlifting out of any cattle that may be raised for sale in the distant national markets. The potential scale of the operations, however, is so large that it already appears to be producing an increased incentive and motivation for the rapid expansion of a road system connecting the new areas of development to the market areas of Brazil. This road system will in its turn further stimulate the development of the cattle raising enterprise. Though some of the capital flowing into these ventures is Brazilian (as a result of the tax advantages noted above), the speed and extent of the development also appears to be a function of an increased flow of foreign, particularly West German, capital to Brazil. Brazil is, indeed, a country which appears to have captured the imagination of those Germans looking for investment opportunities overseas and German entrepreneurs have also been encouraged to make such investment by the existence of favourable German tax laws which, some years ago, were changed to encourage overseas investment in the developing world within which Brazil offers better prospects than most other countries. Thus, as a result of the combination of Brazilian and German fiscal encouragement for investment in the interior of Brazil, it appears that the ventures there will quickly approach the critical minimum size which we have suggested is needed to make the development of a resource frontier an effective and self-sustaining possibility. When this is achieved, then these colonization developments in parts of Brazilian Amazonia could easily turn out to be the largest in terms of areas and the quickest in terms of time of any, anywhere in Latin America. By the middle of the 1980s these new developments could make Brazil one of the world's main cattle producing countries and cattle the most important agricultural enterprise in the country.

However, in spite of such dramatic changes taking place in parts of the Amazon and Paraná basins in Brazil and the formidable trans-Amazonia highway system already well on the way to completion, most of the vast area still remains untouched; or even in some cases, as with Manaus and the now largely-abandoned rubber industry of its region, still looking back with nostalgia to an earlier period of a higher level of economic activity. These were cases in which the higher levels of activity were not sustainable in the face of competition from similar products coming from other more favourably located parts of the world. This description of the situation in the heart of the Amazon basin is valid also for the less extensive basin of the Orinoco and its tributaries and the even smaller and less developed northward-flowing rivers of the Guayanas, where effective occupation is still limited to areas well within 250 kilometres or so of the coast. Brasilia on the South eastern fringe of the Brasilian selva, and Ciudad Guayana, on the fringe of the Venezuelan selva, constitute developments which can be considered separately from the question of the use or otherwise of the continent's 'empty heart'. Their significance will be examined in the next chapter dealing with possible future economic geographical aspects of Latin America's development.

The intention in presenting this brief description and evaluation of the 'empty lands' of Latin America has been to put the situation in the 1970s into perspective. Three aspects need to be stressed. Firstly, one must note that the continent is not quite as empty as it is sometimes made out to be. Secondly, it is seen that many of the 'empty' areas are virtually unpopulated or have a very low density of population for very good reasons and that in many of these cases there is still a trend towards the outward movement of population for social as well as economic reasons, thus further denuding such areas of people. Thirdly, it is clear that the empty areas which could well have potential for development are often proving difficult to develop, if for no other reason (and this is in itself a very good one) than that investment in such areas is less rewarding and less urgent than investment elsewhere in the countries concerned. Only in the special case of Brazil—with a strong non-economic motivation for colonizing effectively all its national territory (a kind of 'manifest destiny' attitude to national frontiers)—have we noted a really strong and effective movement to extend the area of occupied territory. Even there, however, the great bulk of 'empty Brazil' remains empty and seems likely to do so for most of the rest of this century.

However, having evaluated the current position as far as the empty areas and the resource frontiers of the continent are concerned, we must now return to the current and, for the foreseeable future, more important economic geographical problems of the populated and utilized areas of the Latin American nations and so take further our hypothesis that the geographical pattern of economic development for each nation can be effectively described in terms of a centre periphery model.

The Geography of Underdevelopment

Earlier in the chapter we presented a set of factors which, it was suggested, led to Latin American economies becoming spatially concentrated around a central, usually the capital, city location. As part of the same process of the geographical evolution of the economic system, the other parts of the national territories, even those which were effectively occupied, were largely ignored in terms of their development and their developmental possibilities, except for traditional agriculture and for other primary economic activities such as plantation agriculture and mineral extraction. We must now demonstrate that such a description of the geography of secondary and tertiary economic activities in Latin America is justified. Before doing so, however, it appears worthwhile to note briefly that we are dealing here with an issue which is relevant and, indeed, fundamental to the whole problem of economic development and underdevelopment.

An earlier virtually *exclusive* concern by economic planners for nationally aggregated problems of economic growth has now been rejected as an approach which can satisfactorily ensure that the welfare of the population in all parts of a country will benefit from economic development. Thus in Western Europe and elsewhere in the industrialized world we have become increasingly familiar with the additional attention which has been devoted in recent years to spatial aspects of economic development within national boundaries. However, this increasing concern for the geography of economic development in mature industrial countries has not yet been matched by a similar degree of interest in such matters in the developing countries. Even apart from what is, or more usually is not, presented in governmental planning exercises in this field, one must also note that the theoretical and descriptive literature on 'development economics' still largely ignores the problem!

A standard textbook on development planning, written by Professor Lewis, one of the world's leading advisors in this field, devotes a mere seven pages, out of the 121 devoted in total to plan strategies, to the question of 'regional balance' in a developing economy. And in marked contrast with his proposals on other aspects of economic development planning, where recommended strategies are based on a wealth of analysis, his conclusions on strategies for the regional economic problem appear to be extremely tentative and hesitant. For example, he concludes that 'a workable approach to regional balance is to treat suspiciously all proposals for development in towns whose population exceeds 500,000 or has not yet reached 5000.' Such a conclusion appears to be based on little more than preconceived notions of doubtful validity. For example, minimum town-size restraint for the location of new economic activities is a particularly bad indicator of growth potential when one is concerned with countries with a 'resource frontier' and which may have only relatively small parts of their national territories in effective occupation. Such advice given to the United States even less than 100 years ago would have effectively prevented the development of most of its national territory and of many centres of industry and commerce which today exceed the 500,000 population mark! Nor is advice against planning new growth in cities already having over half-a-million people necessarily wise for, as much evidence from the United States and Europe indicates, large cities have been critically important in creating the right conditions for the cumulative growth of secondary and tertiary economic activities in periods of rapid economic growth. Moreover, most Third World countries have already developed—for better or for worse—pre-industrial cities with much larger populations than 500,000 and in the industrialization process advantage needs to be taken of the considerable investment already made in the infrastructure of such cities.

However, while such advice may not be appropriate in its specific recommendations, it does at least recognize that there is a geographical aspect to development planning which needs attention simultaneously with that given to other aspects of the process. There is, however, one school of economists which still argues that developing countries cannot afford the 'luxury' of regional planning. These economists see such regional planning as a device whereby maximum rates of growth are constrained by the need to locate activities in economically unattractive areas. They argue that such uneconomic locations of new activities adversely affect the speed of economic growth because scarce resources (particularly capital) are used less efficiently than would otherwise be the case. In the longer term, these economists suggest, the spatial problems of the developing countries will either 'sort themselves out' or the countries concerned will eventually become rich enough to be able to afford to divert some resources to dealing with their depressed and undeveloped regions.

With reference to Latin America, even if not to other parts of the developing world, such a view seems naïve in the extreme since it appears to ignore both the economic and the socio-political realities of the contemporary situation. Regional disparities in per capita well-being (measured by means of income-per-head or through indices based on social as well as economic criteria) of the order of 10 to 1 exist in most Latin American countries. This is the case even in a country like Mexico where there has been some concern for backward areas of the country over the whole of the revolutionary period since 1910. In other countries of Latin America the regional disparities appear to be even greater, ranging as high as 37.5:1 in the case of the Central American country of Guatemala. Such disparities are not only fundamentally divisive for a country in political and social terms, and hence certain to hinder modernization efforts, but are also significant in economic terms. This is because in economic terms such disparities put almost all the population in the poorer areas of a country outside the ranks of the consumers of anything but the simplest and cheapest goods, and thus act as a major restraint on the creation of an economy which can be diversified away from the production of primary commodities for export into one in which an indigenous manufacturing industry has continued scope for expansion.

One can find many examples of such restraints on industrial growth in Latin American countries over the last two decades. New factories built as part of development plans have not been able to produce to their full capacity because there has continued to be insufficient demand for their output due to the inadequate purchasing power of most people in the poorer parts of the country. This phenomenon of less-than-capacity use of factories has again even affected Mexico, which has proceeded further and faster than most of its Latin American neighbours in the industrialization process. The continuation of this situation, in which there is a lack of a sufficiently strong increase in the growth rate of effective demand for industrial products as a result of the continuation of wide discrepancies in income between the core area and the periphery, would seem to ensure that the degree of industrialization can never rise above a modest level. This must inevitably frustrate development plans: a phenomenon which is not unknown in Latin America where, as we shall see below, there is strong evidence of chronic regional imbalance in the way in which all the national economies have developed.

Dual Spatial Economies in Latin America

It is, however, easy to hypothesize that Latin American countries exhibit the features of a dual spatial economy. Nor is it difficult to suggest that such an economy is marked, on the one hand, by a developed core region of limited areal extent, with an important industrial component contributing to its degree of development, and on the other, by an extensive undeveloped 'periphery' with few secondary economic activities. But it is much more difficult to present adequate quantified evidence to demonstrate the validity of these ideas. A paucity of spatial statistics and of other reliable information creates problems in attempting to describe the situation adequately and accurately even for a single country of Latin America, let alone for all the countries of the continent on a comparable basis.

Even in the case of Venezuela, where the spatial structure of the economy appears to have been more thoroughly subjected to analysis than in the case of any other country of the continent, the presentation of the pattern of regional imbalance has been principally in terms of the degree of urbanization of the population in different regions of the country. But in Latin America, with its phenomenon of pre-industrial urbanization, the degree of urbanization and the distribution of urban population is not necessarily a good indicator of the distribution of economic activities and of regional variations in well-being. Elsewhere in the continent there are usually broad regional figures of incomes per head (generally on a provincial or departmental basis) but these often mask significant spatial variations which occur within the large administrative areas concerned. Moreover, in that the administrative units used for such statistical purposes vary in size and scale within, as well as between, countries, comparisons based on such evidence are often difficult to justify. Statistics of employment by regions and sectors are usually either unavailable or unreliable and, in any case, are not necessarily a particularly good measure of spatial variations in the level of economic activities for they fail to distinguish contrasts in productivity arising from the variable application of capital or energy to the activities concerned.

In an attempt in the mid-1960s to overcome the lack of readily available and comparable data for describing the geography of economic activities within the countries of Latin America, an analysis was made of the spatial distribution of publicly available electricity generating capacity. Continental-wide information for roughly the same period of time (the early 1960s), for each country, was available on the location and capacity of all public-supply electricity generating stations, except the very smallest ones. These have been mapped in Figure 9–2.

It is self-evident that a more appropriate indicator of geographical patterns of economic development at the time would have been provided by a study of the spatial distribution patterns of electricity consumption by industry and other economic sectors, but such data were not available on a sufficiently wide and standardized basis. There are two factors, however, which permit us to assume that the distribution and size of generating stations generally indicate the quantities of electricity consumed in different locations. First, all of Latin America is short of electricity-generating capacity such that where capacity exists, it will be run at maximum possible output. Thus, the quantity of electricity produced (and therefore consumed) depends mainly on the size of each station rather than on a pattern of demand which means that some stations are used more than others. Second, long-distance transmission systems for electricity were hardly developed at all in Latin America by the early 1960s. This meant that electricity consumption was necessarily spatially concentrated around the locations of production facilities. Moreover, as the areal basis for the geographical analysis of the data was by grid squares as large as 100 km × 100 km, there could, in general, only have been a little movement of electricity across the graticule used (see Figures 9–3 and 9–4). And where long-distance transmission systems were known to exist at the time, as in south central Chile and from the hydro-electricity stations on the River São Francisco in eastern Brazil, appropriate adjustments were made to the allocation of generating capacity in the grid squares affected.

For each of the nine largest countries of Latin America, a cartographical analysis of the geographical pattern of electricity production was made and is presented in Figures 9–3 and 9–4. These maps provide a clear visual impression of the high degree of geographical concentration of the production of electricity in all the nine countries. This impression is then confirmed, ranked, and measured by simple statistical analyses of the mapped patterns. For example, each map includes a graph showing the minimum number of grid squares required to account for 25 per cent, 50 per cent, and 75 per cent of the total amount of electricity production capacity in the country concerned. The situation overall for the nine countries is summarized in Table 9–1.

This table shows that in five of the nine countries at least 25 per cent of electricity production was concentrated in but a single grid square and that in three of the remaining four countries in only 2 squares. In four countries half of the capacity was in 1 or 2 squares and in four others in 3 or 4. Even the third quartile of electricity production was spatially highly concentrated, as it was found in no more than four more squares for any country except in the case of Mexico. Taking the analysis a little further, so as to relate the degree of concentration of the production of electricity to the size of each country, and to take into consideration the relative importance of different centres of the capacity, an *Index of*

Table 9–1. Distribution of electricity-generating capacity in the nine largest Latin American countries

Number of grid squares needed to locate . . . / Country	25%	50%	75%	100%	Total number of grid squares to cover the country
		of total national generating capacity			
Argentina	1	2	5	31	299
Bolivia	1	2	4	22	151
Brazil	1	2	6	30	908
Chile	2	4	8	34	134
Colombia	2	4	7	22	160
Mexico	3	8	20	64	217
Paraguay	1	1	1	5	71
Peru	2	3	7	29	178
Venezuela	1	3	6	30	128

Concentration of Capacity around a previously determined Mean Centre of Production was calculated. The index is recorded in the case of each country on the map of the country concerned whilst in Table 9–2 the nine countries are rank-ordered by their indices.

Table 9–2. Ranked indices of the concentration of electricity-generating capacity

1	Paraguay	0.84
2	Brazil	0.73
3	Argentina	0.65
4	Peru	0.60
5	Bolivia	0.55
6	Chile	0.52
7	Colombia	0.51
8	Venezuela	0.45
9	Mexico	0.44

This clearly indicates the very high degree of concentration of production in most of the countries. Indeed, only the indices for Venezuela and Mexico fell just below the mid-point in the scale the limits of which are 0 and 1. (A score of 0 would indicate a perfectly uniform distribution of activities over the national territory whilst a score of 1 would indicate the concentration of all activities within a radius of 50 km of the mean centre.) The highest degree of concentration was found in the case of Paraguay where, as seen on the map, there is only very limited development of electricity-generating capacity outside the Asunción area; that is, outside the capital city core region of the country. Perhaps a little surprisingly, Brazil is in second place in the table of the ranked order of spatial concentration of capacity in spite of the existence of two distinct centres of

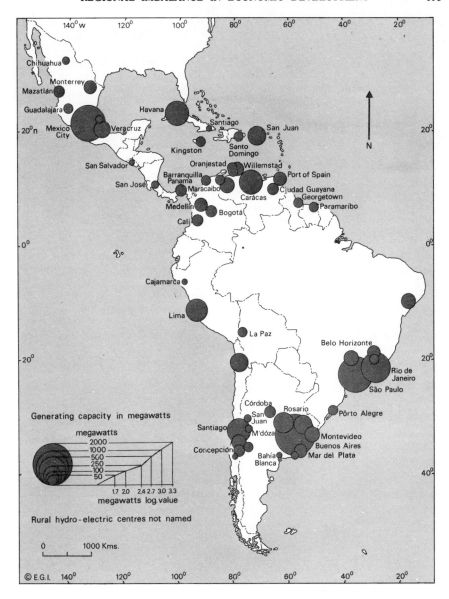

Figure 9–2. Latin America: the distribution of electricity-generating capacity

KEY TO MAPS SHOWING SPATIAL PATTERNS OF ELECTRICITY GENERATING CAPACITY IN LATIN AMERICAN COUNTRIES.

✦ Capital City (point of origin for the 100×100 km graticule)

✱ Mean Centre of Electric Production derived from the formula:

$$\bar{x} = \frac{\Sigma(x_i c_i)}{C}$$

$$\bar{\Delta} =$$

$$\bar{y} = \frac{\Sigma(y_i c_i)}{C}$$

where x_i = vertical co-ordinate of the i'th area
y_i = horizontal co-ordinate of the i'th area
c_i = capacity of the i'th area
C = Total Capacity

Spatial Distribution of Electricity Generating Capacity—The Capacity has been totalled for each square of the graticule and the totals ranked in descending order. Distribution is shown thus:

● Minimum squares required to locate 25% of country's total capacity

◉ Minimum additional number of squares (if any) required locate next 25% of capacity

◉ Minimum additional number of squares (if any) required locate next 25% of capacity

• All other areas with generating capacity

All other squares have no generating capacity

Graph: This plots cumulative capacity by ranked order of squares shows also number of squares required to achieve 25%, 50% and 75% of total capacity

Index: Index of Spatial Concentration of Electricity Generating Capacity. This falls within the range 0 to 1 and is derived from the formula

$$1 - \frac{\sum\limits_{i=1}^{m} c_i r}{\sum\limits_{r=1}^{n} r\left(\frac{C}{n}\right)}$$

where c_i = capacity of i'th square
C = Total Capacity
r = radius in 50 km. intervals from the mean centre

Key page. This refers to Figures 9–3 and 9–4 on pages 195 and 196. Also see text for explanation.

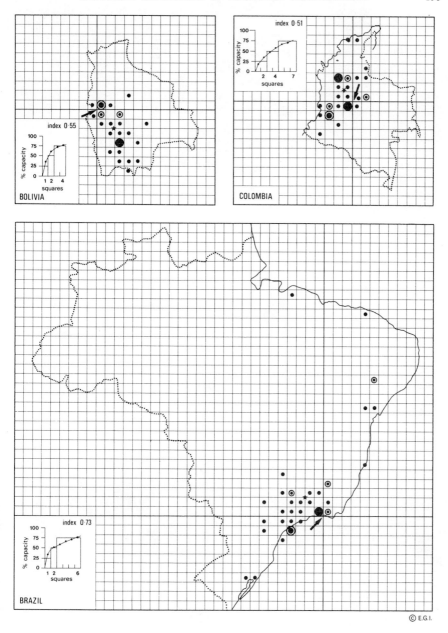

Figure 9–3. The distribution of electricity-generating capacity in three countries

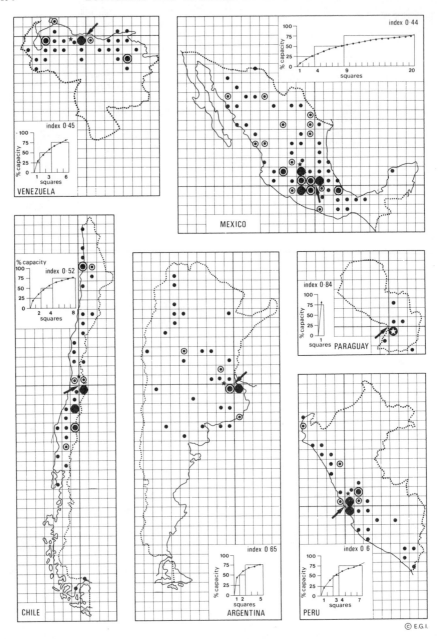

Figure 9–4. The distribution of electricity-generating capacity in six countries

development around Rio and São Paulo. In relation to the total size of the country, however, these two centres can be viewed almost as being next-door neighbours—a relationship which stands out clearly on the map (see Figure 9–3). Between them they completely dominate the electricity production system. Incidentally, even if one excludes the whole of 'empty' Brazil from the calculation of the Index (that is if one excludes those parts of the country with less than three people per square kilometre, or roughly all the country west of a line linking Uruguay and Fortaleza), then the Index of Cencentration for the remaining part is still as high as 0.6.

At the other end of the ranked order of the nine countries Venezuela and Mexico, as already mentioned, have indices of slightly under 0.5. The results for these countries quantify special features in their spatial patterns of electricity generation. In Mexico, a planned programme of rural electrification extends back to the 1930s and there is also a large use of electricity for pumping irrigation water in some of the large-scale agricultural projects in areas along the west coast and adjacent to the boundary with the United States. These factors would seem to account for the much more geographically widespread electricity production pattern in Mexico. In spite of this, however, the heavy concentration of capacity around Mexico City still stands out very clearly and this confirms the other available evidence that we have of the great concentration there of non-agricultural activities.

In Venezuela, the use of electricity in the oilfields of the Maracaibo region and in the large refineries of the Paraguana peninsula, coupled with the first stages in the development of electricity-generation capacity in the Guayana project in the eastern part of the country, introduced an element of countrywide dispersal in the spatial pattern of production. In the light of these aspects of the country's economic geography it is, indeed, rather surprising that Venezuela's index should still have been as high as 0.45. The fact that it is so high emerges from the existence in the Caracas region of about 35 per cent of generating capacity—so giving an indication of the dominance of the capital city metropolitan region in non-oil industry activities.

Thus, the maps and the statistical analyses of the geographical distribution of electricity production within the nine countries clearly indicate the existence and high relative importance of a centre of electricity availability and use in each country. Given the ubiquitous nature of the need for electricity in all types of economic activities—except traditional agriculture—then this geographical pattern of electricity supply appears to provide good evidence for the existence of a set of clearly defined 'core regions' in the Latin American countries examined. And, on the other hand, the absence or the very limited development of electricity supply facilities over much of the national territories appears to suggest the co-existence of a far more extensive peripheral region in each country in which secondary and tertiary activities are so unimportant that little or no publicly available electricity supply facilities had, by the mid-1960s, been called into existence.

Thus, for the nine countries which have been included in this analysis there seems to be little doubt about the ability of the core/periphery hypothesis adequately to describe their geographical patterns of modern development. Later in the chapter we shall return to examine in more detail the nature of the geographical contrasts in some of these countries. Meanwhile, it seems appropriate to try to provide a continental-wide overview of the number, size and geographical distribution of the centres of development: again utilizing the generally available mid-1960s data on the distribution of electricity generating capacity as the means whereby the general picture can be established.

Locations where at least a modest 50 MW of electricity-producing capacity were sited are ranked in Table 9–3 and these locations are designated as the centres of non-agricultural economic activity in Latin America. The descending importance of each centre in the rank order is a function of the quantity of locally located generating capacity. The importance of each centre is, moreover, shown relative to that of the centre in the first position—Buenos Aires. The geographical distribution of these centres over the continent is shown in Figure 9–5. In total it is estimated that about 90 per cent of all the non-agricultural activities of the continent in the mid-1960s are located in the 49 centres shown in the table and map. As a yard-stick against which to measure the degree of concentration of activities which this represents, it is significant to note that these 49 centres contained only about 30 per cent of Latin America's 200 million people at that time.

Looking at the results of the analysis in a little more detail, one is impressed by the degree to which the results confirm the traditional description of the location of Latin America's non-agricultural activities. This can be seen, firstly, in the highly coastally-orientated nature of the pattern. Well over half of the centres (30 out of 49) are on the coast (or tide-water) whilst the mean distance of the other 19 from the nearest port to which there is a railway or paved-road connexion is only 75 kilometres (Figure 9–6). Secondly, it can be seen in the domination of the capital cities, which is very powerful indeed. Capital cities comprise seven out of the top ten in the rank order (excluding Rio de Janeiro which has recently lost its status as the capital of Brazil following the designation of Brasília as the new capital), and there are another twelve capitals in the rest of the list. These nineteen capitals in all account for almost 60 per cent of the activities located in the 49 centres and over 55 per cent of all the continent's non-agricultural activities. One should point out, however, that some of the capitals of Latin American countries do not appear at all in the ranking: for example, Asunción, Quito, and some of the capitals of Middle America countries. However, as we have seen already in the presentation of the country data on electricity generation for Paraguay (see Figure 9–3), this does not necessarily indicate that these countries do not exhibit a strongly geographical concentrated distribution of economic activities. Rather is it a result of the scale at which the analysis has been made (that is, at the continental scale). Thus the development of industrial and commercial activities in these capital cities was, at the period in time for which the information was available, in-

Table 9–3. Ranked centres of economic activity in Latin America

Rank	Centre	Country	Rank within country	Size (when Buenos Aires = 100)
1	Buenos Aires	Argentina	1	100
2	São Paulo	Brazil	1	63
3	Mexico City	Mexico	1	50
4	Rio de Janeiro	Brazil	2	34
5	Santiago	Chile	1	25
6	Havana	Cuba	1	18
7	Caracas	Venezuela	1	17
8	Lima	Peru	1	17
9	Rosario	Argentina	2	15
10	Montevideo	Uruguay	1	13
11	Antofagasta	Chile	2	9.1
12	Mar del Plata	Argentina	3	8.9
13	Belo Horizonte	Brazil	3	8.6
14	Maracaibo Oil Towns	Venezuela	2	8.4
15	Concepción	Chile	3	7.5
16	Veracruz	Mexico	2	7.0
17	Monterrey	Mexico	3	6.8
18	Medellín	Colombia	1	6.6
19	San Juan	Puerto Rico	1	6.6
20	Ciudad Guayana	Venezuela	3	6.5
21	Mazatlan	Mexico	4	6.3
22	Córdoba	Argentina	4	5.8
23	Recife	Brazil	4	5.7
24	Bogotá	Colombia	2	5.7
25	Panama	Panama	1	5.3
26	Cali	Colombia	3	5.0
27	Mendoza	Argentina	5	4.8
28	Paraguana	Venezuela	4	4.7
29	Maracaibo	Venezuela	5	4.5
30	Willemstad	Netherl. Antilles	1	4.5
31	Salvador	Brazil	5	4.4
32	Port of Spain	Trinidad	1	4.4
33	La Paz	Bolivia	1	3.8
34	Porto Alegre	Brazil	6	3.7
35	Guadalajara	Mexico	5	3.6
36	Tampico	Mexico	6	3.1
37	Barranquilla	Colombia	4	2.9
38	Kingston	Jamaica	1	2.8
39	San José	Costa Rica	1	2.7
40	Oranjestad	Netherl. Antilles	2	2.7
41	Santo Domingo	Dominican Rep.	1	2.6
42	San Juan	Argentina	6	2.6
43	Chihuahua	Mexico	6	2.5
44	San Salvador	El Salvador	1	2.4
45	Santiago	Cuba	2	2.4
46	Cajamarca	Peru	2	2.4
47	Bahia Blanca	Argentina	7	2.3
48	Georgetown	Guayana	1	2.2
49	Paramaribo	Surinam	1	2.2

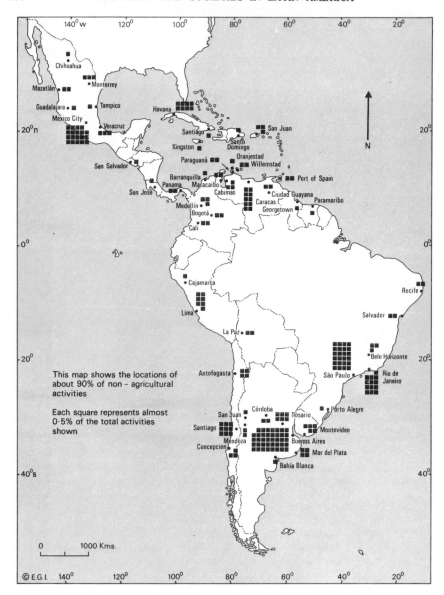

Figure 9–5. Latin America: the main centres of economic activity

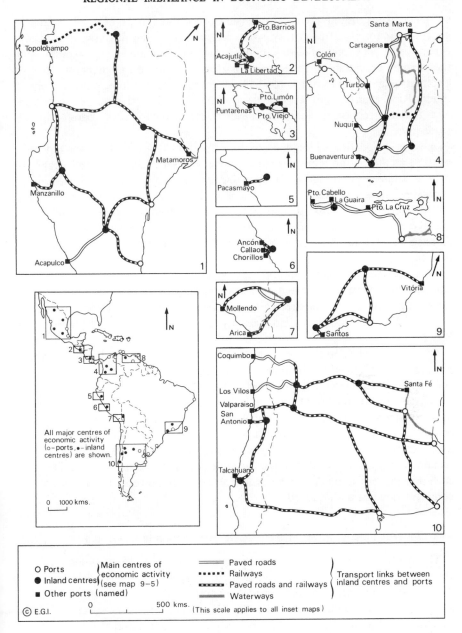

Figure 9–6. Latin America: centres of economic activity and transport facilities

sufficient to necessitate the local provision of as much as 50 MW of electricity-generating capacity. Hence they were excluded from the analysis. Subsequent expansion in the supply of electricity has brought the remaining capital cities, with the possible exception of Tegucigalpa in Honduras, up to this minimum level of electricity supply. Indeed, as we shall see later, when we look more closely at Puerto Rico, even the smallest countries, with a limited development of secondary and tertiary economic activities, nevertheless exhibit strong core/periphery tendencies.

A general updating of the analysis based on the data used here has not been possible as there is no more recent comprehensive set of data available such that only incomplete information is available on the later growth of electricity-generating capacity in Latin America overall. However, what later information is available does suggest that the pattern as it had evolved is in general terms being still accentuated rather than weakened. Details of recently developed or newly planned generating capacity show much of it to be in areas of existing high capacity.

This includes the first developments in Latin America of nuclear power stations, all of which are located in or near centres of high electricity demand: as, for example, in the case of Brazil's first nuclear station which is under construction (in 1977) at a location almost exactly halfway between Rio de Janeiro and São Paulo.

On the contrary, hydro-electricity has to be developed at locations where physical geographical conditions are suitable. However, in this case the geographically concentrated pattern of demand for electricity acts as a constraint on the hydro-potential that can be exploited as development is restricted to locations from which the electricity can be economically transmitted to centres of demand—currently to locations not more than about 600 kilometres from the using centres. Thus, as shown in Figure 9–7, actual hydro-electricity developments remain geographically related to the pattern of existing electricity demand centres such that most of Latin America's potential for hydro-power in the interior of the continent remains undeveloped.

The Continued Geographical Concentration of Economic Development

This continuation of the process of the spatial concentration of non-agricultural economic activities indicates that limited and modest attempts to date by Latin American countries to achieve a broader geographical spread of economic growth and employment opportunities have not, in general, been very successful. This suggests that the 'play of market forces', relatively unhampered as far as location policies are concerned in most Latin American countries, is, indeed, having the effects that the Swedish economist, G. Myrdal, suggested it would have. He hypothesized that such market forces would have a tendency to increase inequalities between the regions of a country as industrial production, commerce,

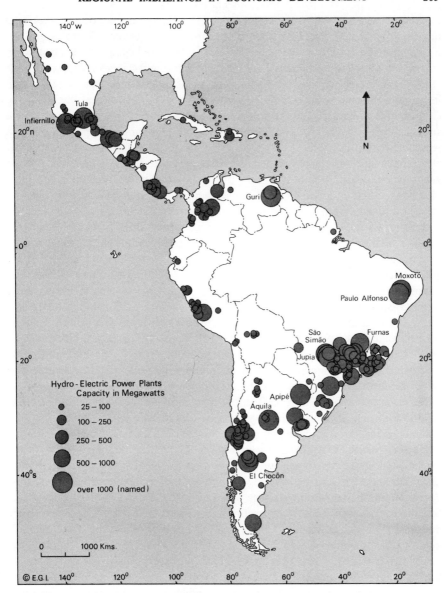

Figure 9–7. Latin America: hydro-electricity developments

banking, insurance, shipping and, indeed, all those economic activities which tend to give a higher than average return, cluster in certain localities. At the same time, he argued, the expansion of activities in the favoured locality has 'backwash effects' elsewhere in the countries concerned. These effects include denuding the other localities of capital, of their resources of skilled labour and of benefits from intra-regional trade. In other words, there is a continued evolution of the core/periphery spatial pattern of economic development; the pattern which, we suggested earlier, typifies the geography of the contemporary economies of Latin American countries.

We have since attempted to define the 'favoured localities' by reference to the geographical distribution of electricity production and have noted the high degree of concentration of economic activities in these localities in almost every country of the continent. More detailed studies of particular situations serve to confirm and elaborate this general view. In Argentina, Greater Buenos Aires, already the foremost centre of the whole continent (see Figure 9–5 and Table 9–3), continues to grow as it attracts much of the new secondary and tertiary industries that are created in the country. It has thus increased its estimated share of the total national value added in manufacturing and commerce to almost 60 per cent. Around Buenos Aires, relatively proximate cities such as Rosario and Mar del Plata (both about 300 kilometres from Buenos Aires) have also achieved expansion through 'overspill' tendencies from the 'core city' as some entrepreneurs decided that the benefits of a Buenos Aires location could be more than offset by the costs likely to be incurred by a location in a city of over 6 million people with its serious transportation and congestion problems. Further away, however, Córdoba, some 600 kilometres from Buenos Aires, only succeeded in securing a share of the expansion of industry in Argentina by dint of considerable local efforts on the part of the city authorities, local businessmen, trades union leaders and other influential parties. They formed a group for stimulating new investment in the locality and attempted to achieve this aim both by publicity for the city's advantages for industry and by offering help over the provision of sites and their development for industrial purposes. The fact that Córdoba succeeded in attracting industry—most notably by securing important factories connected with the motor car industry and so more than doubling its share of national value added in manufacturing and almost doubling its industrial workforce—seems to have been due more to its own efforts than to any really positive commitment on the part of the national government to the expansion of the city and its region. In less favourably located parts of Argentina for industrial development, for example, Misiones, Formosa and Patagonia, there have been no similar concerted local efforts to secure development. Nor had the national government before 1970 paid little more than political lip-service to the need for, and the desirability of, stimulating local regional economies through their diversification away from agriculture and other primary activities. Thus, as shown in Figure 9–8, manufacturing in such regions was very little developed. Thereafter, however, in the

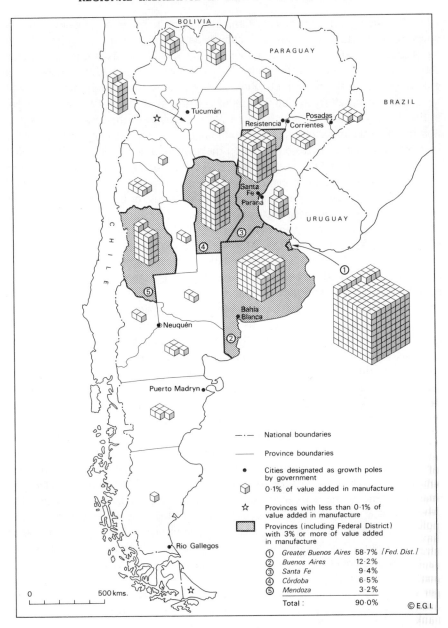

Figure 9–8. Argentina: the distribution of manufacturing industry

1970–75 National Development Plan, a number of regional industrial growth poles were nominated—with the choice based on the local availability of mineral/energy resources or on labour availability. These growth poles are also shown in Figure 9–8, together with Bahia Blanca which was nominated as a growth centre for the province of Buenos Aires. Some success appears already to have attended the effort to stimulate industrial growth in Bahia Blanca. Elsewhere in the country, however, there is, as yet, little evidence of the creation of a situation in which the other designated growth areas have achieved any propensity for sustained economic expansion based on the growth of economic activities 'which tend to give a higher than average return'. This seems to be specially true of the relatively heavily populated centres in the north of the country (see Figure 9–8) which cannot be viewed as 'resource frontier' locations for industrial development and which are not otherwise particularly attractive locations for private industry given their distances from the main markets of the country. And so far government aid has been much to limited to overcome the disadvantages.

The inclusion of proposals for regional development in the election programmes of political parties and statements by national governments that such development is, indeed, a fundamental part of their economic—and often strategic—policies are very common throughout Latin America. For Mexico, regional development, albeit directed from the centre, was virtually a 1910 revolutionary warcry. In terms of the spatial patterns of infrastructure development since then, as, for example, in the provision of rural electricity, the nation-wide supply of oil and natural gas, the construction of roads and the spatial extension of welfare services, attention to parts of the country away from the capital city can be numbered among the achievements of successive Mexican governments. In spite of such achievements, however, these same governments did not take any really effective steps over the same period either to encourage the dispersal of established manufacturing and other secondary and tertiary economic activities away from Mexico City, or even to discourage its further concentration there. In fact, their policies in respect of the geography of economic activities evolved such that they have had exactly the opposite effects and have thus tended to strengthen the already strong market forces which favour the location of everything in the centre! The consequential strong geographical concentration of industry and commerce in Mexico City is apparent from all the available indicators. With about 16 per cent of the country's population, it enjoys over 36 per cent of total employment in manufacturing, 34 per cent of value added in industry, 60 per cent of all bank loans, 63 per cent of national investment in higher education and over 36 per cent of the country's gross national product. If one includes the areas immediately adjacent to Mexico City then the share of the 'centre' becomes even greater (e.g. 46 per cent of industrial employment).

The strength of the degree of geographical concentration has emerged from government policies which have deliberately aimed to keep down the costs of the factors of production in Mexico City. Amongst these are, first, the subsidization of freight rates on foodstuffs and agricultural and other raw materials which have to be moved to Mexico City from other parts of the country. (Note that there has been no compensating subsidization of the cost of transporting manufactured goods in Mexico, thus effectively discouraging location of industry away from Mexico City which, for most such goods, provides some 80 per cent of the total market.) Secondly, the 'Law of New and Necessary Industry' (dating from 1941 and revised in 1946 and 1955), which was designed to stimulate the growth of import substituting industry, was applicable even to the permitted industries which planned to locate in and around Mexico City which thus received 65 per cent of the total investment (and 40 per cent of the jobs created) in such new, highly productive activities. Third, there has been government subsidization of certain items of consumption (particularly basic foodstuffs and gasoline) in Mexico City, aimed at containing the pressures for wage increases which might otherwise have priced the location out of the market for certain industries.

In taking such action successive Mexican governments concerned, and they are by no means the only Latin American governments to act in this way, indicate their acceptance of the importance of two separate considerations which together outweigh even a declared belief in the idea of a more equitable pattern of regional development. First, they tend to accept that it is entirely 'natural', and more than fully expected, that any industrialist would want to locate in Mexico City. If the industrialist cannot do this with a reasonable chance of success, then he may decide not to proceed at all with his plans for building a factory. In other words, governments have generally believed that they have no ability to make industrialists locate elsewhere in the country away from Mexico City. If they did choose to try to force a factory away from the capital city region to another location then the entrepreneur concerned would, in turn, so it has been thought, choose not to build his plant in Mexico at all. This is a risk that governments considered they could not afford to take.

Secondly, in spite of all the political platitudes expressed about the need for, and the desirability of, ensuring that citizens in all parts of the country have an opportunity to participate in the nation's development, national leaders know that they are 'made' or 'broken' by their ability or otherwise to sell themselves to the most articulate, the best organized, and the politically most conscious pressure group in the country. National leaders are fully aware that this group occupies the tenements and shanty towns, as well as the elegant suburbs, of the Federal District and its immediately surrounding area. If there is legislation, or threat of legislation, that seems likely to reduce the ability of Mexico City to continue to attract jobs and income, then large numbers from this group can be outside the parliament buildings or the presidential palace within a matter of few days, at most, or even a few hours, if necessary. Their abilities so to pressurize governments are clearly recognized. By contrast, the failure of a government to match its electoral promises on regional development to less articulate, less well-organized and less politically conscious (and much smaller) groups in the distant states is unlikely to produce anything much more serious than a spot of local trouble outside the offices of the government's representative in the area concerned, or possibly the 'threat' of a delegation which will travel from the area affected to Mexico City in order to present the grievances of the people it represents. Such a delegation can, on arrival in Mexico City, easily be overawed and overshadowed by the appropriate Minister and his city-based experts who will, if it is necessary, usually be able to convince the delegates that all will be well within the 'foreseeable' future. Politico-economic reality in other words, even in Mexico, and much more so in most other Latin American countries, lies in the dominance of the central government whose actions can easily and usually have the effect of strengthening the development of the core region at the expense of the country's unprivileged periphery: a phenomenon recognized, for example, in the case of Chile where, from 1920 to 1960, there was a steady increase in the urban concentration of economic activities in Santiago, the primacy of which increased from 2.33 to 5.18 over this period. Similarly in Brazil, for which Figure 9–9 clearly shows the contrasting per capita income results emerging from the concentration of higher value added industrial and commercial activities in Rio de Janeiro and São Paulo and adjacent cities.

The Role of Transport Facilities

We return to Mexico, however, to illustrate another important aspect of the regional development problem which is created within the framework of the core/periphery model of the spatial economic organization of society. Transportation developments, especially the construction and improvement of roads, have frequently been held to be the key to the regional dispersion of economic activities and hence to the possibilities of a more equitable distribution of economic activities over a country. In that the absence of transport facilities, or the existence of very inferior ones, obviously means that any economic activity which depends on contact with the outside world (for example, for obtaining supplies of raw materials and components, and/or for marketing the goods produced) will never be located in areas so affected, this is something of a truism. Even in this context, however, one should recall that the development of certain economic activities in isolated locations does in itself sometimes produce the transport infrastructure required. We saw examples of this in the previous chapter, when we were examining the growth of plantation systems and of extractive industry in Latin America and we have seen another example in this chapter in our discussion of the early growth of a cattle-raising industry in the interior of Brazil. Apart from this relationship between transport facilities and the growth of new economic activities, however, the hypothesis stated above on the role of transport in developments appears to imply that if only the road and/or rail facilities in those parts of a country which lie beyond the boundary of the developed core were to be improved, then the development gap between 'core' and 'periphery' would start to

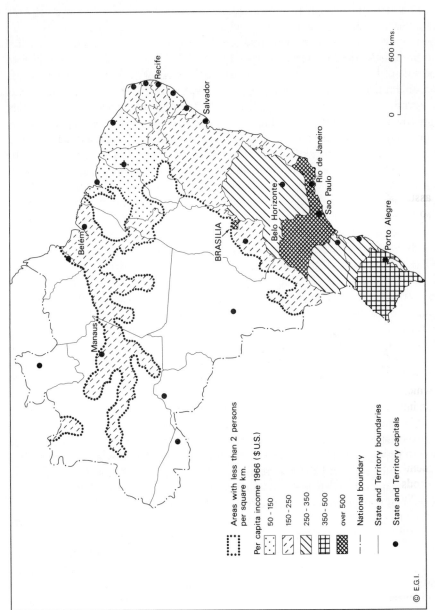

Figure 9–9. Brazil: Per Capita Income by state

Areas with less than 2 persons
per square km.

Per capita income 1966 ($ U.S.)

50 – 150

150 – 250

250 – 350

350 – 500

over 500

National boundary

State and Territory boundaries

State and Territory capitals

© E.G.I.

close as entrepreneurs rush to locate their investment in the latter area rather than in the former.

This 'law' of development, however, assumes that all else is equal, whereas from our knowledge of the contrasts between core and periphery we know that this assumption is as far from being realistic as it is possible to get! And because it is so unrealistic, the hypothesis as stated is invalid. There would, in fact, appear to be sound theoretical reasons, as well as much empirical evidence, to suggest that an alternative, almost in fact a contradictory, hypothesis more nearly represents the truth of the situation as far as transport expansion and economic development are concerned. This can be stated as follows: where there is a development or an improvement in a transportation infrastructure within a country already marked by such a strong regional imbalance in development that it amounts to the existence of a core/periphery situation, then the immediate effect is to strengthen the market forces which favour the development of the core region at the expense of the periphery—unless it is accompanied by strong government action designed and intended to protect the latter. This is because the cost of getting raw materials and other factors of production into the centre, and the cost of getting the finished goods back to whatever markets may exist in the periphery, are both reduced. Thus the products of the centre can now compete more easily with alternatives which had previously been locally made. So small-scale industries, using primitive or intermediate technology only and located in the towns of the 'periphery', fall victim to the products of the more advanced technology located in the 'centre'. Similarly, the marketing and wholesaling functions of the peripheral towns can now be superseded, in part at least, by similar activities in the centre where increasing economies of scale in the growth of these functions are such as to enable them to more than offset the additional transport costs involved in delivering goods to a much wider area. This is so because the improvement of transport facilities leads to a reduction in the per kilometre transport costs, whilst increasing size of shipment arising from the greater throughput also reduces the unit transportation cost. Such consequences seem to have arisen from the considerable investment of funds in Mexico's road network, the development of which has significantly enhanced the competitiveness of many activities of the capital city, the influence of which has expanded to cover a larger area of the country in respect of consumer goods' markets and the provision of central place services.

Similarly in Venezuela, where, until the 1960s, virtually the only large element of investment of government revenues from oil, apart from the money spent in Caracas and its immediate region, was in the field of road construction. But all the roads built led to Caracas which could thus be fed with its import requirements more cheaply (so reducing the costs of the factors of production in Caracas) whilst the outward-bound lanes of the same roads could carry mass-produced articles from the factories in the Caracas area to larger and larger areas of the country: to the detriment of the level and range of economic activities in the country's smaller towns.

Even more recently the same process appears to have been at work in Colombia. Here the linking of the capital, Bogotá, with the other main cities and towns of the western part of the country has provided an important stimulus to industrial development in the capital at the expense of industry in other locations. The latter previously enjoyed some degree of protection by virtue of their relative isolation from the products of the larger factories in Bogotá. Now a process of geographical concentration of production facilities appears to be under way to the detriment even of industry in cities like Medellín and Cali which previously more or less matched Bogotá in their degree of industrial development. And for new industry the capital, with its larger local market, generally appears to be the preferred location with road transport along the new trans-Andean roads able to deliver the products into all other subsidiary market areas of the country.

This preceding argument and the associated examples could be interpreted as an attack on the utility of transport-infrastructure improvement in helping economic development. To attempt to sustain such an argument would obviously be ludicrous in the face of all the evidence that better transport facilities not only encourage growth but are, indeed, a prerequisite for it. This, however, is not the point at issue. What remains to be determined is *where* the main economic growth will occur, given transportation improvements in a developing country. It will, of course, be readily accepted that the degree of growth will certainly be locationally related to the new facilities. Thus, within the periphery, areas near to the new road or railway will do better than those further away. There is evidence of this from Venezuela, for example, where there have been differential rates of growth between those towns in the periphery on or near one of the new roads, and those still remote from them. But this distinction is a relatively minor one compared with the unequal division of benefits arising from the new transport facility as between the favoured core city and its region, on the one hand, and the undeveloped periphery, on the other. In this relative inequality in sharing the benefits of new transport facilities we see the real role of those facilities which connect a pre-existing core region with the lesser-developed peripheries within an underdeveloped country already exhibiting strong geographical contrasts in levels of economic and social well-being. Such new facilities further accentuate these contrasts between the rich and the poor regions—in the absence of appropriate government intervention designed to change the geography of the economic system.

Clearly then, investment in roads or railways to 'improve' the accessibility of the periphery to the centre is not enough in itself to secure the objective of economic advance in the depressed regions. Such investment, though necessary in itself, must be accompanied by other measures designed to ensure that the benefits of transport construction flow into those areas lagging so far behind the centre in well-being per capita. One effective way would be to introduce physical controls on the *use* of the road: prohibiting, for example, any flow of certain consumer goods along the road from the centre towards the periphery in the hope thereby of stimulating the development of factories to make the goods at some point in the periphery itself. But such physical controls tend to create more problems than they solve, as well as being difficult to administer. Indeed, they almost inevitably invoke an ever-widening degree of direct control over economic decision-making, something which only Cuba among the Latin American nations has, so far at least, incorporated into its economic system. A more acceptable and hence a more practical possibility within Latin America arises from the introduction of positive measures of various kinds to encourage the dispersal of economic activities away from the core region. The implementation of such measures could ensure that the new road, or other new transport facility concerned, was used as a determinant of the geographical directions and patterns that such dispersal shall take. But such an approach implies a comprehensive evaluation of the propensity for, and the need of, development in various parts of the 'periphery' before the transport development programme is finally determined. To date, however, few Latin American governments have had enough real interest in, or effective motivation for, the introduction of a more dispersed geographical pattern of non-primary economic activities so as to ensure that an approach to the problem of priorities in investment in transport facilities based on these considerations will outweigh the many other interests in, and the motivations for, improved transportation facilities.

Looking around Latin America in the late 1970s one sees much evidence of the vast investment that has gone into transport facilities over the last 30 years. These include the improvement and electrification of the railways of the central valley of Chile centred on Santiago; the reconstruction to modern standards of the highway system radiating from Buenos Aires; the creation of an intensive network of new roads in the Brazilian states of Rio de Janeiro, São Paulo and Minas Gerais; the building of the Atlantico Railway designed to give Bogatá a direct connection with the Caribbean coast; the linking of the capitals of the Central American countries by the Inter-American highway; the construction of a super-highway system in between Mexico City and its port of Veracruz; and the building of airports equipped for the latest intercontinental jets at every capital city in the continent. In other words, no matter where one looks in the continent, one sees that almost all of the investment in transport developments has been made in capital city regions or in locations leading to and from the core areas. If our foregoing argument is valid, then such investment can only have had the effect of further strengthening the position of the core regions relative to other parts of the national territories. Thus, such transport investment will have made it even more difficult to make a start in reducing the wealth and welfare gaps between the richest and the poorest regions of most Latin American countries.

It is, therefore, hardly surprising that there is little evidence to date that the gap between average per capita well-being in 'core' and 'periphery' is starting to close; and some evidence, as we have seen, that it is continuing to widen. This seems to be the case, for example, since the early 1960s in the 'battle' between north-east and south-east Brazil for economic development. The south-east core region continues to forge ahead, in part because it appears to secure a net gain from intra-regional trade with the north-east, which is obliged by national regulation to buy its industrial goods requirements more expensively from the factories of south-east Brazil than if it had the freedom to buy them in foreign countries, but which in return is required to sell its agricultural production to the industrializing core region of the country at government-controlled prices.

On the other side of the continent the same sort of relationship emerges between the core region of Lima and the country's periphery set in the harsh conditions of the Sierra. The 'backwash' effect on the Sierra of the continued development of Lima through the migration to Lima of higher-quality labour and capital from the Sierra has been accompanied by the latter's lack of choice in buying its import requirements of consumer and other goods. These can only be bought from the factories of Lima rather than from potential lower-cost suppliers overseas. These factors have, it has been calculated, been sufficient to reduce the rate of growth in the Sierra by some 4 or 5 per cent per annum. This has depressed the Sierra's rate of growth in many years to one even below the rate of growth of the population, so ensuring a stagnating income per capita. Meanwhile, that of Lima's inhabitants continues to move ahead at a not unreasonable rate.

The hinterlands (or peripheries) of Latin American countries are, in other words, even subsidizing the growth of the centres and producing a situation in which Latin America is becoming a continent of widely-scattered developed zones, feeding on and keeping down standards of living in the remainder of the national territories. There are a few significant exceptions to this situation and they will be examined in the next chapter, together with future possibilities for geographically more extensive and nationally integrated patterns of economic development. Meantime, in the late 1970s, the hypothesis that the economic geography of Latin America's secondary and tertiary activities can still be described adequately by the core/periphery model appears to have a virtually general application throughout the continent from Mexico, in the north, right through to Chile and Argentina up to 10,000 kilometres away to the south.

Bibliography

a) The approach to the contemporary economic geography of Latin America followed in this chapter is not one which is compatible with most of the best-known geographical literature on the continent. Moreover, for those readers without an appropriate background in and/or knowledge of developmental economics the first requirement will be additional background literature on the hypotheses of regional imbalance in economic development. In this respect the following books and articles are recommended:
FRIEDMANN, J., *Regional Development Policy*, M.I.T. Press, Cambridge, Mass., 1966. Note that the sub-title to this book is *A Case Study of Venezuela*. This provides the most comprehensive study of regional imbalance for any Latin American country.
GINSBURG, N., 'From Colonisation to National Development': Geographical Perspectives

on Patterns and Policies, *Annals of the Association of American Geographers*, **63,** (1973).

HILL, A. D. (ED.), *Latin American Development Issues*, Clag Publications Inc., East Lansing, 1973.

This collection of papers by North American geographers contains a number of contributions which are significant for their discussion of the 'regional development' issue.

HOYLE, B. S. (ED), *Spatial Aspects of Development*, J. Wiley and Sons, London, 1974.

JOHNSON, E. A., *The Organisation of Space in Developing Countries*, Harvard University Press, Cambridge, Mass., 1970.

This general text on the spatial structuring of developing economies argues against rapid and over-urbanization and for the establishment of a nationwide system of market towns in which relatively small-scale and geographically dispersed industrial growth can occur.

STÖHR, W., *Regional Development—Experience and Prospects in Latin America*, Mouton and Co., Den Haag, 1975.

Note that this is one of many publications sponsored as part of the Regional Development Programme of the United Nations Research Institute for Social Development in Geneva. Many of the other publications of this Institute are highly relevant.

UNITED NATIONS: *Economic Bulletin for Latin America*, **18,** (1973).

This particular issue of the Bulletin is concerned especially with regional and geographical problems.

b) The geographical 'core' areas of national economies have involved the development of very large cities and city regions and an understanding of their structure and problems is important. See

BEYER, G. H. (ED), *The Urban Explosion in Latin America*, Cornell University Press, Ithaca, 1967.

FRIEDMANN, J., *Urbanisation, Planning and National Development*, Sage Publications, Beverley Hills, 1974.

GEISSE, G. and HARDOY, J. E. (EDS.), 'Regional and Urban Development Policies', *Latin American Research Review*, **2,** (1972).

HARRIS, W. D. and RODRIGUES-CAMILLONI, H. L., *Growth of Latin American Cities*, Ohio University Press, Athens, 1971.

HAUSER, P. M. (ED.), *Urbanisation in Latin America*, UNESCO, Paris, 1961.

MORSE, R. M., 'Latin American Cities: Aspects of Function and Structure', in Friedmann, J. and Alonso, W. (Eds.), *Regional Development and Planning: a Reader*, M.I.T. Press, Cambridge, Mass., 1964.

c) There are also useful case-studies on particular Latin American cities and city regions. These include the following:

BIRD, R., 'The Economy of the Mexican Federal District', *Inter-American Economic Affairs*, **17,** (1963).

CLARKE, C. G., 'Urbanization in the Caribbean', *Geography*, **59,** (1974).

FITZGIBBON, R. H., 'The Economy of "Montevideo" ', *Inter-American Economic Affairs*, **6,** (1952).

FRIEDMANN, J. and LACKINGTON, T., 'Hyperurbanisation and National Development in Chile', *Urban Affairs Quarterly*, **3,** (June 1967).

MORSE, R., 'São Paulo in the 19th and 20th Centuries', *Inter-American Economic Affairs*, **5** (1951) and **8** (1954).

SARGENT, C. S., *The Spatial Evolution of Buenos Aires, 1870–1930*, Arizona University Press, Temple, 1974.

SEMPLE, R. K. *et al.*, 'Growth Poles in São Paulo', *Annals of the Association of American Geographers*, **62** (1972).

SNIDER, D. E., 'The Metropolitan Nodality of Montevideo', *Economic Geography*, **38** (1962).

d) Some of the books listed under a) above include case-studies of the patterns and problems of regional development in Latin American countries. In addition the following articles (listed alphabetically by author rather than by country) provide readily accessible descriptions and analyses of these aspects of the economic geography of many of the largest countries of the continent.

BAER, W., 'Regional Inequality and Economic Growth in Brazil', *Economic Development and Cultural Change*, **12** (1964).

BERRY, B. J. L., 'Relationships between Regional Economic Development and the Urban System: the Case of Chile', *Tijdschrift voor Economische en Sociale Geografie*, **LX** (1969).

DICKENSON, J. P., 'Imbalances in Brazil's Industrialisation', in Hoyle, B. S. (Ed.), *Spatial Aspects of Development*, J. Wiley & Sons, London, 1974.

GILBERT, A. W., 'Industrial Location Theory: its Relevance to an Industrialising Nation' (Colombia), in Hoyle, B. S. (Ed.), *Spatial Aspects of Development*, J. Wiley & Sons, London, 1974.

LAVELL, A. M., 'Regional Industrialisation in Mexico; some Policy Considerations', *Regional Studies*, **6** (1972).

MORRIS, A. S., 'Regional Problems and Argentina's Economic Development', *Geography*, **57** (1972).

SEMPLE, R. K. and GAUTHIER, H. L., 'Spatial–Temporal Trends in Income Inequalities in Brazil', *Geographical Analysis*, **IV** (1972).

SLATER, D., 'Underdevelopment and Spatial Inequality', *Progress in Planning*, **4** (1975). (Part 2 on Peru.)

SMITH, C. T., 'Problems of Regional Development in Peru', *Geography*, **53** (1968).

e) The problems of the peripheral areas of various Latin American countries arising from overpopulation (relative to resources), outmigration, and the absence of job opportunities and social and economic infrastructure affect the majority of the population of most Latin American countries. These sorts of problem are treated specifically in the following books and papers (though they are, of course, also dealt with in most of the references under d) above).

ACKERMAN, W. V., 'A Development Strategy for Cuyo, Argentina', *Annals of the Association of American Geographers*, **65**, (1975).

BARKIN, D. and KING, T., *Regional Economic Development: the River Basin Approach in Mexico*, Cambridge University Press, Cambridge, 1970.

BUTLAND, G. J., 'The Human Geography of Southern Chile', *Institute of British Geographers*, Publication no. 24, 1957.

CARVAJAL, M. J. and GEITHMAN, D. T., 'Economic Analysis of Migration in Costa Rica', *Economic Development and Cultural Change*, **23** (1974).

EIDT, R. C., *Pioneer Settlement in North East Argentina*, University of Wisconsin Press, Madison, 1971.

FITCHETT, D. A., 'Irrigation Agriculture and Regional Development in Southern Argentina', *Annals of Regional Science*, **8** (1974).

FLORES, E., 'The Significance of Land Use Changes in the Economic Development of Mexico', *Land Economics*, **XXXV** (1959).

KIRBY, J., 'On the Viability of Small Countries; New Zealand and Uruguay Compared', *Journal of Inter-American Studies*, **17** (1975).

ROBOCK, S. H., *Brazil's Developing North-East*, Brooking Institution, Washington, 1963.

UNITED NATIONS, 'Rural Settlement Patterns and Social Change in Latin America', *Economic Bulletin for Latin America*, **10** (1965).

UNITED NATIONS, 'Geographical Distribution of Population in Latin America and Regional Development Problems', *Economic Bulletin for Latin America*, **8** (1963).

WEBB, K. E., *The Changing Face of North East Brazil*, Colombia University Press, New York, 1974.

WHETTEN, N. L., *Guatemala: the Land and the People*, University of Florida Press, New York, 1961.

f) Efforts which have been and are being made to colonize the empty heartland of Latin America have attracted much attention, mainly on the basis of studies of particular projects or groups of projects. See, for example,

BARRETT, T., 'Colonisation of the Santo Domingo Valley', *Annals of the Association of American Geographers*, **64** (1974).

CRIST, R. E. and GUHL, E., *Pioneer Settlement in Eastern Colombia*, Smithsonian Institute, Washington, 1956.

CROSSLEY, C. R., 'Santa Cruz at the Cross-Roads: a Study of Development in Eastern Bolivia', *Tijdschrift voor Economische en Sociale Geografie*, **52** (1961).

EDELMAN, A. T., 'Colonisation in Bolivia, Progress and Prospects', *Inter-American Economic Affairs*, **20** (1967).

EIDT, R. C., 'Pioneer Settlement in Eastern Peru', *Annals of the Association of American Geographers*, **52** (1962).

FRIEDMANN, J. and BANCHI, H. S., 'Forestry Enterprise in Three Zones of Southern Chile', *Tijdschrift voor Economische en Sociale Geografie*, **61** (1970).

FLETCHER, G. R., 'Santa Cruz: a Study of Economic Growth in Eastern Bolivia', *Inter-American Economic Affairs*, **29** (1975).

KIRBY, J., 'Agriculture Land-Use and the Settlement of Amazonia., *Pacific Viewpoint*, **2** (1976).

KLEINPENNING, J. M. G., 'The Integration and Colonisation of the Brazilian Portion of the Amazon Basin', *Nijmeegse Geografische Cahiers*, No. 4, Nijmegen, 1975.

SIEMENS, A. H., 'Recent Spontaneous Settlement in Southern Veracruz', *Canadian Association of Geographers' Occasional Paper*, No. VI, 1964.

STEWART, N. R., 'Japanese Colonisation in Eastern Paraguay', *Publication 149, N.A.S.*, Washington, 1967.

WAGLEY, C. (ED.), *Man in the Amazon*, University of Florida Press, Gainesville, 1974.

WOOD, H. A., 'Spontaneous Agricultural Colonisation in Ecuador', *Annals of the Association of American Geographers*, **62** (1972).

g) The role of transportation in the structuring and re-structuring of the geographical pattern of societies is of fundamental importance. The following publications present in more detail some of the issues involved.

BARBER, G. M., 'A Mathematical Programming Approach to a Network Development Problem' (the Colombian Highway System), *Economic Geography*, **51** (1975).

GAUTHIER, H., 'Transport and the Growth of the São Paulo Economy', *Journal of Regional Science*, **8** (1969).

MOMSEN, R. P., *Routes over the Sierra do Mar*, Rio de Janeiro, 1964.

SOBERMAN, R. M., *Transport Technology for Developing Regions: a Study of Road Transport in Venezuela*, M.I.T. Press, Cambridge, Mass., 1966.

STANN, E. J., 'Transport and Urbanisation in Caracas 1891–1936', *Journal of Inter-American Studies*, 17 (1975).

STOKES, C. J., 'The Freight Transportation System of Colombia', *Economic Geography*, 43 (1967).

STOKES, C. J., *Transportation and Economic Development in Latinn America*, Praeger New York, 1968.

WILSON, G. W. *et al.*, *The Impact of Highway Investment on Development*, Brookings Institution, Washington, 1965.

CHAPTER 10

Emerging Themes: Towards a New Economic Geography of Latin America

In the two preceding chapters an attempt has been made to isolate, describe and explain the major components in the contemporary economic geography of Latin America. We turn now to indulge in some geographical prediction on the likely trends in the spatial patterns and ordering of the economy of Latin America, based on our understanding of the processes out of which the current economic geography has emerged and on an interpretation of the way in which these processes will work in the future, when they will undoubtedly also be influenced by new forces and new restraints.

In descending order of probability we can predict four distinct, but not altogether unrelated, prospects for the future geography of the Latin American economy. Firstly, we may confidently expect the geographical expansion of the 'core areas' at their fringes; secondly, we anticipate a strengthening of the potential for development in second-order cities and even in other lower-order towns; thirdly, there seems likely to be the deliberate encouragement of major, new growth areas within the framework of national development planning which pays greater attention to spatial aspects of economic development; and fourthly, there is some chance that more effort will be directed towards the opening-up and colonization of parts of the empty heart of the continent. This chapter will be devoted to an examination of these likely developments and their implications for Latin America's economic geography. Thereafter, in a final chapter of the book we shall discard the assumption of continued full national sovereignty on the part of the continent's many individual nations and evaluate the possible spatial impact of Latin American economic integration, in whole or in part.

The Geographical Expansion of the Core Areas

To predict the geographical extension of the core areas at and around their fringes does not involve a very intensive use of the 'crystal ball'. Such a prediction implies no more than the continuation of the process of central city growth which has been readily apparent for periods of up to 100 years in some Latin American countries and for at least a generation in all the rest. The process has already produced some of the world's largest urban agglomerations. This is an aspect of the human geography of Latin America which has been discussed at length elsewhere in the book in the sections on the urban environment and urbanward migration (see Chapters 5 and 6). As shown too, in Chapter 8, the growth process has, in part, been a function of the concentration of secondary and tertiary economic activities in these cities and this continues to be a phenomenon of great current importance, given the almost continental-wide adaptation of large scale industrialization as the most appropriate policy for achieving development. It is, moreover, a geographical growth process which will continue to be important unless and until there is very positive government intervention in the location decision-making processes of both private entrepreneurs (both domestic and foreign) and of state capitalists.

In the meantime, however, there is great pressure of demand for land in and around these cities. This arises not only from the need for space in which to carry out the economic activities themselves, but also from the derived demand for land for new residential areas, for wholesaling and retailing functions, for educational, social and medical facilities, and for transport developments, particularly new roads. All this creates physical, as well as technical and economic, problems in the expansion of the continuously built-up areas. This is demonstrated time and time again in the great cities of the continent.

The continuing expansion of Mexico City, for example, has created problems arising from the difficulty of building on badly-drained land susceptible to flooding during the rainy season. Caracas, the capital of Venezuela, lies in an elongated intermontane basin and its expansion has literally 'filled up' the limited space available. Similarly, Rio de Janeiro has come to occupy all the suitable, and even some inherently unsuitable, terrain in its hill and mountain-girt location around the Bay of Guanabara. Even a much smaller city such as La Paz, the capital of Bolivia, high up in the Central Andes, is finding that the expanding needs for living and working space are necessitating new developments up on the general plateau level (at around 3700 metres) in valleys below which the city has traditionally sheltered as its inhabitants sought out an altitude for living and working somewhat less demanding on the abilities of both men and machines. Similarly, San José in Costa Rica has had its growth potential adversely affected by the high probability of repeated pollution in and around the city by volcanic ash from one of the several nearby still-active volcanoes.

Such physical problems associated with particular sites do not, however, frustrate the geographical expansion of all Latin American core cities. Buenos Aires and Montevideo, for example, the two major Latin American cities which developed more rapidly than any others in the late nineteenth and early twentieth centuries, could carry on expanding outwards from the centre over the pampas for as far ahead as one can possible visualize. Even Bogotá, the highland capital of Colombia and which by way of contrast has grown rapidly only over the last 30 years, still has the bulk of its intermontane basin to cover with the paraphernalia of urbanization! But even for these cities—as well as for the others which are affected directly by the problems of the physical attributes of the site in which they are located—there are immense technical and economic problems associated with growth. These problems, although they have so far been insufficient in themselves to overcome the lethargy and/or unwillingness of governments to take sufficient action to restrain the growth of the primate and other large cities, are now causing many governments to think more seriously of the possibilities of the dispersal of population and other time-honoured physical planning approaches to the phenomena of congestion and overcrowding. Unfortunately, in this respect, as in the process of industrialization and urbanization, the efforts at physical planning have usually been copies of measures taken in the quite different economic and social circumstances of North American cities and hence not very appropriate for tackling the problems of the much poorer cities of Latin America.

The provision of urban motorways on a grand scale, à la Los Angeles, in cities like Caracas and Mexico, is probably the most blatant example of the misuse of foreign technology and of a most inappropriate approach to investment priorities in the capital-scarce situations of most Latin American countries. Such urban motorways do little to improve the lot of the overwhelming majority of Latin American city dwellers who are forced to make increasingly difficult journeys to and from work in generally inadequate public transportation facilities. In these two cities, where urban motorways have been a favourite way of using up scarce capital resources over the last 25 years, without their having made much difference to urban congestion, attention and resources have only recently been directed to the construction of rapid mass-transit facilities. So far, the development of such mass public transport facilities has been on a very limited scale though, increasingly, the sheer pressure of demand for urban transport from the rapidly growing populations now seems likely to lead to their continuing expansion into city-wide systems.

Increasing government interest in physical planning approaches to the problems of the core city is one reason for the attention that is now being given in several Latin American countries to the concept of the 'Greater Metropolitan Region' as a means of taking the pressure off the centre itself. Another reason for this, and probably an even more important one in present circumstances in Latin America, emerges from concern for the increasing inefficiency of the core cities as locations for secondary and tertiary industry. This inefficiency, which is, of course, reflected in higher costs of production and lower profits for the entrepreneurs concerned, arises from infrastructure deficiencies of a serious nature in most of the cities concerned. These include the inadequate provision of water and drainage facilities; an excessive pressure of demand on public electricity and gas systems with consequential off-loading of some consumers at peak periods;

and an unpunctual work-force as a result of traffic congestion and overcrowded, inefficient public transport facilities. Thus, on the part of both public authorities and private employers there is now a recognition of the need for the core city to be geographically converted into a core region. This involves either the creation of a multi-nucleated metropolitan region or the development of a linear form of urbanization along the main lines of communications from the city: particularly along inter-urban motorways in which large investments have been made in recent years in many Latin American countries.

Three examples of this type of spatial transformation of the core area stand out already in Latin America. The first is in Mexico where the country's capital has already expanded outside the area that was designated for it after the revolution of 1910, viz. the Federal District of Mexico with its area of about 4000 square kilometres, some of which, however, is too mountainous to be useful for urban development. As the combination of demands for living, working and recreational/cultural space rose rapidly under the impact of Mexican industrialization and a burgeoning bureaucracy in the 1940s and early 1950s, so a greater Mexico City spilled over into the surrounding state with the same name. Expansion has since continued until the continuously built-up area of the capital city now extends out over a radius of up to 20 kilometres from the city centre in most directions with all the inevitable problems for mass-transport facilities and from deficiencies in the public utilities as mentioned above. This expansion, moreover, occurred even before the local industrialization process moved into a later phase in which manufacturing plants, with a need for extensive areas of land, were built in Mexico for the first time. These are the modern, single storey plants which are concerned with the assembly of consumer durable goods ranging from the simplest, such as mass-produced cooking pans, through commodities like cookers and refrigerators, and up to the most complex, the motor car assembly plant. In addition to their land-in-plenty requirement, however, the nature of the organization and the successful operation of such factories demands first-class access to good transport facilities so that they can be constantly fed with the components needed in their assembly-line techniques. Some of these types of plant managed to find adequate space for establishing their production facilities and good transport connexions on the fringe of the built-up area of Mexico City. Many others, however, became convinced that, given the problems of Mexico City itself, an extra-Mexico City location was essential to efficient operation.

Coincidentally, but fortunately, by this time, the first stages in Mexico's superhighway system were approaching completion (see Figure 10–1). As these new roads were essentially capital-city focused, rapid freight transport facilities to and from Mexico City in several directions became possible. This meant that a continuing flow of component parts to new assembly plants from older established component suppliers in the city would be assured. Thus, several large towns, notably Puebla, Cuernavaca, and Querétaro, all within two hundred kilometres of the capital, could then be considered as possible locations for this type of industry.

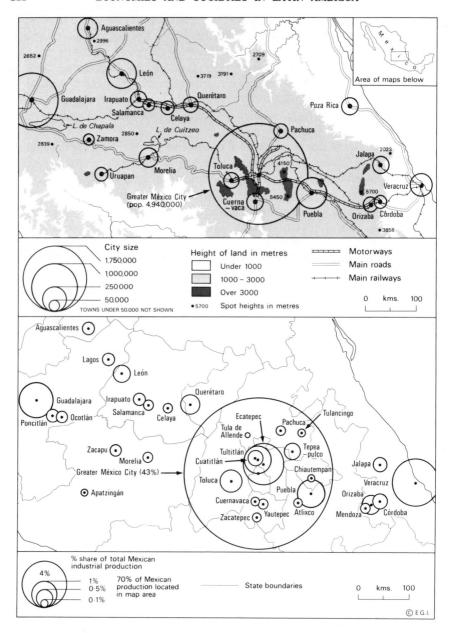

Figure 10–1. Aspects of the economic geography of Mexico's Core Region

Puebla, for example, was particularly well-favoured as it was served by one of these new highways and it lay, moreover, on the route between Mexico City and Veracruz, the country's main port through which the imported components for the French and German cars (to be built in Mexico under licences from the firms concerned) would be shipped. This combination of favourable location factors resulted in Puebla's choice as the site for the country's largest assembly plant for motor vehicles.

This decision was perhaps the single most important one for producing a major geographical 'breakthrough' in the geography of industrial activity in Central Mexico. This breakthrough consisted of the response to the prospects for opening up a spatially much more extensive economic growth zone (based on the development of secondary and tertiary activities). This could be extended over much of the eastern part of the Central Valley of Mexico and so link up, over the mountainous eastern edge of the plateau, with the coastal industrial region based on oil refining and petrochemicals as well as on other processing activities based on imports through Veracruz, Mexico's main port. This geographical development now achieved the potential to replace the geographically much more limited growth zone of Mexico City and its immediate environs (see Figure 10–1).

In that motor vehicle assembly plants have strong backward linkages to component suppliers, the opportunities for further related industrial development in Puebla and its vicinity were obviously good, and other factories, functionally related to the assembly plant, have decided to locate there. Veracruz, at the end of this line of development from Mexico City, has, on the other hand, started to enjoy the development advantages of forward linkages from its traditional port industries which could be associated, as already indicated above, with the industries based on locally produced oil and gas. Thus, Mexico City, Puebla and Veracruz are becoming nodes of development along the main axis of transportation facilities, including both modern road and rail systems, in the eastern part of central Mexico. This could mark the early stage of the evolution of an urban–industrial region of a kind similar to many which already exist in the industrialized world.

The extension of this economic growth zone westwards from Mexico City has, to date, been less apparent but some industrialists have already chosen locations in Querétaro, León and even as far west as Guadalajara, some 400 km from Mexico City. Such locations are attractive on the basis of a more readily available and a lower cost labour force and by virtue of their having fewer problems of services and space than in Mexico City. In addition, however, promotional efforts by the states and cities involved have created certain advantages for industrialists locating in this region. These include the remission of local taxes for new industry over periods of up to ten years, a greater willingness by the local authorities to provide the kind of infrastructure that the companies need, and the provision of factory buildings in industrial estates. The Federal government, too, is now also participating in the provision of such facilities and is, moreover, encouraging the location of industry in such new centres.

It must be emphasized, however, that the Central Mexican growth zone described here is not yet in existence except in a tentative or, at best, an embryonic form. The concentration of secondary and tertiary economic activities is still very much Mexico City-orientated (see Figure 10–1) and there are still powerful forces at work to keep it that way. But the dice are no longer loaded quite so heavily in its favour and it now seems highly likely that we shall be able to talk in general terms about a Mexican Central Valley Urban–Industrial Region stretching for over 800 kilometres from Veracruz to Guadalajara by the late 1980s with, by then, about as many inhabitants, if not as much industry and commerce, as in the present-day Boston–New York–Washington region of the United States. It should, however, be remembered that this developing more-extensive industrial growth zone, as compared with the hitherto almost exclusive concentration of industrial activities on Mexico City itself, still represents an excessive degree of spatial concentration of high-value economic activities when viewed in the Mexican national context. The whole of the Veracruz–Mexico City–Guadalajara region, shown in Figure 10–1, constitutes only about 12 per cent of the land area of the country. The region presently contains about 40 per cent of the national population—and about 70 per cent of the country's industrial production.

A second example from present-day Latin America where a spatial transformation of the core area is occurring is in Venezuela (see Figure 10–2). In Venezuela, as already indicated above, the capital city, Caracas, has grown to such an extent that it fills the small intermontane basin in which it was first established as a colonial town. Possibly more so than any other Latin American city, except for the new creation of Brasília, the urban form of Caracas approaches most closely that of a modern, motor-car-orientated North American city. It lacks an effective centre (the plaza and the immediate neighbourhood of the Spanish colonial town have been overwhelmed by post-1940 developments) and the urban functions that traditionally assemble in and around the city centre are scattered along the urban motorway which runs the length of the intermontane basin in which Caracas lies. In addition an airfield (for private flying), a large university campus, the extensive grounds of the military officers' club, and the big houses in extensive gardens of the relatively large numbers of wealthy Venezuelans and foreigners eat up the remainder of the desirable spaces along the bottom and lower slopes of the valley. On the flanking hills the modern flats, as well as the shanty towns of the workers and the unemployed take up much of the rest of the land on which building is possible.

Manufacturing industry has developed more recently in Venezuela than in Mexico, partly because of contrasting governmental policies in the first half of the twentieth century and partly because American manufactured goods gained and maintained preferential entry to Venezuela after 1940 in return for certain preferences which were extended to Venezuelan oil in U.S. markets. These factors inhibited the effective development of other than small-scale industry until the late

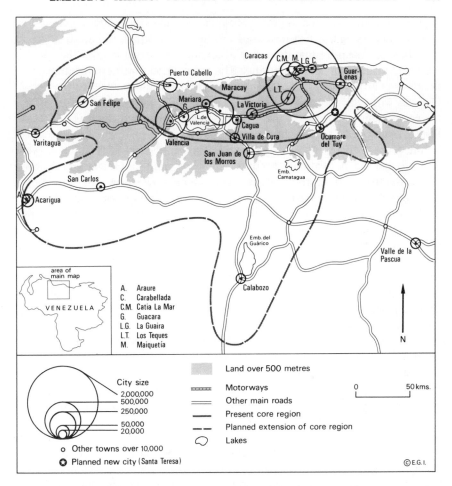

Figure 10–2. Venezuela: its Core Region and possible expansion

1940s. It was only since then, as government incentives were introduced in order to encourage the substitution of imported manufactured goods by domestically produced products, that industry started to expand rapidly (employment in manufacturing was only about 60,000 in 1941: by 1966 it had increased to over 200,000). Most of the new industry naturally sought Caracas locations, for reasons given in the previous chapter, and the city quickly achieved a manufacturing sector making goods for consumption in the dominant market of the country, viz. the Caracas region itself. Thus, in 1963 Caracas contributed over 44 per cent to the national total of value-added in manufacturing. However, the dispersal of industry soon became something of a necessity because of the physical problem of the lack of room for expansion. Industrial development thus spilled over into adjacent locations in the state of Miranda and by 1963 these locations were almost as important as Caracas itself for their contribution to industrial production: between them by that date they accounted for 55 per cent of the country's total value-added in manufacturing. The most important new location in this period was at the port of La Guaira—on the coast immediately to the north of Caracas with which it was connected by a super-highway running through the intervening mountains. (The primary purpose of the new highway was to provide a fast route between Caracas and the new international airport which had to be built on the coast as there was insufficient room for it in the city itself: it did, however, also provide the motivation for industrial expansion in La Guaira which now, in effect, became part of the Caracas conurbation.) However, the mountainous physiography of the immediate environs of Caracas prevented expansion on the periphery of the city to anything but a limited degree, so, as industrial expansion continued, potential industrialists had to seek more distant locations for their enterprises. The formerly important colonial towns of Maracay and Valencia, 80 and 130 kilometres respectively to the west of Caracas, were given direct access to the capital in the early 1960s by a new motorway which opened up significant possibilities for their industrial development. They have since become industrial growth poles, closely connected with Caracas but nevertheless with their own local multiplier effects, in a region hitherto relatively undeveloped.

Thus, the core area of Venezuela has been extended from being identified geographically simply with the capital city itself to one of a zone, roughly 200 kilometres long (but without any significant depth), stretching from the coast at La Guaira, through Caracas, over the intervening mountains to the shore of Lake Valencia along which the former colonial towns are being converted into manufacturing cities, and then back to the coast at the now rapidly growing oil refining and petro-chemical cities of Puerto Cabello and Morón. It is worth noting that the oil and petro-chemical industries of these two cities are geographically integrated to the demands for such products in the Venezuelan economy. In this respect they provide a locational contrast with the earlier development of oil industry related activities on the Paraguana peninsula, where the locational choices for refineries were related to external markets and, as we argued in Chapter 8, came to constitute 'enclave economies' in the Venezuelan context, geographically as well as economically isolated from the mainstream of the country's development.

As in the case of the central valley of Mexico, it is a motorway which forms the axis of this new extended growth zone. This provides a facility for the fast interchange of products by interdependent firms and for the low cost marketing of articles for final consumption as well as for the receipt of raw materials and other inputs imported into Venezuela through the ports at the two ends of the zone. However, as shown in Figure 10–2, a massive geographical expansion of the core region is now envisaged. This is to take care of Venezuela's rapid population growth and the equally rapidly rising living standards consequent upon the wealth generated by the country's petroleum export industry. Thus, the infrastructure (of modern highways, of communication systems, of energy availabilities and even of railways—which Venezuela has so far done without, except for a few isolated mineral lines) of this larger region is being developed, and expansions of the pre-existing centres of population are being planned. The expanded region will, as shown, be over 300 kilometres from north to south and up to 400 kilometres from east to west and thus also constitute a 'growth region' on a geographical scale similar to that of 'Boswash' in North America or the 'Golden Triangle' in N. W. Europe. If things eventually work out as envisaged, then the fully-structured region of industrial and commercial developments with a large number of cities and towns constituting a hierarchy of central places all inter-connected by modern transport and communication systems will provide another prime example of effective geographical expansion of a previously very small core region. One final note of warning, however. As the inset map on Figure 10–2 clearly shows, even the expanded core region constitutes a small part of the country as a whole, such that other elements of the spatial aspects of Venezuela's development remain to be reorganized.

The third main example of this core region-expansion type of development in Latin America is in Brazil (see Figure 10–3). Brazil's post-1920s pattern of development produced a clearly defined bi-nuclear core region, focused on Rio de Janeiro and São Paulo. Using a Western European geographical scale we would be inclined to describe these two multi-million cities as widely-separated poles of growth. In Brazilian terms, however, as seen from Figure 10–3, the 400 kilometres between them makes them virtually next-door neighbours. Their inter-urban connections by rail, modern highways and air services (the Rio-São Paulo link is one of the 10 busiest air routes in the world) are close and effective and a new coastal highway between the two cities (and which will also open up hitherto relatively inaccessible parts of this very beautiful coastline for tourist and recreational activities) will be completed in 1978. Referring back to Figure 9–15, however, one can also see that a third city, Belo Horizonte, located inland and about the same distance of 400 km from both Rio and São Paulo, also emerges as one of the main centres of economic activities in Latin America. It has, however, remained well behind the other two in its scale of development. Since the 1960s, however, the locational attractions of Belo Horizonte, particularly for the metal industries including iron and steel developments and for other producers' good industries, have been significantly enhanced as a result of the establishment of Brasília as the new capital of the country (replacing Rio de Janeiro). Brasília's growth—to be discussed later in the chapter—as a centre of the 'government industry' (an important part of the tertiary economic sector) has had the effect of 'pulling' some development inland and this has been most important in the case of Belo Horizonte, which was a 'natural' location for such new activities. Given that it had already achieved importance as the main inland centre of industrial development, the much improved transport facilities from Rio and from São

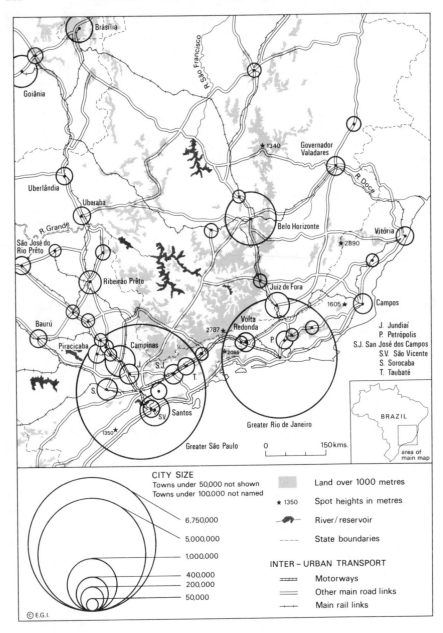

Figure 10–3. Brazil: cities and transport facilities in the Core Region

Paulo which joined at Belo Horizonte en route to the new capital, greatly enhanced its locational attractions.

Thus, Belo Horizonte has become the apex in the emerging triangle of Brazil's core region of development. Indeed, it now seems likely to increase its size and standing, and its ability to attract industry, more quickly than either Rio or São Paulo where diseconomies of scale are emerging in these cities with populations of almost 5 and over 7 millions respectively. Following on from this geographical pattern of development in south-east Brazil, it seems reasonable also to hypothesize that urban industrial development will, in the future, not be restricted to the three nodes in the network, but will also tend to locate along the routes connecting them as well as in a further extension of the region to the west and north to take in Vitória (on the coast) and Governador Valadares which was, indeed, even in the 1960s one of Brazil's fastest growing cities at the crossing points of important east–west and north–south routes to and from the core-region proper.

This produces the chance, therefore, of a geographically much extended, multi-node core area to absorb the developments that might otherwise have been almost entirely concentrated on Rio and São Paulo. It is interesting to note that the geographical scale of this potential multi-node core region is also roughly the same as that of 'Boswash': the United States great north-east coast urban industrial area. By the year 2000 there is an even greater chance, than in the case of the core regions of Mexico and Venezuela, that 'Sãoriobelo' could be a megalopolis of equal importance. Paradoxically, in the shorter term of the next decade or so, the spatial structuring of this 'development triangle' seems likely to be the main economic geographical effect of the establishment of Brazil's new capital. Only after that is the geographical impact of Brasilia itself on the interior likely to become the more important element in Brazil's changing economic geography.

Elsewhere in Latin America the dynamics of the geography of the core regions are still basically expressed in the continued peripheral expansion of the primate cities which simply grow outwards and so overwhelm smaller surrounding settlements; as demonstrated very clearly in the cases of greater Buenos Aires and greater Montevideo. There is an exception in the case of Chile, where the separation of the capital from its port by a distance of some 100 kilometres suggests the likelihood of developing an axis of development with major nodes at each end. So far this seems to have happened hardly at all, for Valparaíso has achieved little more than the maintenance of its status based on handling the country's external trade and on the limited development of port industries. Greater Santiago continued to secure the bulk of activities and employment in the country's industrialization efforts: this was recognized by a previous government which introduced some planning mechanisms which aimed to stimulate expansion elsewhere in the region outside Santiago itself. The overthrow of the Allende government in 1974 seems, however, to have put a stop to even those modest efforts to interfere in the location decisions of industry and commerce.

Growth Possibilities in Second-Order Cities

A second trend which appears likely to be important in re-shaping the economic geography of Latin America lies in the strengthening of development possibilities for second-order and other cities and towns, apart from those which enjoy the benefits of expansion as a result of 'spread' or 'overspill' effects from the primate city. As we have previously tried to demonstrate, there has not usually been much national concern for the fate of second-order and other cities at an official level: for good political reasons. In spite of the lack of official encouragement of such development, however, they have sometimes managed to achieve economic success by attracting some modern manufacturing and tertiary industry. One notable case of this has been the success of Guayaquil in Ecuador in challenging the earlier dominance of Quito. It should be noted, however, that the economic advantage it enjoyed of a coastal location was, in itself, not sufficient to give Guayaquil the edge over Quito. Its local élite group also had to involve itself in efforts to achieve sufficient political power at a national level to curb the influence of the capital. This it did so successfully that the government has been run over long periods of time essentially by Guayaquil-sponsored politicians for, of course, the benefit of Guayaquil. Thus, its achievement of a parity of status with, and even of more rapid economic growth than, Quito lies fundamentally as much in political considerations as in economic ones. Had it also been the capital city then it is not difficult to imagine that Guayaquil would have readily achieved as high a degree of primacy within Ecuador as Lima has in neighbouring Peru; or as Buenos Aires did in Argentina, following the mid-nineteenth century success of the porteños (the inhabitants of Buenos Aires) in winning quite convincingly their political struggle with the rival inland cities which were the more important colonial period centres.

In Argentina the country's other cities have had the almost imposible task of keeping up, even relatively speaking, with the expansion and development of the capital. As shown in the previous chapter, even Córdoba's success in attracting industry has depended to a large degree on the significant local efforts which its leading groups of citizens made to achieve this end without much encouragement from Buenos Aires. But now, with the attraction to Córdoba of part of Argentina's motor-car industry, the city has been propelled into what should be a period of self-sustaining industrial growth—assuming that this is possible in the context of Argentina's rather stagnant economic situation.

However, Córdoba has been something of the exception in respect of its success in attracting modern industry, for although Argentina has a number of quite large, second-order cities, mainly the provincial capitals, they remain for the most part as essentially marketing and administrative centres (Figure 10–4). The industrial components of their economies are mainly limited to processing locally available raw materials (for example, sugar, as in the case of Tucumán) and/or to producing bulky products required locally but which have to be made from im-

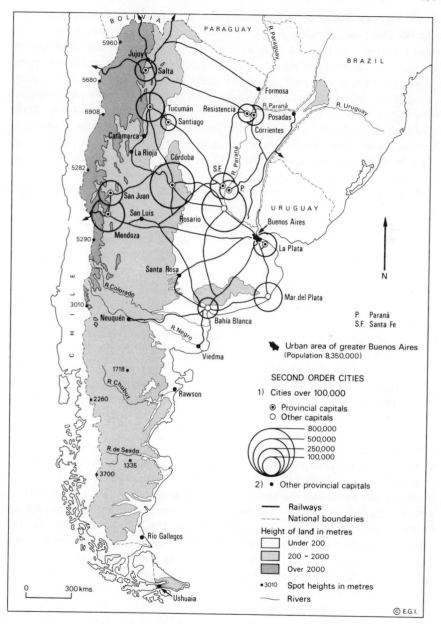

Figure 10–4. Argentina: the system of cities

ported raw materials of much smaller bulk: for example, the ubiquitous coca-cola bottling plant. Rosario and, to a lesser degree, Bahía Blanca have enjoyed some industrial growth; but even so and rather surprisingly, little until recently beyond the industries engendered directly by their exporting functions in respect of Argentina's food and agricultural raw materials production and by their status as important railway centres. In that even these two advantageously located cities have largely failed to participate in the more fundamental process of Argentina's industrialization based on the growth of industries producing goods to substitute for imports over the past 25 years, it is quite clear just how much difficulty has stood in the way of the industrialization of the country's other provincial capitals and other leading towns and cities.

However, there are now some indications that the real costs of the continued expansion of Buenos Aires beyond the seven million inhabitants' level are, at last, being recognized and the first effective governmental measures to inhibit the location of new industrial activities in and near the capital city have recently been taken. There is, as yet, however no accepted national strategy for implementing a fundamental change in the geography of Argentina's economy but industrial 'growth poles' have been designated, including some in the geographical periphery of the country, and, in a general revival of Argentina's economic fortunes, these could well be locations for new and expanded activities, particularly in a situation in which the government was able to refurbish the country's rail transportation system which nominally provides good inter-urban connections throughout most of the country. (Figures 9–8 and 10–4)

A country showing a major contrast in respect of the geography of industrial development is Colombia, where, indeed, the overall spatial patterns of economic and social development in the post-independence period have diverged markedly from the model which has been demonstrated to apply to Latin American countries in general. The Colombian economy has developed with a group of quite distinct and geographically separate centres of secondary and tertiary activities. Although the capital, Bogotá, has always been the largest centre in terms of population, it has never had the same degree of primacy as has been usual in Latin America. In fact, as Table 9–3 shows, in terms of economic activities as opposed simply to population size, it did not even in the 1960s stand in first place. The primary centre in this respect was still occupied by Medellín, the provincial capital of Antioquia, the economy of which, for reasons which have never been very adequately explained, developed an industrial component, initially in textiles and then in a range of other goods, from the third quarter of the nineteenth century onwards. Historically, it thus stood well ahead of Bogotá which remained without a significant modern industrial sector until the 1930s. Since then both cities have attracted new industry, though Bogotá, starting from the lower base, has enjoyed a more rapid rate of increase and, in particular in the 1960s, appears to have secured the largest share of the expansion in the country's newest industries, possibly because rapidly improving transport facilities during this period have made much wider areas of the country accessible to Bogotá (Figure 10–5).

But in this period the rivalry between Bogotá and Medellín has also been accompanied by other major developments in the geography of the Colombian economy. Cali, the country's third city, was, until the earlier 1950s, mainly functioning as a departmental and regional centre and as the centre for the sugar-refining and other agricultural-processing industries of the fertile Cauca Valley. Thereafter, however, it succeeded in establishing itself as a significant alternative centre for the location of industrial activities. During the 1950s and the early 1960s it was particularly successful in attracting many new industries which were established for the first time in Colombia by foreign companies, including pharmaceuticals, paper, rubber and other similar industries. Its location gave it better access to major port facilities than either Bogotá or Medellín (see Figure 10–5) and this seems to have been an important factor in attracting foreign industry. Moreover, as its industrial sector was less developed, it was more susceptible to the adoption of new methods of production (particularly high levels of mechanization) which the foreign companies wanted to employ. Thus, in this period, Cali became Colombia's most rapidly growing industrial city. More recently, however, it too seems to have fallen behind Bogotá in the industrial growth rate achieved.

The geographical dispersal of industrial and associated expansion in Colombia, however, has gone even further than to this trio of cities. Two other cities, Barranquilla on the Caribbean coast, and Bucaramanga, in the Middle Magdalena valley, have also both enjoyed rapid industrialization, thus contributing to a rather complex spatial industrialization pattern which, moreover, also includes some components in smaller centres like Cartagena, Pereira and several other towns located between the main cities themselves (see Figure 10–5).

Why is it that this unusual spatial pattern of industrial development for Latin American conditions has emerged in Colombia? It is certainly true that the difficult physiographic conditions of Western Colombia (see Figure 10–5) contributed to the ability of some of the provincial centres to maintain a degree of independence from Bogotá. These physiographic conditions made the improvement of the bad transport facilities between the different parts of the country expensive and difficult to achieve so that many industries had to be orientated to local rather than national markets. But Colombia was not exactly unique in Latin America in these respects. Elsewhere, however, the transformation of the industrial sector from small-scale to larger-scale manufacturing—with one firm often given a monopoly for supplying the whole of the national market—meant location in the single, central core region. The fact that this did not happen in Colombia appears in large part to be a reflection of the greater political importance of regionalism. Such regionalism was institutionalized in the political system and thus had to be recognized by successive national governments which did not, therefore, as in other countries of Latin America, create conditions in which a capital city location for industrial development was made almost inevitable. It also reflects the

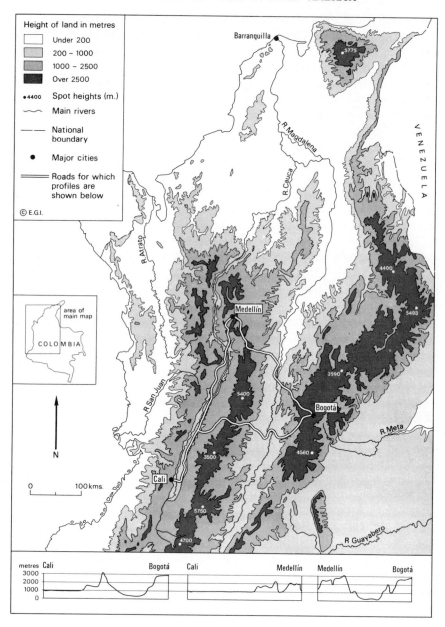

Height of land in metres

- [ ] Under 200
- 200 – 1000
- 1000 – 2500
- Over 2500

●4400   Spot heights (m.)

～～   Main rivers

— —   National boundary

●   Major cities

═══   Roads for which profiles are shown below

© E.G.I.

area of main map

COLOMBIA

N

0   100 kms.

Barranquilla

R. Magdalena

R. Cauca

R. Atrato

VENEZUELA

5775

4400

Medellín

5493

3590

5400

Bogotá

R. San Juan

R. Meta

3800

4560

Cali

5750

4700

R. Guayabero

metres | Cali   Bogotá   Cali   Medellín   Medellín   Bogotá
3000
2000
1000
0

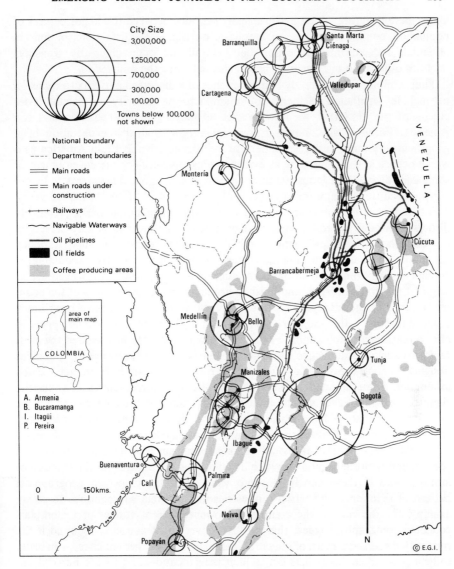

Figure 10–5 (a) and (b). Colombia: the physical and human geography of its Core Region

longer period during which bad transport facilities between the major centres of population continued to put an emphasis on regional satisfactions of market potential. Indeed, interconnection between all the main cities, by transport facilities other than air, has only been achieved since the mid-1950s.

Thus, Colombia has already had experience of a dispersed pattern of expansion to include significant elements of manufacturing activity in second-order cities—of the kind that we now predict as more generally possible in Latin America. Paradoxically, however, one must note that this expectation of a geographically more dispersed pattern of industrialization in Latin America as a whole occurs at the same time as evidence presents itself for the development of some centralization of industrial development in Colombia. This seems to be occurring because of major improvements of transport facilities in the last 15 years. This means that entrepreneurs are now finding that the national market, relatively dispersed through several centres though it is, can be most profitably served by the concentration of production activities in one centre. By such a policy economies of scale in the manufacturing process at one centre produce large enough savings to more than offset the additional transport costs involved in getting raw materials in from, and finished products out to, other parts of the country, given that the transport costs which have to be incurred have been much reduced through better and more reliable facilities. This argument would appear to offer a reasonable explanation for the way in which Bogotá has secured the most rapid expansion of activities over the last ten years. However, not all industries designed to serve the national, rather than a regional, market have, in fact, located in Bogotá. Some selected one or other of the alternative centres of industrial significance. This suggests that a multiplicity of centres in the country can now be accepted as the 'norm' from which further developments in the spatial ordering of society can proceed. Each of the five main individual centres is, indeed, sufficiently large and diversified that it should be able to sustain continued growth even in competition with the capital city with its additional advantages for the location of industry etc. If these conclusions are valid, then the dispersed geographical pattern of secondary and tertiary industries in Colombia will continue to set an example for the rest of the continent. However, recent studies of Colombia's economic geography suggest that positive government action is required if the relatively dispersed pattern of industrialization is to be further enhanced—in order to help persuade industrialists not to limit their locational sights too narrowly to Bogotá, the centre of government. Second-order cities elsewhere in the continent have an even greater need of similar government action to help them to achieve a continuing prepensity for self-sustaining industrial growth.

At this stage one needs to remind oneself that the phenomenon of a national territory divided into a 'core' and 'periphery' occurs at strongly contrasting geographical scales in Latin America. For instance, it will be noted that Brazil's core area triangle of Rio de Janeiro, São Paulo and Belo Horizonte extends over an area which is almost as large as the area covered by the more complex system of growth towns and cities in Colombia. Whereas the former can still be described as a core region, in that it leaves most of Brazil's occupied territory outside its limits, the Colombian case involves a system of centres which are geographically dispersed over almost all parts of the country which are populated to any large extent. (Compare Figures 10–3 and 10–5.) This contrast in geographical scale is even more clearly demonstrated in the cases of Puerto Rico and Venezuela. The small Caribbean island territory of Puerto Rico has a total area which fits easily into the Caracas/Maracay/Valencia 'core' region of Venezuela (see Figure 10–6).

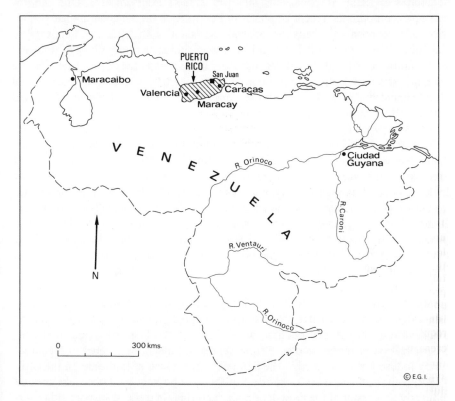

Figure 10–6. Venezuela and Puerto Rico: contrasts in geographical scale

Thus Puerto Rico, by the geographical standards of the Latin American countries which we have examined so far, could hardly be considered as likely to have a regional development problem of any great significance! However, this is not so, for even Puerto Rico considers itself to have a regional problem arising from the propensity of San Juan, the capital, to attract most of the new developments in the economy at the expense of development everywhere else in the island.

Puerto Rico's rapid economic development in the period since the early 1950s had been based on industrialization under particularly favourable circumstances: viz. a position inside United States tariff barriers, but without U.S. tax and other obligations. Though this has meant a speed and ease of development which is un-matchable by other small nations of Latin America, the latter are, nevertheless, almost without exception, aiming at the same end of diversification into manufac-turing industry to increase employment and to raise per capita income. Puerto Rico's experience of spatial problems associated with industrial expansion, therefore, is not without importance for another dozen or so nations and territories of Latin America, most of them in the Caribbean area. One can, for example, compare the recent emphasis in Puerto Rico on the geographical disper-sion of new economic activities around the island with what has happened in Jamaica. Puerto Rico and Jamaica have many similarities, in both environmental and cultural terms, but they differ markedly in respect so far of the latter's failure to establish any effective programme of comprehensive and co-ordinated spatial development planning. As a result there has been consequential continued marked concentration of activities in Kingston, its capital city.

The somewhat earlier decision to industrialize by Puerto Rico at first seemed certain to enhance further the already dominant status of the island's capital, San Juan, which enjoyed a virtual island monopoly of central city services and amenities. This was because few investors would wish to look, or even think of looking, beyond its metropolitan areas as a location for their factories in a situa-tion in which the industrialization programme was based essentially on the impor-tation of raw materials and semi-manufactures and the export of the finished products of the markets of the United States. Such trade to and from Puerto Rico could only be handled through the port of San Juan as the smaller ports of the island could offer neither the capacity nor the facilities (e.g. container berths) required by the traffic. Thus, to locate a factory elsewhere in the island would in-crease transport costs above the level incurred in a San Juan location and in addi-tion would isolate the enterprise from professional, technical and other services available only in the metropolitan area. Thus, in the first few years of the in-dustrialization programme over 55 per cent of all new jobs created in manufac-turing industry were located in the San Juan area which at that time, in the early 1950s, contained less than 20 per cent of the total population. Other jobs created indirectly as a result of the growth of manufacturing (in trade, transport, other ser-vices and government etc.) were even more heavily concentrated in the metropolitan zone, which thus seemed set to become a classic example of a core area. Its further development would then have the effect of gradually denuding the rest of the island of economic growth potential as it attracted population in in-creasing numbers from the provincial towns and the country areas whose in-habitants sought better opportunities in the capital (see Figure 10–7). Such a developing geography of the island's economic activities was, of course, fully in keeping with the general model for Latin American countries as presented in Chapter 9.

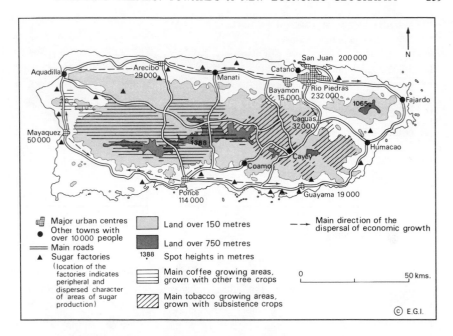

Figure 10–7. Puerto Rico: aspects of its economic and social geography

However, in 1953 the Puerto Rican government recognized the need to establish a positive industrial location policy designed to contribute to the 'orderly'
regional development of the island. The policy, as first defined, laid principal
emphasis on establishing as many factories as possible in the smaller and more
remote towns which, it was argued (from the sort of evidence presented above),
had not been getting their proportionate share of the new industrial jobs. Thus, an
Industrial Decentralization Programme was formally launched and has since
remained the basic principle for guiding the development of Puerto Rico's spatial
economy. A variety of means have, however, been selected to implement the
programme. In the early stages most attention was given to the improvement of
the infrastructure outside San Juan, but such physical planning developments (for
example, new and improved roads and a factory construction programme) are
effectively only disincentive-minimization measures. In themselves they could do
nothing to ensure that a factory's profits were at least as great when it is located
away from San Juan as when it is in the metropolitan area itself. Thus, it was later
accepted that positive financial inducements were necessary to persuade industrialists to accept that profit maximization could arise from their choice of a
location for their factory outside San Juan.

Three forms of financial incentives designed to decentralize industry were
evolved and are illustrated in Figure 10–8. In general, the incentives were intended

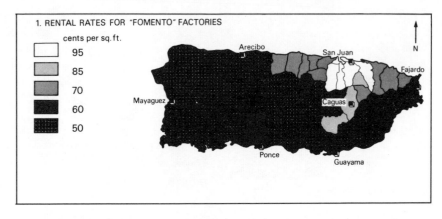

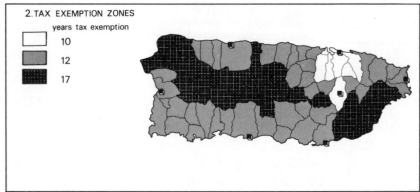

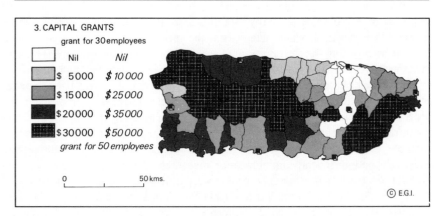

Figure 10–8. Puerto Rico: government incentives for industrial decentralization

to be inversely proportional to the probability of a location securing industrial development based on entrepreneurial choice and thus they reflect the early aim of the programme to secure at least one factory in each municipality. This aim was always seen as one which would not necessarily secure an optimum economic solution to the spatial pattern of secondary economic activities, but it was considered to be desirable in order that all parts of the island could be positively involved in the growth sector of the economy and so ensure the programme of the widest possible support. Though politically attractive, however, it was soon recognized that such an approach to the location of manufacturing activities was economically untenable.

Since the middle 1960s, therefore, a second aim of the programme has become the dominant element in the government's industrial decentralization efforts. This second aim involved the achievement of major industrial expansion in the island's main regional centres: viz. Arecibo, Mayaguez and Ponce. Efforts in this direction have proved to be much more successful, and that success, as shown in the contrasts between the 1950–60 and the 1960–70 changes in the distribution of population and of manufacturing industry (see Figure 10–9), now provides the basis for a more balanced geography of Puerto Rico's economic progress. It is one, moreover, which appears likely to offer net gains to the economy when compared with both other alternatives; viz. concentration of development in San Juan, on the one hand, and its dispersal around all the municipalities, on the other. This net gain arises because the relatively small provincial cities can be expanded cheaply; when compared, that is, with the high marginal costs of expanding the infrastructure of San Juan and the high social costs inherent in further growth of industrial and associated traffic in its already overcrowded streets. Expansion of the provincial cities not only has the effect of giving higher rates of returns on the funds invested by the government in infrastructure improvements, but it also enables the industrialists themselves, on locating in one of the regional centres of concentrated development, to count on some, at least, of those external economies which they could have expected to achieve by a location in San Juan. In such circumstances, the additional financial help given by the government to industrial investors through the incentives seems to have been more than sufficient to offset the extra costs to an industrialist of a location away from the metropolitan region. Thus, the enterprise is more profitable in the out-of-San Juan location. At the same time the cost of the incentives made available to the private investors by the government appears to have been less than the additional amounts of public investment which would have been required for expanding the capital city's infrastructure and other services, has all the plants concerned opted for a San Juan location. In other words, there is good *prima facie* evidence that the Industrial Decentralization Programme has been of new overall economic advantage to the economy.

In terms of the actual developments which resulted from the decentralization policy, the most significant breakthrough was achieved by the initial establishment

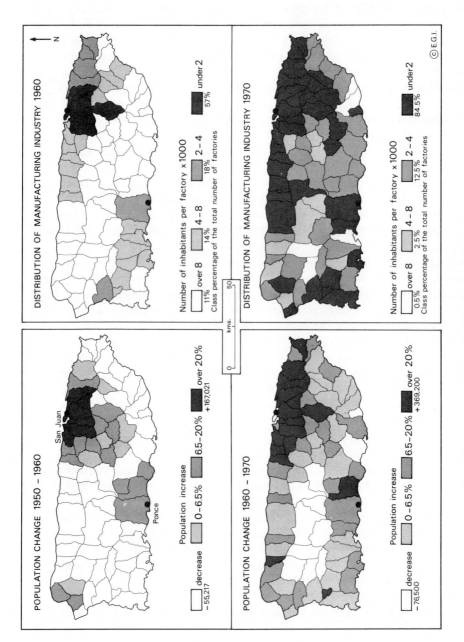

Figure 10–9. Puerto Rico: the Distribution of Population and Manufacturing Industry 1950–70

of an oil refinery at Ponce, on the south coast, in 1962. This has since provided the basis for a later development of an associated petrochemical complex which is now in a period of strongly self-sustaining growth. The conclusion that this development represents a major success for the Industrial Decentralization Programme lies in the fact that without financial incentives to locate elsewhere, the oil refinery would almost certainly have gone alongside an earlier oil refinery which had been located on the outskirts of San Juan. Its location at Ponce and the subsequent other developments which have taken place around it have created a viable south coast complex. This is important not only in itself, but also as a countermagnet to the San Juan/Caguas node at the other end of the main north–south route across the island. Arecibo, Mayaguez and Fajardo (see Figure 10–7) have provided other centres for development. Their expansion, which has also been realized through the location there of major industrial enterprises, has ensured that most of the island's working population now lives within daily commuting distance of job opportunities in the growing secondary and tertiary sectors of the economy. The development has certainly reduced the incentive for migration to the capital and it created the basis for reorientating Puerto Rico's spatial economy so as to produce a better 'balance' between San Juan and the rest of the island. Significant social, as well as economic, advantages also flow from this new pattern, for most of the population has also been put within reach of centres on which an island-wide availability of educational, cultural and medical facilities can be effectively based.

It should perhaps be made clear that none of these developments has meant that San Juan itself has not continued to grow. Quite apart from its industrial functions, San Juan is the centre of the island's expanding tourist industry and it remains the centre of administration and government and the highest-ranking commercial and professional services. Because of these service functions there is inevitably some new growth of job opportunities in San Juan, no matter where on the island a factory is established. All the Industrial Decentralization Programme has done is take away from San Juan the additional industrial growth element that it would otherwise almost inevitably have had. This, of course, makes the problem of metropolitan growth that much easier to handle: a consequence with very obvious advantages.

In the meantime, the direct and indirect job opportunities created in the second-order centres through their effective industrialization will eventually bring these towns to a size and degree of affluence at which they can begin to offer competition to San Juan in the provision of a widening range of services. The speed with which this can be achieved, and so create an ordered and integrated hierarchy of central places in Puerto Rico, depends essentially on the continuing success of the Industrial Decentralization Programme, for only a significant industrial sector in the economies of the towns concerned can provide the economic base on which a development of their other functions will follow.

And what is true in this respect for Puerto Rico applies in general to most other

Latin American countries. The need to get industry into the second- (and third-) order cities and towns is a pressing geographical need which is gradually being recognized in most parts of the continent, and the examples of Colombia and Puerto Rico on this issue are not without importance for other parts of the continent. This is starkly demonstrated in the case of Uruguay.

There, structural economic change, involving industrialization and an expansion of tertiary activities, started much earlier than in most other Latin American countries. Since then, however, continued centralization of development has produced an entity more like a city-state than a nation (Figure 10–10). Thus, today many of the country's available resources have to be devoted to sustaining Montevideo. The costs of doing this clearly seem to exceed the benefits arising for the Uruguayan economy as a result of diseconomies of scale and the inefficiency with which the services of the city are organized. This means that too few resources are available to invest in the effective development of the country's periphery. Thus much of this remains almost devoid of activities other than an insufficiently capitalized agriculture making less than optimum use of the land's capabilities and from which migration to Montevideo still continues as a result of the lack of opportunities and of a reasonable level of service facilities. In light of this, one is perhaps justified in hypothesizing a relationship between the willingness of successive governments to allow Montevideo to secure almost all the development that the country has achieved since the commercialization of agriculture and the country's poor economic performance over the last 40 years. It certainly appears possible that an alternative spatial structure for the Uruguayan economy, whereby the total costs of providing the goods and services required by the community could have been reduced (by eliminating the high marginal costs involved in expanding the public services in the capital city), might well have created conditions in which continued economic growth was still possible. By the introduction and implementation of a policy to provide sufficient incentives to get some of Montevideo's economic activities out into selected growth points in the rest of the country, the spatial pattern could be turned into one with strongly developing, dispersed centres of activities around which the rest of the national economy could be successfully integrated into a structured, coherent whole. Indeed, the development of a system similar to that in Denmark or New Zealand, for example, where agricultural and non-agricultural activities jointly produce expanding economies whose benefits are enjoyed by inhabitants of all parts of the national territories, could alter the outlook for Uruguay.

Meanwhile, Uruguay can perhaps be seen as a warning to other Latin American countries which, in their early decades of structural economic change, largely seem content to 'let things happen *where they will*', rather than *where they ought to be*, in the interest of maximizing short-term economic growth. However, the high rate of growth thus achieved will soon fall away as the country has to pay for the diseconomies and the heavy social costs of highly centralized geographical patterns of development. The Puerto Rican approach, with its emphasis on

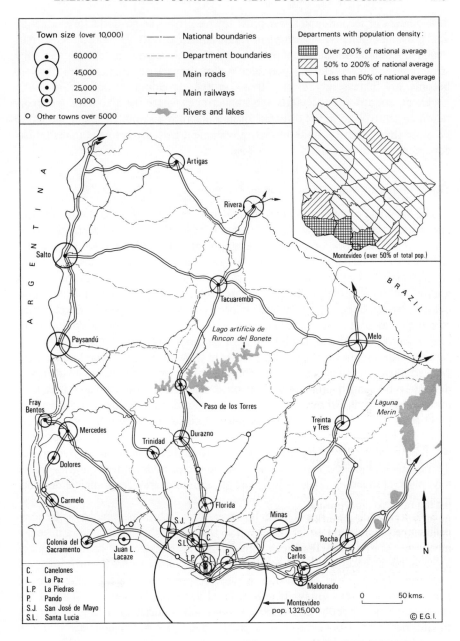

Figure 10–10. Uruguay: a spatial economy dominated by Montevideo

development in second- and lower-order towns, provides one model for evaluation and possible emulation elsewhere in Latin America, after its adjustment to particular conditions within a national territory. Such moves to secure more fully structured and more closely integrated national space economies seem likely to become an increasingly strong trend in the development policies of Latin American countries, particularly the smaller ones where the additional transportation costs involved in the dispersal of manufacturing should be small enough to be more than offset by quite modest government help given to the industrialists concerned, as in the case of Puerto Rico.

The Planning of Major New Growth Zones

The third line of evolution of the future economic geography of Latin America arises from the deliberate fostering of major new urban/industrial growth zones within the framework of national development planning. To some extent, this represents an alternative strategy to the one which has just been discussed. The two strategies are alternatives for two reasons. Firstly, because investment funds are limited, both in the public and private sectors, such that there may well be a choice between financing either one major new growth centre or the development of some or all of the second-order cities; and secondly, because the choice of the one or the other tends to involve different attitudes and outlooks towards spatial aspects of development. It is not that either of these reasons necessarily makes the two strategies mutually exclusive, for available funds could be divided and differently persuaded pressure groups on development strategies could each be partially successful. To date, however, in Latin America the two strategies seem in practice to have turned out to be alternatives and so they appear likely to remain. There are certainly strong possibilities that a few more Latin American countries will follow the major new growth zone philosophy so whole-heartedly embraced by Venezuela and Brazil over the last decade or so, whilst other countries, as we have seen, are tending towards the more structured overall geographical development efforts.

Both Venezuela and Brazil have, however, already been persuaded of the compelling need to incorporate into the spatial structure of their economies a development representing a marked break with the past in terms both of its nature and of its location in relation to the previously effectively-used part of their national territories. Out of their persuasion in these respects have emerged the cities of Brasília and of Ciudad Guayana in Brazil and Venezuela respectively. Though the latter name is probably one hundred times less familiar than the former, its significance is probably several times greater and hence will be considered here in somewhat more detail. But first we must present a brief evaluation of Brasília in terms of its relationship to the existing and the future economic geography of Brazil.

In Chapter 9 we saw that the area in which Brasília is located cannot be considered part of the 'empty heart' of the continent. Nevertheless, Brasília's location was remote, and quite deliberately so, from the pre-existing centre of gravity of Brazil's population and economic activities. (see Figure 10–11a where, on the right-hand map, we see the relationship of Brasília's location to that of all Brazilian state capitals.) The intention in this choice of location for the new Federal Capital of Brazil was quite openly and deliberately to switch the country's geographical focus of attention from the coast and the world overseas to the interior of the country. However, it could not be so far in the interior as to make the whole project ludicrous and impracticable. The project can, therefore, be differentiated geographically from the idea of Brazil's 'manifest destiny'—a development which will be considered later in this chapter.

Brasília might have been conceived and built 'merely' as a major new city on the fringes of the effectively settled part of the country. As such it could, in the long term, have been expected to achieve an important role in various central place functions in the system of Brazilian cities and to serve as the new centre for the developing west. But the 'west' was not really developing all that strongly, and in respect of its needs for a centre it already had its own central places of a size, and with ranges of functions, appropriate to the level of development achieved. These included towns like Goiania, Goias, and Uberaba, each of some 50,000 to 100,000 inhabitants. Instead, Brasília was intended to be and was, indeed, built specifically as the country's new capital city. It was to be the capital, moreover, of one of the world's largest nations and one which had visions of its own potential for future growth and development. Brazil's new capital had, therefore, to provide a foretaste of what that potential would be like when finally fulfilled. And because it was to be the capital city, it would have a population of civil servants and foreign nationals with all that that implies in terms of high per capita purchasing power (by Brazilian standards). Therefore the city could not be allowed gradually to develop from a frontier-style, 'hicktown' entity into a multi-functional city as time passed by. On the contrary, it had to be planned and laid out in the style that would be expected by these high-income inhabitants and by its visitors. This motivation for Brasília carried, of course, implications for the scale of public investment which would be required in housing, in the city's social and economic infrastructure and in the necessary provision of facilities for access by land and air. Similarly, there were scale-of-investment implications for those private-sector institutions, both national and foreign, which had to do their business in the nation's capital. The scene was thus set for a high and continuing rate of investment in the 'device' which had been evolved to alter the shape of Brazil's economic geography.

The extent to which the concept and the plan, as formulated along the lines set out above, have been implemented in the period since 1961 is a far more significant and outstanding phenomenon than the degree to which Brasília has not yet, in social or cultural terms, approached the status of the former capital of the country, Rio de Janeiro. In a physical sense Brasília has emerged according to the master plan (see Figure 10–10a). This plan, however, did not envisage something else that has also emerged: namely, a series of shanty towns around the periphery of the designated area, serving the needs of the tens of thousands of unplanned immigrants who have moved to Brasília to find jobs and other opportunities created by the immense programme of construction (see Figure 10–11b). But this unplanned phenomenon, though perhaps embarrassing to the architects and politicians, is one measure of the success of the project in an economic sense. The scale of the undertaking has been so great that a self-sustaining economic entity has quickly been created and as a consequence has attracted migrants who would otherwise have moved to the south-east of the country. Brasília, in other words, has already succeeded in deflecting away from the core area of the country around Rio and São Paulo part of the population flow into it that would otherwise have occurred.

At the same time Brasília's connections with the rest of the country have gone ahead as planned. A national highway network, which is well on the way to completion, will link Brasília with all the other populated parts of the country. These highways have also enhanced the value of land with access to them and, in spite of an undue indulgence in land speculation rather than in serious efforts at effective land-use, they have created the beginnings of what could turn out to be powerful corridors of economic growth. Even agricultural activities have developed in response to the opportunities presented by the rapidly developing markets in Brasília and by the lower transport costs on foodstuffs made possible by the highway development programme. Brasília has, moreover, even started to fulfil the functions for which it was planned, and both law-makers and the civil servants have begun to participate in the relocated activities of governments switched from Rio de Janeiro. Again the pressures *against* change have been turned by the magnitude of the forces *for* change which have been created in the building of the new capital.

It is, however, still too soon to evaluate the likelihood of Brasília becoming a second Canberra which, having relatively quickly reached a level of activity and of size consequent upon the relocation of governmental activities, then achieved little further growth based on the multiplication of activities and functions, for several decades. Such a 'fate' for Brasília is still possible and, if it occurs, will inevitably make the city an isolated enclave of modern activities within an area of stagnation whilst 'all the action' remains in Rio and São Paulo. Should this happen, then Brasília, in spite of all its architectural splendours, could only be described as a failure.

However, by the second half of the 1970s the odds seem to be heavily weighted against such a failure, whilst there is a significantly higher probability that Brasília will become an active component in the spatial ordering of the Brazilian economy. It will function in this respect as the counter-magnet to Rio and São Paulo and thus create the chance of firmly establishing long, and strong, corridors of economic growth between itself and the older centres. All this will, of course, serve

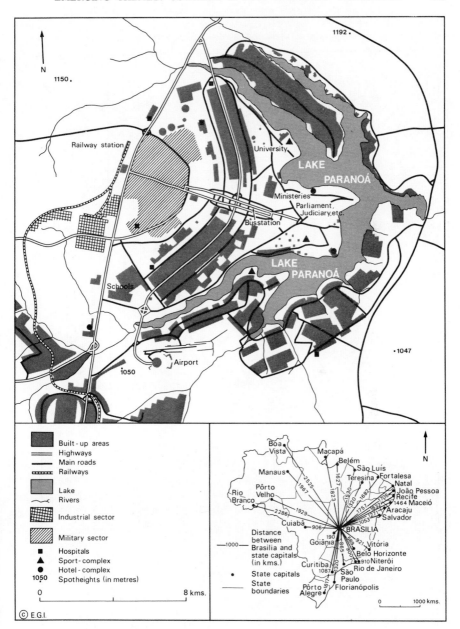

Figure 10–11a. Brasília: urban structure and its national location

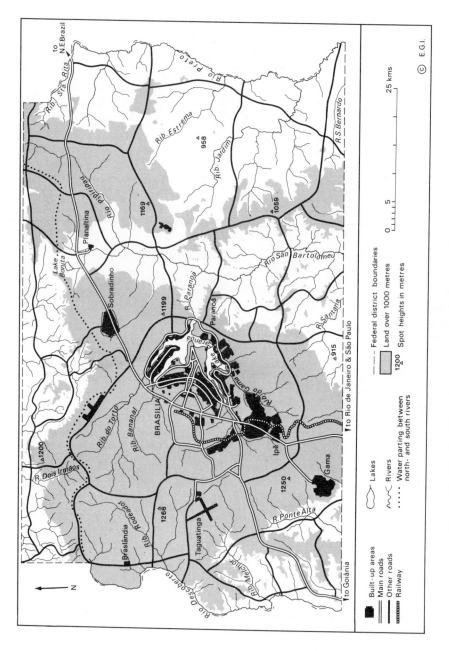

Figure 10–11b. Brasília: urban and transport developments in the federal district

to reduce the pressure of population and industry growth which would otherwise have occurred on the core area. This type of spatial re-development has, however, yet to start and will be dependent upon the establishment of manufacturing industry in Brasília. But an effective start to the much more recently considered industrialization process of the new capital may well necessitate positive financial penalties to inhibit the location of industries in the Rio/São Paulo/Belo Horizonte triangle of growth. The possibilities of such penalties being introduced seem, at the moment, to be rather remote and thus Brasília will have a much harder task to achieve self-sustaining growth in this hitherto undeveloped and, indeed, unplanned sector of its economy.

A similar concern for the lack of a planned manufacturing industry component in its economy cannot be expressed about the other major Latin American example of a deliberately fostered, new growth zone: Ciudad Guayana in Venezuela. Its establishment and expansion has, in marked contrast with the plan for Brasília, been predicated mainly on the basis of the development of large scale manufacturing industry ranging from iron and steel through to consumer goods and it stands, therefore, as a markedly different kind of project from that of the better-known Brasília.

Ciudad Guayana has emerged out of a fundamental restructuring of what was originally a 'resource frontier' type of development based on the exploitation of iron ore (for export) and the production of hydro-electricity which was at first intended mainly for transmission to the Caracas Metropolitan region. These resource frontier developments, coupled with a high-cost iron and steel plant in its embryonic stages in the eastern part of Venezuela (see Figure 10–12), gave the post-revolutionary government of Acción Democratica, which was elected to power in 1958 following the overthrow of the long-lived dictator Jiménez, a chance to redeem one of its electoral pledges. Acción Democrática had sought and obtained its main support outside Caracas 'by courting the regional forces that had always been latent in Venezuelan history.' Thus the new government stood committed to the development of provincial resources rather than the further accumulation of wealth and power in Caracas: a somewhat fundamental change in the outlook for the country given that the chief concern of governments for the previous thirty, or even 300, years has been Caracas first and the rest of the country nowhere!

Acción Democrática's decision to redeem its promises in this respect, or rather to show that it was attempting to do so, persuaded it to make the so-called Guayana project the initial cornerstone of its regional planning policy. This emerged in the first place, simply because it was the obvious thing to do in that plans had already been worked out, and secondly, because of a deliberate political calculation that the Guayana project presented a somewhat easy (though certainly a bold) initial step towards effective regional planning in Venezuela. One is entitled to describe it as a 'somewhat easy' first step because the resource base for its development was so outstanding and its long-term economic viability appeared to

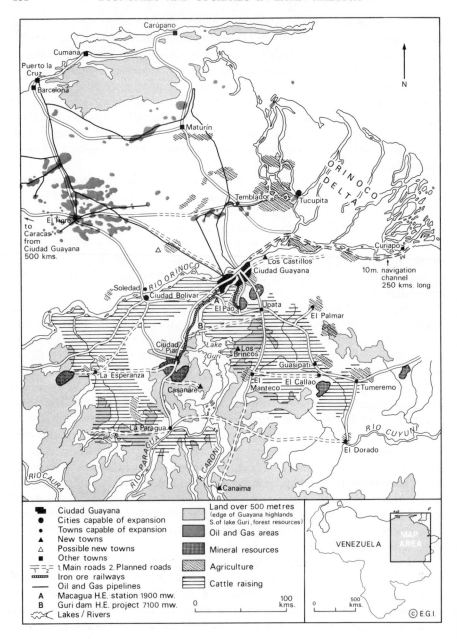

Figure 10–12. Venezuela: the growth region of Ciudad Guayana

be so apparent. In addition it presented a 'growth point' unhindered by pre-existing social and economic problems in that it was to be located in what was virtually an empty area of the country. This meant that thè Guayana development could therefore be handled from the politico-economic centre of the country as a Caracas-based and controlled project. It thus posed no political problems of devolved decision making and control (the similarities with Brasília in this respect are clear). Thus, decisions at the centre, on the type and the tempo of development, could be determined on the basis of technical and/or national considerations only. Such considerations have involved not only an evaluation of what industries were possible in the new region, given the market demands both within Venezuela and in possible export markets, but also calculations as to what mix of industries would produce the appropriate local multiplier effects at the right times in order to match the planned development of the associated urbanization and populating of the growth pole.

Comprehensive and detailed plans for the industrialization of the Guayana region (originally named Santo Tomé de Guayana and only later Ciudad Guayana), based in part on the mathematical modelling of the location factors and of inter-industry relationships, both locally in terms of forward and backward linkages and nationally in respect of market potential, were specified. These, however, have not worked out entirely as anticipated because of several unforeseen problems. These included, first, the prior existence at the location of significant overinvestment in tube-making facilities in the iron and steel plant. This had been developed in the 1950s when the Venezuelan oil industry was in a period of rapid expansion but, by the 1960s, there was a much lower rate of demand for pipes given the virtually stagnant state by then of the country's oil industry, which at that time was losing markets to lower cost producers elsewhere in the world. Second, there were initial difficulties in persuading private investors, in industries like aluminium smelting and pulp and paper plants, that the opportunities at Guayana were quite as good as the planners suggested. In addition to these factors which, of course, reduced the rate at which job opportunities were created, there was, as at Brasília, a demand for housing in Ciudad Guayana which moved ahead much more quickly than the planned rate of urbanization allowed for. There was, in other words, a greater than expected rate of immigration and so there were consequential squatter and shanty town problems as well as problems of unemployment and underemployment. In spite of these difficulties, however, employment at Ciudad Guayana has, nevertheless, moved ahead very rapidly indeed. Both industrial and urban developments are well under way and it is not an exaggeration to suggest that the overall project represents the largest and most significant development of a new growth pole anywhere in the world outside the Soviet bloc. Its continued expansion is set to transform the economy of eastern Venezuela and the description of the region as the 'Ruhr of South America' is probably wrong only in its timing. The massive industrialization of the Caroni and Lower Orinoco rivers seems only to be a matter of the one or two more decades that are needed to have it become fully operational. One can be reasonably confident about this eventual success of the venture given the continuation of rapid population growth in Venezuela and the country's ability to find the continuing flow of investment funds required to keep the development moving ahead. In this respect, of course, the quintupled revenues of the government, arising from the post-1973 changes in the price of oil underpin the venture's likely success—especially as oil revenues are now also available to finance the new railway which will link Ciudad Guayana with the Caracas region and so ensure closer geographical integration of the country's two growth zones.

Thus, a project of this scale and with such wide implications in many development fields necessitates the long-term commitment of many thousands of millions of dollars. Without the Guayana project the money might otherwise have been invested in different parts of the country in various growth points, whose scale of development could have been made suitable to provide local solutions to local problems of overpopulation and underdevelopment. The scale of the spending on the Guayana project has not gone unnoticed in the Andean states of Venezuela with their problems of access, of population pressure on land resources, and of the out-migration of their most active citizens. Nor has it been ignored in the State of Zulia which has been suffering from the relative decline of the oil industry especially in respect of the run-down of employment (due to the increasing mechanization and automatization in the industry). These are areas with large populations, many problems and also astute politicians and for them the Guayana development programme had a demonstration effect. Why not, they argued, get it copied in every part of the country where additional economic opportunities are required for rapidly growing populations and work forces?

How to deal with these areas and their claims came to represent a set of serious problems arising out of Venezuela's particular approach to the question of regional development. Guayana cannot, of course, be repeated elsewhere in the country. Not only is it a resource frontier-based project dependent on the availability of flows of various natural resources which happen to coincide in their locational availability in Guayana, but it is also the sort of planned development which, because of its size and complexity, demands centralized decision taking of a kind which is impossible for areas of the country with both people and politicians. Until recently the concentration of Venezuela's regional development efforts on the Guayana project meant that these other areas have been left as unaided as it was possible to leave them without running the risk of major local explosions. Calculations that an expanding Guayana would ultimately be able to absorb the surplus resources of labour that exist elsewhere in the country produced a relatively high-risk strategy which seemed unlikely to succeed because pressure of population elsewhere was building up too quickly. It also implies that those Venezuelans lacking opportunity elsewhere would be prepared to move to Guayana to better themselves and to leave behind, in their areas of origin, local populations whose reduced size is more appropriate to local opportunities. This was also a high-risk strategy in that it tended to assume that people could be forced to behave in an economically rational way. Given doubts over all these preconditions for the concentration of regional development efforts on Guayana, then the massive development of the new growth pole was certainly not going to solve the spatial problems of Venezuela at one fell swoop, or even indeed, present much more than a second-best alternative to the expansion of the Caracas metropolitan region which seemed likely to be preferred by most people from elsewhere in the country who had to move to find jobs anyway.

On the other hand, the Guayana project gave the national planners some feel for the spatial component in national economic planning and it has brought them up against the need to employ appropriate techniques in dealing with it. Forecasts for the future of the Guayana region necessitated forecasts of what was likely to happen elsewhere in Venezuela, so that the flow of information on regional planning throughout the country has been significantly increased. Thus, perhaps somewhat ironically, the Venezuelan decision to go for a major new regional development project did produce a situation in which the interest in spatial planning throughout the country, and in ways of carrying it out, was greatly increased. Since 1974, moreover, the fortunes of Venezuela have taken a turn very much for the better, given the greatly enhanced foreign exchange earnings and government revenues which could be secured from oil at $12–15 a barrel instead of $3 or less. In light of this, even the Guayana project no longer absorbed the resources the country could make available for regional developments—and since then it has been possible to strengthen other regional planning programmes and so take some of the 'steam' out of the anti-Guayana projects lobbies in other parts of the country.

Brasília and Ciudad Guayana thus represent a significant type of development in the changing geography of Latin America's economic activity and though they have, as shown above, been successful in many of their aims, the complete validity of them as instruments of regional development has still to be finally proven. Nevertheless there are now possibilities that the approach will be emulated elsewhere in the continent, even in the much poorer Central American region where preliminary studies have been made by the Inter-American Development Bank of such sorts of growth centres for the Gulf of Honduras, the Gulf of Fonseca and the Rio San Juan region of Costa Rica. However, the most notable new possibilities occur in southern Argentina and in Eastern Peru. In the former case, there is an outline plan for an industrial complex approach reminiscent of that of Ciudad Guayana and based in this case on the oil and gas resources of Patagonia. In the case of Peru the plan exists with respect to a frontier development along the so-called 'Marginal Highway', to which reference has already been made (see page 185). The concept of the 'Marginal Highway', however, leads us on to the fourth possible line of future development in Latin America's economic geography: that of the 'opening up' of the continental interior, and it is to this that we turn in the last part of this chapter.

The 'Opening-Up' of the Continent's Empty Heart

We have previously, in Chapter 9, noted the types of effort already made to open up parts of Amazonia. We saw then that, with the exception of recent large-scale agricultural colonization development schemes in Brazil based mainly on cattle raising in areas cleared from the jungle, little impression has so far been made on this massive region. We also hypothesized that economic motivations for increasing levels of food production in Brazil, whose population is now approaching 100 million (and still increasing at about 3 per cent per annum and becoming increasingly urbanized), could well provide sufficient incentive for massive clearance and development schemes; especially if the promoters of such schemes continue to enjoy favourable fiscal incentives. The 'jungle' is, in other words, becoming profitable not only in respect of land clearance for cattle raising but also for large-scale forestry and for mineral exploitation—especially, so far, for iron ore and for bauxite. Thus, given the continuation of a social and political structure in Brazil which accords not only status on entrepreneurs but also guarantees them the right to keep the profits they make more or less intact (without too large a slice being taken by government), then the rate of exploitation of this frontier region may well become a surprising feature of Latin America's economic geography in the 1980s. This possibility is further strengthened by the very firm policy of Amazonia development which is being followed by successive Brazilian governments. Thus, the political belief in the 'need' to integrate Amazonia into Brazil has begun to be operationalized by the extensive highway system which is being built in the region (see Figure 10–13). Furthermore, the development of the northern part of the Amazon is seen officially in terms of the opportunity it offers for the resettlement of migrants from the overcrowded and poverty-stricken dry north-east of the country. Over thirty million Brazilians live in the north-east and out-migration is inevitable if living standards are to rise from their currently very low levels (see Figure 9–9): the northern part of the Amazon basin is considered to offer an alternative to migration to the south-east of the country and the government is thus prepared to invest heavily both in official colonization schemes and in helping with spontaneous and private enterprise ventures. Such political and economic motivations for the development of Brazil's empty heart have now become powerful enough to overwhelm the fears of some scientists that such development will irrevocably upset the delicate ecological balance of the region with incalculable consequences, not necessarily only for, and within, the region itself. The warnings have been made but are not being heeded and thus, in respect of Brazil's Amazonia, the economic geographical question remaining to be answered is whether the resources of capital and manpower now being put into development will be sufficient to conquer the jungle on a permanent base and so add a new dimension to the economic map of Latin America.

The current likelihood of similarly-inspired transformations of other parts of the Amazon basin of the interior of Latin America are remote, with the possible

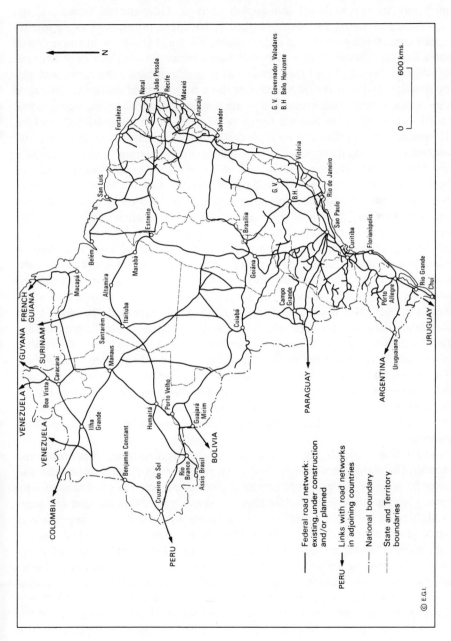

Figure 10–13. Brazil: the national road system

exception of developments in the northern fringes of the region. These lie immediately to the south of the growth zone of Guayana in Venezuela, the significance of which has been described above. Here, in response to the market openings created by successful establishment in Ciudad Guayana and its region of metallurgical, chemical, and pulp and paper industries etc., privately financed exploitation both of forest reserves and of probable mineral resources could well be stimulated. It is also conceivable that those large parts of the interior basins of the Amazon and other rivers which are potentially petroliferous may become worth exploiting by companies requiring oil supplies for international markets. However, sufficient incentive for such costly operations have arisen only as a consequence of the major upheaval in the traditional oil-producing world, particularly the Middle East, whereby a large part of the world's currently proven reserves have become so uncertain—for both political and economic reasons—that it has become worthwhile to look for alternatives. Even so, however, and this also demonstrates very well how the scale of development efforts in a region like Amazonia depends on exogenous factors, the successful exploration for oil in one of the world's two remaining frontier regions, viz. the Arctic reaches of Alaska, Canada and the U.S.S.R., on the one hand, and off-shore continental shelfs and slopes, on the other, will probably have the effect of postponing the likelihood of a really major search for oil in the Andean forelands of eastern Colombia, Ecuador, Peru, and Bolivia beyond the 1980s. Until after that, therefore, Latin American petroleum developments in the interior of the continent, such as those in the Putamayo region of Southern Colombia, and in adjacent areas of Ecuador, seem likely to remain rather small-scale and to develop only at a very modest rate. This is because, when compared with the two other frontiers for oil potential development, both of which promise supplies in the countries which need the oil, the potential supply from the Amazon basin would not necessarily be seen as being any more secure than oil from the Middle East—for very obvious political reasons.

Apart from possible commercial interests for exploiting and developing the frontier, the main alternative method is by means of government-sponsored and financed projects. As explained previously, however, there are good reasons why most government projects to date have not been successful in the past and seem unlikely to be much more successful in the future. In particular, it is impossible to envisage the economies or the political structures of any of the Andean nations concerned becoming strong enough in the next decade to enable them to face up to the awe-inspiring amount of capital investment needed to bring about the incorporation of their eastern provinces into their nationally integrated spatial economic and social systems. A former Peruvian President, Fernando Belaúnde Terry, nailed his political future to the development of his country east of the Andes. As an architect/planner by training he had the right sort of training and background to be able to conceive, and to see the immense implications for, the Upper Amazonian Marginal Highway running from Venezuela in the north to link up the Andean countries as far south as Bolivia in their regions of more or less zero development (see Figure 10–14). He was also able to demonstrate that the scheme was 'practical', in a physical sense, and that it would, when implemented, fundamentally change the economic geography of the nations concerned. Construction of parts of the road in Peru—together with a system of feeder roads designed to provide access for opening up new land for settlement—was started during Belaúnde's period as Peruvian President.

Unfortunately, however, neither the political nor economic motivation for its full implementation were strong enough to bring it anywhere near the point of really serious consideration by all the countries concerned. Politically not even the Peruvians, and especially not the largest sections of Peru's population living in the barriadas of Lima and other coastal cities or eking out an existence in the difficult physical and social conditions of the altiplano, saw the concept as being of more than theoretical validity for strengthening the Peruvian economy. In their ranking of priorities for investment funds they put it far below investment which would bring some shorter-term improvement to their difficult lot. Similar attitudes prevailed in the other countries concerned, though elsewhere not even minorities as large as that in Peru saw the Marginal Highway as a reasonably attractive proposal: possibly because the idea came from a neighbouring country with, no doubt, an eye to the chance it would give for national aggrandizement! The overthrow of Belaúnde has enabled the Peruvian politicians to dismiss the development from the range of alternative possibilities for capital investment, though, of course, the chances of its being taken up again by some aspiring politician always exist. Moreover, it does seem one of the obvious starting points for the economic development programme of the internationalists of the Group of Andean Countries, the work of which led to the Andean Pact for Economic Integration in 1969. However, the political reality of this international programme has yet to be tested against the strength of the diverse national forces in the Andean region—a topic for examination in the final chapter of this book.

Economically, the development of the interior by means of a capital-hungry marginal highway, or some other similar projects, appears likely to be well-nigh permanently postponed by two factors: first, by the size of the capital requirement. This was estimated, even in the late 1960s, at a minimum of $500 million spread over 10 years, a sum which was equivalent, at that time, to about 10 per cent of the total anticipated rate of availability of public investment funds in the four countries affected. Given the many other demands for capital resources in the countries concerned, the project is fairly obviously a non-starter without a prior agreement to get it financed overseas. And this introduces the second factor which works against the possibility of implementing the project. This is the high degree of probability that the investment will produce a very unsatisfactory rate of return given the need to discount future revenues (which are much more remote in time than the associated costs) at a rate approximating to the opportunity cost of capital in Peru and the other countries: at, say, a rate of the order of 25 per cent.

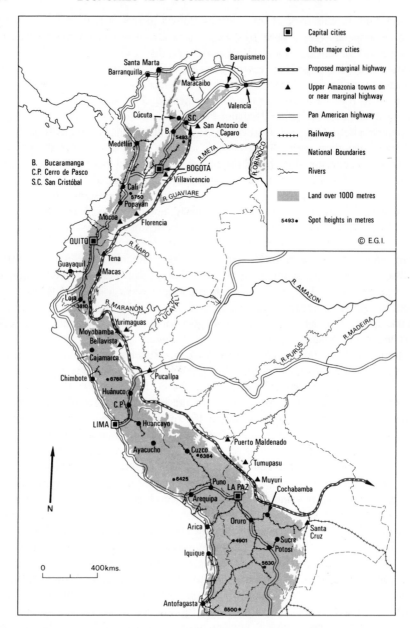

Figure 10–14. Andean South America: the Marginal Highway project

In as far as overseas investment in these countries is always likely to be concerned with financial returns on capital and not on intangibles like social and political benefits, then it seems likely always to be able to find better investment opportunities than that presented by the Marginal Highway Scheme. Yet, without a marginal highway, or some equally big public investment in the area, the chance of opening up the interior appears remote. Hence the low-order status which we must confer on this sort of development, amongst the various possibilities which can be seen as leading to the evolution of a more dispersed geography of Latin America's economic activities over the rest of the century.

Figure 10–15 is an attempt to represent cartographically the four separate development possibilities that have been briefly described in this chapter as the ones which could, over the next two decades, lead to important changes in the economic geography of Latin America. The trends have generally been presented in appropriate national contexts—based on the assumption that the continent will, in political terms, remain made up of a series of sovereign nation states each in full control of its own affairs and each largely concerned with its own development problems, irrespective of international considerations vis à vis its Latin American neighbours. Given the powerful forces of nationalism in all Latin American countries (as, indeed, in almost all countries around the world) and given the degree of physical separation of most Latin American nations (see Figure 9–1), then this is hardly an unreasonable assumption.

However, as shown in Figure 10–15, there are elements at a supra-national level which enter into the calculations on the future economic-geographical patterns of the continent—in respect, particularly, of trade between the countries. There have also been significant political developments over the past 20 years which are important for inter-Latin American potentials for growth and change. In light of this it would be inappropriate to conclude this book without indicating the geographical implications of such economic and political integration in Latin America. The question is considered in the last chapter—Chapter 11—though it must be made clear that its inclusion does not imply more than a recognition that there is some probability of effective integration in the continent which, if it occurs, will contribute to changing the geographical patterns of development. In the context of 1977, however, it is difficult to see this as anything more than another possible development trend, the implications of which one would only rank-order in fifth place behind the other four dealt with in this chapter.

Bibliography

The extensive bibliography at the end of Chapter 9 listed much of the literature from which the ideas set out in this chapter initially emerged. Careful study of books and articles mentioned in that bibliography provide further background to the geographic predictions made in this chapter and will help to persuade the reader of the reasonableness or otherwise of the author's ideas on the likely

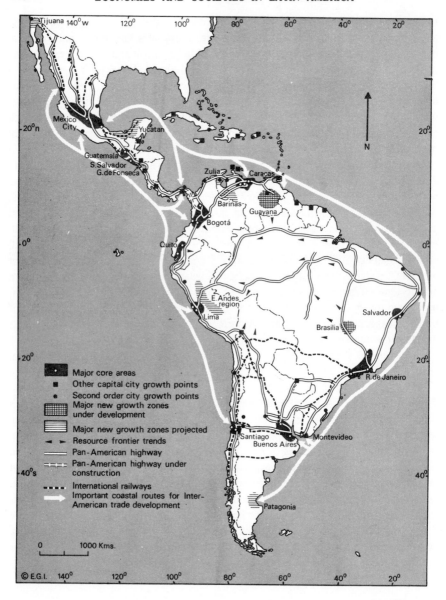

Figure 10–15. Latin America: a summary of its main spatial development trends

development in economic geography of Latin America. The following additional books and articles are also concerned with the geography of Latin America's development potential:

BELAÚNDE, T., *Peru's Own Conquest*, Lima, 1965.
The case for the development of Peru's oriente by a former President of Peru.
BROMLEY, R. J., 'Agricultural Colonisation of the Upper Amazon Basin; The Impact of Oil Discoveries', *Tijdschrift voor Economische en Sociale Geografie*, **63** (1972).
CURRIE, L., *Accelerating Development: the Necessity and the Means*, McGraw Hill, New York, 1966.
The case for urbanization as a policy instrument in Colombia.
DUSANT, E. R., 'Cibuco: A New Regional Growth Centre in Puerto Rico', *Ekistics*, **36** (1973).
A description of a development of a second-order growth centre.
FRIEDMANN, J., 'Urban-Regional Policies for National Development in Chile', in Rabinovitz, F. F. and Trueblood, F. M. (Eds.), *Latin American Urban Research*, Vol. 1, Sage Publications, Beverley Hills, 1971.
HILL, A. D., *Latin American Development Issues*, Proceedings of the Conference of Latin American Geographers, Vol. 3, C.L.A.G. Publications, East Lansing, 1973.
Most of the 18 papers in this volume are important for an understanding of geographical development problems.
KEARNS, K. G., 'Belmopin, Perspective on a New Capital', *American Geographical Review*, **63** (1973).
The location and development of Belize's new capital city: hardly a Brasília, but geographically significant in the context of Belize.
LYNCH, E., 'Propositions for Planning New Towns in Venezuela', *Journal of Developing Areas*, **7** (1973).
This specifies some of the urban aspects of the expansion of Venezuela's core region.
NELSON, M., *The Development of Tropical Lands, Policy Issues in Latin America*, Johns Hopkins University Press, Baltimore, 1973.
PICÓ, R., 'Geography and Development in Latin America', in Hill, A.D. (Ed.), *Latin American Development Issues* (see above).
This was the keynote address at the Conference. It is by a Puerto Rican geographer who was largely responsible for the geographical planning of Puerto Rico as described in this chapter and sets out the issues concerned very clearly.
POSADA, A. J. and DE POSADA, J., *The C.V.C., Challenge to Under-development and Traditionalism*, Bogotá, 1966.
Describes the plans to transform the Cauca Valley of Colombia.
POLEMAN, T. T., *The Papaloapan Project; Agricultural Development in the Mexican Tropics*, Stanford University Press, Stanford, 1964.
An evaluation of an integrated river basin development in a hitherto little populated part of Mexico.
RICHARDSON, H. W., 'The Relevance of Growth Centre Strategies to Latin America', *Economic Geography*, **51** (1975).
RODWIN, L., *Planning Urban Growth and Regional Development: the Experience of the Guayana Programme of Venezuela*, M.I.T. Press, Cambridge, 1966.
SACHS, I., 'Population, Technology, Natural Resources and the Environment: Eco-Development, a Contribution to the Definition of Development Styles for Latin America', *U.N. Economic Bulletin for Latin America*, **18** (1973).
STOUSE, P. A. D., 'Instability of Tropical Agriculture: The Atlantic Lowlands of Costa Rica', *Economic Geography*, **46** (1970).

VOLSKY, V. V. *et al.*, 'Regional Problems of Multipurpose Utilisation of National Resources in Latin America', *Soviet Geography*, **6** (1965).

YOUNG, R., 'The Plantation Economy and Industrial Development in Latin America', *Economic Development and Cultural Change*, **43** (1970).

CHAPTER 11

The Economic Geography of Latin American Co-operation and Integration

The Spanish and Portuguese empires in Latin America provided an organizational superstructure for the early development of the continent within the framework of which there were important elements of continental-wide similarity in spatial patterns and control systems which established a well-ordered hierarchy of, for example, cities and towns. After independence the new nations each went their own way with, as we showed earlier, the geography of development emerging first and foremost out of what the Spanish and Portuguese systems of government, administration, and economic development left behind. The physical separateness—even isolation—of most of the then rather limited enclaves of settlement and development quickly produced the break-up of the multi-national entities which emerged in the immediate post-independence period, viz. the failure of Gran-Colombia and of the United States of Central America to survive. Thereafter, economic colonialism tended to widen the gaps still more as the external ties of most Latin American countries were orientated very strongly to their trading partners in Europe and North America and away from each other.

By and large the physical separateness of the limited economically active regions of individual Latin American countries (see Figure 9–1) inhibited the need for close economic ties with neighbouring countries and, more favourably, the 'need' for territorial disputes with each other. It was only Brazil, already with a feeling for its 'manifest destiny' for controlling the heartland of the continent, that worried very much about its frontiers in regions of more-or-less emptiness as far as social and economic developments were concerned and as a result Brazil extended its frontiers time and time again into regions which for its neighbours seemed to be of zero importance. There were, and are, boundary disputes elsewhere—also in largely empty regions—as, for example, between Venezuela and Guyana and between Argentina and Chile, but in most of these cases, too, few people were involved. Sometimes rival claims to areas which were considered to be economically significant erupted into serious disputes: as in the conflict between Peru, Chile, and Bolivia over the desert region rich in nitrates; or as in the dispute between Chile and Argentina over territory in the southernmost part of the continent where oil resources had been discovered; or in the Brazilian, Paraguayan, and Argentinian dispute over territory in the upper sections of the Paraguay–Paraná river system with its potential for colonization. Sometimes, as in the dispute between Bolivia and Paraguay over territory lying between and far-distant from the core regions of the countries, it has also been suggested that it was not really the reported mineral wealth as such which motivated the dispute, but more the backing given to the two countries by Shell and Exxon which wanted to ensure that they could exercise the agreements they had made with their respective states over the largest possible areas with oil potential.

Relatively few that such disputes over potentially economically attractive territory have been in Latin America, such conflicts still unhappily outnumber the agreements which have been made by two or more countries jointly to develop the resources of a region divided between them and the overall potential of which could only be achieved by collective rather than individual action. Mexico and the United States have achieved such co-operation over the utilization of the waters of the Rio Grande to the benefit of agricultural developments on both sides of the river frontier. But away at the other end of the continent, it was not until the 1970s that an effective overall international agreement was signed for a joint effort to tap the potential of the massive Paraguay/Paraná river basin, the collective development of which would enhance the levels of welfare in some of the poorest regions of the countries concerned. This River Plate Basin Agreement (see Figure 11–1), calling for the physical integration of the member countries through appropriate joint public works' projects, followed a period in which some specific agreements were reached between two or more of the countries concerned in respect of international river crossings for transport facilities' developments and for the joint use of the waters of a river at a site where the banks of the river lie in different countries for the joint development of hydro-electricity potential—as, for example, in the joint Brazilian/Argentine agreement on a massive 2000 MW hydro-electricity plant at the falls on the Iguaçu river. On a smaller scale potential for such joint developments exists in Central America in, for example, the Gulf of Fonseca, shared between El Salvador, Honduras and Nicaragua and for which, as mentioned in the previous chapter, the Inter-American Development Bank has already made a preliminary survey. More important in December 1977 a decision was finally reached by the countries concerned for the study of a possible Amazon River Basin Agreement.

The fact that so few such joint projects between Latin American countries have so far been undertaken indicates, first, the lack of resources of capital and of know-how for undertaking them successfully, in situations in which most Latin American countries have more than enough projects on which to use their limited resources without getting involved in the complications of having to agree what is to be done with neighbouring countries—especially in a situation in which most of

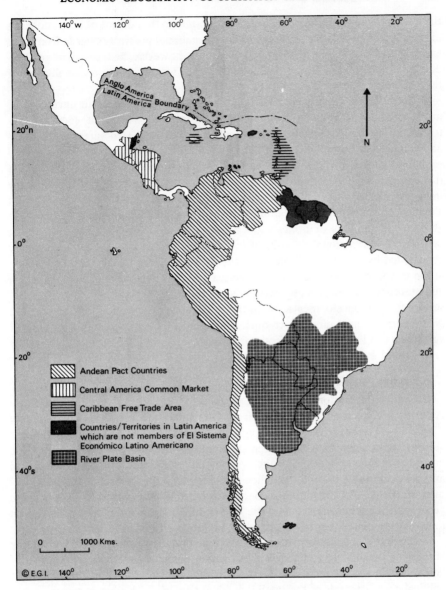

Figure 11–1. Latin America: economic integration groupings

the international projects are, almost by definition in the context of the continent's distribution of population, in areas where the national political rewards from such expenditures would be rather limited. Secondly, however, the lack of progress indicates a more general lack of interest for actions which are internationally, rather than domestically, more significant.

In light of this, what is somewhat surprising is that there should have been so much consideration given to much more formal questions of economic integration—within the context, that is, of organizational structures at the international level in Latin America which imply a willingness to move towards overall economic integration in a free trade or a common market sense. It could be that this emerges simply from a propensity of Latin American countries to follow the trend established elsewhere—as with the European Common Market—or that Treaties of Economic Integration provide a splendid opportunity for rhetoric about a communality of interests that is not expressed in anything more concrete; or that the international theories of economic integration have been so strongly propagated by Latin American economists, as a result of their academic training in the free-trade schools of North America and Western Europe, that politicians and statesmen were, at least, persuaded of the need to pay the appropriate lip-service to such developmental advantages. Whatever the reason, or combination of reasons, Latin American countries have, so far, achieved more by way of agreements to integrate their economies than they have in respect of bi-lateral or multi-lateral agreements to develop their frontier regions.

The Central American Common Market

Economic integration is, indeed, in a legal sense, already a fact as far as Central America is concerned. The nations from Guatemala to Costa Rica inclusive (see Figure 11–1) signed a Treaty of Economic Integration as long ago as 1960, and in various ways since then have been theoretically working towards creating one unified economic system out of the five national economies. The economic, social and political problems, and the difficulties of forming the Central American Common Market (C.A.C.M.), do not concern us here. What we need to look at is the geographical background to, and the spatial implications and results of, the steps towards economic integration that have, so far, been taken.

In the first place, its formation has given a stimulus to studies and evaluations of the area's problems as a geographical whole, compared with the previous situation in which studies tended to be made within the framework of the watertight political compartments of the small individual countries. This has been particularly important for considerations of infrastructure development, notably in the field of transport. This has already been reflected in an enhanced degree of attention to those facilities—roads, ports, railways, telecommunications and air services etc.—the improvement of which could mean a higher degree of opportunity for the five separate economic systems, as a result of their being able to make physical contact with each other at a much lower cost than hitherto. In that the

United States has been the main provider of funds for such transportation projects, and in that the U.S. has had the integration of Central America as one of its policy aims for many years, then the reason for the importance of this consideration can easily be appreciated. Moreover, priority by the U.S. in providing funds for transportation and communication facilities which have Central American, rather than just national significance, may be confidently expected to continue. Such dependence on American aid in this respect means that decisions in this sector of the economies of the Central American countries are beyond the competence of the national governments to determine; unless, of course, they are prepared to forgo the foreign grants and loans which are essential for the successful financing of all major projects—and this is difficult given the limited resources for such developments which these countries can otherwise lay their hands on.

In the second place, there are, or rather could be, geographical implications flowing from the decision to integrate into an effective common market the five previously separate national markets for industrial products (agricultural products are, by and large, excluded from the provisions of the common market arrangements). Each of the five countries has typically developed a small range of similar industries consisting, apart from those concerned with the initial processing of primary products, of import-substitution developments. By and large these industrial developments have, in each case, been located in, and immediately around, the five capital cities concerned. Thus, each capital has functioned as the core element in a typical core/periphery situation (Figure 11–2). However, had Central America been integrated at a stage preceding this degree of industrialization and, as a result, been better served by transportation facilities through the isthmus, then it is highly probable that most industries would have selected a single location for serving the whole of the central American market. The consequence of this would have been the emergence of a single core region for the whole of the isthmus, with the unlucky other four capitals becoming the equivalent of provincial cities in a nation-state and thus, on the evidence from most other Latin American countries, likely to find themselves lacking industrial components in their economies.

A fear that an industrial locational pattern along these lines, as far as industries to be newly-established were concerned, could well be a consequence of economic integration clearly lay behind the protocol on 'Integrated Industries' which was attached to the main treaty. In this protocol an integrated industry was defined as an industry which could only be attracted to Central America because the existence of the larger, integrated market made production possible at or above a minimum scale of operation. Such an industry could not, in other words, have established itself previously in any one of the national markets because no single one of these offered a large enough demand to make the minimum scale of operations possible. The protocol then went on to specify a severe locational restraint on such industries. It said that no one member country of the Central American

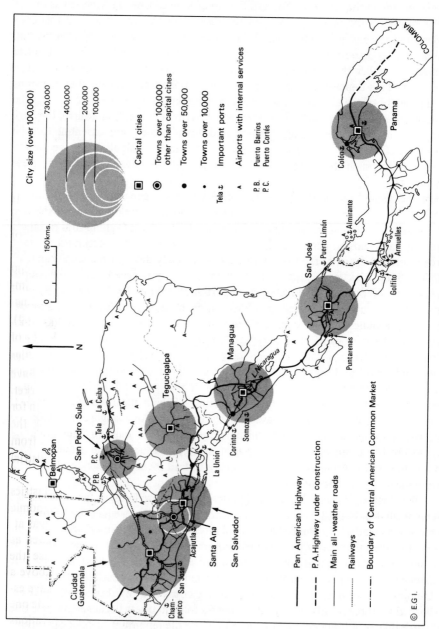

Figure 11–2. Central America: its urban and transport infrastructure

Common Market should secure a second integrated industry until each of the five member countries had attracted one. This was thus a measure firmly designed to prevent the centralization of industry at any one location to which, without such control, all new industry would tend to gravitate in order to take advantage of particularly favourable cost conditions for production and transport and in order to achieve possible external economies arising from its location in an industrial complex. In theory, therefore, the Central American Common Market set up a system in which at least the five pre-existing centres of industry should roughly maintain their positions relative to each other—and so avoid the political problems which would clearly arise from the concentration of such high value-added economic activities in one or two locations.

What was intended by the protocol has, however, not exactly worked out in practice for, as was expected, some locations, such as San Salvador, have been preferred over others, such as Tegucigalpa, the capital of Honduras, for the location of new industrial activities and great pressures developed to circumvent the intention of the protocol. The avoidance by an industry of formal designation as an integrated industry was one obvious way out. Thus many new industries which would probably never have found it worthwhile going to Central America with the prospects of marketing their products in one country only, have located there with the intention of selling freely throughout the region under the free trade provisions of the Treaty for industrial goods. In that these industrial plants have not located in Central America under the rules of the integrated industries' protocol, they have, of course, been quite at liberty to choose their own locations. In as far as many of them have calculated that San Salvador and Guatemala City are better (that is, higher-profit) locations than elsewhere in Central America, they have enhanced the status of these cities as industrial locations relative to that of the other capitals.

Quite apart from attempts to avoid the intention of the protocol in this way, however, other industries which have been designated as integrated industries nevertheless appear to have been accepted and located without the original regulations of the protocol being applied. Guatemala, which had already attracted an integrated industry, was able to secure a second one, even though other member countries of the Common Market did not, at the time, have their first integrated industry plant. Thus, the ability of the protocol to control effectively the geographical pattern of industrialization arising from integration was put in considerable doubt. As a result, the continued ability of an integrated Central America to attract new industries (arising out of the continued expansion of markets for industrial goods from the rapidly rising populations and increasing per capita incomes) started to produce an unbalanced rate of industrial growth in the five centres. Consequently, considerable pressures were brought to bear against the whole idea of the economic and political wisdom of the Common Market arrangements by those member countries which found themselves losing out in competition for new industrial activities with more favoured localities.

Thus, in order to avoid the possible break-up of the organization it was necessary to re-allocate official—or semi-official—bodies which also offered employment opportunities and relatively high value-added economic activities to those locations which were not doing so well in the competition for industrial development. Plans were, moreover, also drawn up—and are illustrated in Figure 11–3—for a rather complex pattern of infrastructure and trading developments which, it is thought, could help to inhibit such a tendency towards the centralization of development. To date, however, there is little evidence to suggest that the countries concerned have either the means or the will to create such general conditions for a spatially more dispersed pattern of development and most of the plans remain on paper only. It is, paradoxically, those developments—such as the road system between the countries—which could have been organized without the formality of the Common Market Treaty etc. which constitute the main success in Central American integration efforts to date.

The Latin American Free Trade Area

But, of course, even an integrated Central America, in terms of its geographical area and its total population, amounts to no more than a small to medium-sized Latin American country. This fact has been recognized in the proposal that only an integrated Central America, and not individual Central American countries, shall be eligible to become the member state for the Central American region of an economically integrated Latin America. Steps towards the economic integration of the whole of Latin America date back to the mid-1950s but so far the only concrete institution to emerge out of the countless discussions which were initiated within the framework of the U.N. Economic Commission for Latin America (E.C.L.A.) is the limited-in-scope, and even more limited in practice, Latin American Free Trade Area. Its efforts to stimulate intra-Latin American trade, particularly in industrial goods, have so far been only very modestly successful. The continued hope, however, that it, or a successor organization, will eventually begin to work effectively, makes it necessary that we evaluate possible geographical implications of such continental-wide economic integration.

A prime motivation for economic integration between sovereign nations is the greater opportunity that it gives for industrialization. This is because it introduces possibilities of reductions in unit manufacturing costs as producers take advantage of increasing economies of scale and of interdependencies between industries, given the existence of larger markets for their products. Thus, many studies have been undertaken to determine the most appropriate industrial structure for an economically integrated continent. But within the framework of the evaluation of the continental requirements for, and the possibilities of, industrial growth by sectors (iron and steel, non-ferrous metals, motor vehicles etc.), little official attention has been given to determining the most likely, or the most appropriate, spatial patterns of industrial development. Until the late 1960s advice on location was

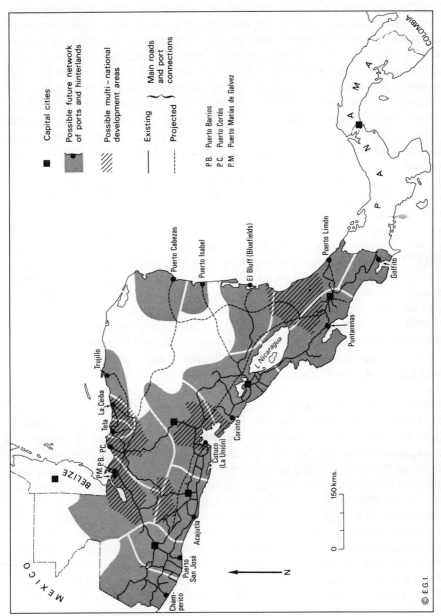

Figure 11–3. Central America: spatial structure for an integrated region

largely restricted to comments such as, 'industrial expansion should take advantage of suitable siting' and 'regional investment policy for industry should concentrate on the countries that are relatively less developed'. These comments were more than inadequate to cover the complexities of the location issue. They were also mutually contradictory in that it is virtually impossible to conceive of a situation in which the most suitable sites (determined presumably by the relative economic advantages of alternative locations) would be found in the relatively less developed countries of the continent. More realistically, the present pattern of the geography of economic activities in Latin America and the determinants of this pattern (see Chapter 9) suggest that the economic integration of the continent could well act as yet another cause for the further concentration of activities on existing core areas, in the absence of any positive measures to prevent this happening.

The existing coastal, or near coastal, locations of almost all the main centres of economic activity (see Figure 9–5) seem likely to act as magnets for new investment in industrial plants designed to serve a wider-than-national market. This is not only because these locations are immediately recognizable as industrial growth centres, equipped with the kind of economic and social infrastructure required, but also because the locations have easy access by sea to the main markets for industrial goods located at or near the coast in other member countries of the economically unifying continent. The advantages of sea transport over land transport for trade between the various centres of activity are largely self-evident for, in many cases, land transport facilities are either inadequate or non-existent or provide even less direct routes than does coastal shipping.

In such circumstances Buenos Aires will have its existing advantage over Córdoba and other inland locations in Argentina still further enhanced. In Brazil, the existing industrial centres of the south-east will be more advantageously located, in respect of transfer distances and costs, in relation to most of the main market areas of Latin America, than will the north-east of the country and inland locations. Mexico is geographically eccentric to the main areas of demand in Latin America anyway, and thus, with a view to minimizing additional costs which are incurred in getting goods to the point of export offering the lowest cost and most frequent shipping services to the rest of Latin America, it is unlikely that any industrialist would look far beyond the Mexico City–Veracruz axis of development (see Figure 10–1). This reduces the chances of success for the proposed economic growth zones to the north and north-west of the capital. There is a similar difficulty for the smaller west coast countries, where any industry aiming to serve the Latin American market as a whole suffers a cost penalty because of the distance involved in shipping goods to the major markets of Argentina, Brazil and Mexico. Thus, it is unlikely that entrepreneurs in these countries will seriously look beyond the existing centres of manufacturing activity in the Lima and Santiago areas, for there at least they can achieve economies in processing costs through linkages with other firms and take advantage of the more developed infrastructure in these centres. Thus, their claims on public funds for infrastructure improvements will be even further strengthened to the detriment of claims from other, less well-developed, parts of the countries whose relative ability to attract industry will fall even further in competition with the core regions.

On the basis of these arguments it seems that any moves towards Latin American economic integration have possible adverse consequences for the spatial ordering of economic activities in most countries. The traditional economists' answer to this argument would be that the stimulus to economic growth arising from economic integration will be so great that the favoured, and geographically limited, industrialized 'core' areas will distribute the benefits of integration to other parts of the national territories of the member countries. Any tendency for a prolonged division of a country into expanding and depressed areas will, so they would argue, be remedied by the economic pressures which arise in the processes of rapid development in the expanding areas. Such pressures include the economic and social effects of congestion in the cities of the core region and the requirement for economic policy makers to take a clear look at the development potentials of the depressed areas as it becomes apparent that the country is failing to utilize the resources in such areas.

But the evidence to date of the effects of congestion and of the 'clear looks' of economic policy makers is not very encouraging, as we have seen in previous chapters. Indeed, the empirical evidence available so far suggests, in fact, that exactly the opposite is happening. Economic pressures are still producing concentration. And the impact of free trade in industrial goods in Latin America seems more likely to accentuate the pressures in favour of concentration at most of the existing growth centres than it does to reduce them. These pressures come from the cost savings secured by plants in such concentrated areas of development through economies of scale in production, by external economies through linkages and infrastructural development, and through locational advantages which give lower transport costs to and from existing industrial areas. In that congestion costs are not internalized to the firm, but remain a charge to the national economy as a whole, there is no reason why individual entrepreneurs should worry at all about them in their decisions to locate in the core areas.

A Latin American common market involving free trade in industrial goods could, moreover, also have an adverse effect on the chances of geographical dispersion of economic activities in another way. This could arise from the effect that a common market has on the size of the market available to an industry. Within an individual nation-state, an important factor ultimately leading to a decision to do 'something' about underdevelopment and low living standards in the periphery of the nation is the curb on the continuation of industrialization in the core area which results from the insufficient size of the home market. In order to stimulate the effective demand for nationally manufactured goods and to ensure the continuation of the industrialization process, it ultimately becomes necessary to increase the purchasing power of the population in the areas of the country away from the core region. This increasing economic pressure from the industrial sector implies a need for a country to face up to the problems of adjusting economic and social policies, such as taxation and land tenure, so as to ensure that a larger and geographically more dispersed part of the total population could be converted into effective consumers of goods that the core areas are increasingly able to produce. Some Latin American countries had arrived at that point in their industrialization programmes and others were approaching it. Now, the introduction of free trade in industrial goods produces a strong possibility that these economic pressures for reform will be reduced, even though the protagonists of economic integration argue that integration is not an alternative to reforms in the economic and social structure of member countries. The danger, however, arises because the economic integration of many nation-states ensures that the capital-city-orientated industrial sectors can survive on the basis of new export opportunities opened up in the markets of the other member countries of the integrating area—so reducing or eliminating the pressure for internal redistribution of wealth to bring more consumers onto the market for the industrial products.

Thus, though it is certainly not intentional on the part of most of the proponents of Latin American integration, most of whom recognize the need for change in the structures of Latin American societies as part of their general dissatisfaction with the existing politico-economic system, the economic integration of the continent could well present an easy way out of the economic, political and social dilemmas involved in the process of creating sufficient new domestic demand for the increasing industrial output of the 'core' areas among the populations of the depressed peripheries of the Latin American countries. Overall, there is a danger that an economically integrated, or even a merely free-trading, Latin America will become little more than a series of interconnected 'core' areas feeding on and having close economic and political relationships with each other. And as an inevitable concomitant of this development, each core area will turn its back even more effectively on the opportunities for mutually beneficial contact with the remainder of the national territory within which it is situated. Recognition that such a danger exists in the Latin American moves to economic integration is the first step towards formulating appropriate counteraction to inhibit its development: indeed, one can see this as one element in the 1969 decision to postpone until 1980 the declared aim of the organization to establish a Free Trade Area. In this decision the choice of 1980 for implementation of the aim appears likely to have been related most strongly to the fact that 1980 was so far in the future that no government of the time really had to think seriously about the possibility and its implications.

The Andean Pact

It was with the dangers described above in mind, together with more general fears of the domination by Mexico, Brazil, and Argentina of the industrialization of the continent, that the Andean countries of Latin America—from Venezuela to Chile—decided to come together in the Andean Pact for the mutual benefit of its member countries (see Figure 11–1). The declared aims of this Andean Group of countries closely paralleled those of the Central American Common Market including the establishment of internal free trade in locally produced goods, a common external tariff, the jointly agreed establishment of new industries to serve the needs of the whole region, and the improvement of the transportation and communications' infrastructure of the Andean area to facilitate the planned expansion in trade and other exchange. Over the years many decisions in these spheres have been taken and the enthusiasm of the members seemed at one stage as though it would be sufficient to overcome the economic and political problems associated with an attempt to integrate so diversified and dispersed a group of countries. After six years, however, there is little to show for the efforts. There has certainly been a decision on an Andean trunk-road system, but its implementation is a matter for the various countries involved. On the industrial side only two programmes for integrated development have been approved—for engineering and petro-chemicals—and even the latter, by the end of 1976, had still only been approved by Peru. And in 1977 Chile virtually withdrew from the Group, following the decision of its military government to introduce a liberal foreign-investment law and so requiring freedom to use tariff policies to regulate the investment. Moreover, Chile has followed its withdrawal from the Andean Pact by indicating an interest in associating itself with the group of nations which formed the River Plate Basin Agreement, the essential element of which was, as indicated earlier in the chapter, to get things moving on the physical, rather than the economic, integration of its member countries in terms of transport and electrical-energy facilities etc. The geographical extension of this agreement to include trans-Andean projects might prove to be a significant development for a region of Latin America in which the physical barrier of the Andes has for long seen little by way of new infrastructure developments to ease the contacts betwen east and west. It could well be that such technically orientated and politically pragmatic joint public works' sorts-of-efforts, designed to overcome, for example, the barrier of the Andes or the challenges of multi-national river basin developments, will prove to be much more significant over the rest of the century in changing the economic geography of the region than the politically and economically much more sophisticated integration attempts epitomized by the Central American Common Market and the Andean Pact.

Indeed, given the fact that the latter are becoming increasingly recognized as devices which, if implemented, can have unexpected, undesirable and even uncontrollable effects on the geography of national development (as well as on other aspects of national development planning), then the intentions of the governments supporting them may be nothing more than a strictly political expression of regional solidarity. In Latin America such expressions of solidarity are needed to provide a rallying cry against the continuing fears of domination by the United

States and other parts of the industrialized world. Such domination is still thought likely from direct governmental intervention, but nowadays the influence of the United States, in particular via its multi-national corporations whose activities still count for so much in most countries in Latin America, is perhaps considered to be the more dangerous.

El Sistema Económico Latino Americano (Sela)

The convention establishing *Sela* was signed in Panama City in 1975—almost 150 years after Simón Bolívar had convened the *Congress Anfictiónico* in the same city, in his unsuccessful attempt to establish a Federation of Latin American States. It is perhaps back to the failure of that effort in 1825 that many Latin Americans would date the beginning of their dependence in the world economic system in which Latin America came to be dominated by the industrializing world. In the context of the New International Economic Order and the now serious efforts to change the relationships of the hitherto dominant and dependent nations of the world, *Sela* is perhaps the most appropriate expression of the regional solidarity that most countries of Latin America think they need with each other in order to be able to adopt a more effective bargaining stance with the outside world. And though it represents a kind of regional integration, no one seriously supposes that it will start to try to implement the kinds of developments which affect national decision-taking in respect of industrialization and fiscal and monetary policies. In this context of Latin American nationalism—a powerful force for changing the geography of the economies and societies—*Sela* will not intervene and is thus not the same kind of dangerous organization in these respects as the C.A.C.M. and the Andean Pact were proving to be. At the same time neither will it inhibit the integration of national systems of transport, communication, and energy facilities whereby, through bi-laterally or multi-laterally agreed programmes of joint public works, the efficiency and effectiveness of these basically essential elements for the geographical expansion of Latin American economies can be improved. Such developments will give possible new shapes to the geographical patterns of economic activities in the continent which as a whole, possibly through *Sela* or a similar institution, can present a collective image of the continent's efforts to the rest of the world. In the context of progress towards a New International Economic Order, Latin America—with its generally higher degree of development and of organization than in Africa or Asia—ought thus to be able to play a very positive role.

Bibliography

In this chapter we have been concerned with two aspects of integration in Latin America. First, with developments which are, in themselves, trans-national in that they affect two or more countries. As shown, such developments in Latin America are not frequent and there is not much literature specifically concerned with the topic. See, however,

BROWN, R. T., *Transport and the Economic Integration of South America*, Brookings Institution, Washington, 1966.

This is concerned with the most important infrastructural element in such multi-national developments.

DOXIADIS ASSOCIATES, 'The Rio Plata Basin: a Methodological Study for its Integrated Development', *Ekistics*, **34** (1972).

The second aspect of integration considered is that which is based on the concepts of supra-national organizations such as Common Markets and Free Trade Areas. These are much studied in international economics and they have, of course, become a common phenomenon in many parts of the world. A basic text which sets out the theoretical framework as well as presenting an early picture of the Latin American efforts at integration is

WIONCZEK, M. S. (ED.), *Latin American Economic Integration; Experiences and Prospects*, Praeger, New York, 1966.

See also the following books and articles either on specific aspects of economic integration and/or dealing with particular organizations:

CARNOY, M. (ED.), *Industrialization in a Latin American Common Market*, Brookings Institute, Washington, 1972.

CASTILLO, G. M., *Growth and Integration in Central America*, Praeger, New York, 1966.

CLAPP and MAYNE, INC, *A Strategy of Regional Economic Development for the Caribbean*, Caribbean Economic Development Corporation, San Juan, 1968.

KEARNS, K. C., 'International Co-operation for Development: The Andean Common Market', *Focus*, **24** (1973).

ODELL, P. R., 'Economic Integration and Spatial Patterns of Economic Development', *Journal of Common Market Studies*, **6** (1968).

ORANTES, I. C., *Regional Integration in Central America*, D. C. Heath, Lexington, 1972.

RAMSETT, D. E., *Regional Industrial Development in Central America*, Praeger, New York, 1969.

SCHMITTER, P. R., 'Autonomy or Dependence as Regional Integration Outcomes: Central America', *Institute of International Studies, University of California Research Series no. 17*, 1972.

UNITED NATIONS, 'Impact of the Caribbean Free Trade Association', *Economic Bulletin for Latin America*, **18** (1973).

YUDELMAN, M., *Agricultural Development and Economic Integration in Latin America*, Allen and Unwin, London, 1970.

Finally, a recent article which summarizes what has happened and what current problems there are in respect of economic integration and which puts the integration question in the context of the 'Latin American system':

ANON., 'The Sistema Economico Latino Americano; Its Antecedents and Prospects', *Review of the Bank of London and South America*, **10**, No. 12, December 1976 and **11**, No. 1, January 1977.

This monthly review of the London based Bank of London and South America is, incidentally, a convenient way of keeping up to date with economic developments in Latin America. In addition to information on specific developments in industry, trade and commerce etc. there are also articles on particular problems and countries to provide necessary background understanding.

Index